two purposes. The first is
is more phi-
contri-

LAW AND APOCALYPSE:
THE MORAL THOUGHT OF LUIS DE LEÓN
(1527?–1591)

ARCHIVES INTERNATIONALES D'HISTOIRE DES IDEES
INTERNATIONAL ARCHIVES OF THE HISTORY OF IDEAS

44

KARL A. KOTTMAN

LAW AND APOCALYPSE:
THE MORAL THOUGHT OF LUIS DE LEON
(1527?-1591)

LAW AND APOCALYPSE:
THE MORAL THOUGHT OF LUIS DE LEON
(1527?-1591)

by

KARL A. KOTTMAN

MARTINUS NIJHOFF / THE HAGUE / 1972

© *1972 by Martinus Nijhoff, The Hague, Netherlands*
All rights reserved, including the right to translate or to
reproduce this book or parts thereof in any form

ISBN 90 247 1183 5

PRINTED IN THE NETHERLANDS

With love to my parents, Karl and Dorothy,
and my wife, Mary.
And with respect to:

Ernest J. Burrus, S.J.
Claudio Guillén
James T. Monroe
Stanley Moore
Carlos G. Noreña
Francisco L. Peccorini
Richard H. Popkin
John R. Quinn
Paul Saltman
William L. Shipley
Avrum Stroll

TABLE OF CONTENTS

PREFACE

This book has two purposes. The first is clearly historical, the second is more philosophical and interpretive. Its success in the former will be less arguable than its attainment of the latter.

The contribution to the history of Spanish letters consists in critically establishing the fact that the sources of Fray Luis de León's moral and spiritual thought are Hebraic and that he can be seen to stand as one in a long line of Christian Hebraists, both scholastic and humanist. His philosophical views are cast in an Hebraic tradition, not in an Hellenic one as supposed by nearly every other commentator.

I have stressed the presence of a living Hebrew culture in Spain after 1492, and I have suggested that this and the Jewish parentage of Fray Luis are very significant. I have also identified an intellectual debt Fray Luis owed to non-Jewish Orientalists such as Egidio da Viterbo and Girolamo Seripando. But, even they learned from exiled Spaniards. I want to present Fray Luis as a most characteristic thinker in the world of Baroque Spain. I think most will agree with the picture I have outlined.

The more audacious aspect is my wish to show the importance of the Jewish heritage as found in the literary and philosophical production of this remarkable genius. It is, of course, my contention that today knowledge about Fray Luis and what he stood for is extraordinarily important. I do not insist that his contribution to thought was altogether unique, or that he was solely responsible for all the good things he was capable of saying. Like all great teachers, Fray Luis was a follower of mentors and had faithful students of his own. But, it is apparent that he was an extraordinary and gifted student of humanity. He was one of the early, and perhaps the most significant, of all the interpreters of the discovery of America and its implications for mankind.

First, what is new about Christians recognizing the importance of Jewish culture? Of course some have rejected Israel's rich history as of no special significance. Others, like St. Paul, while insisting that grace is from Jesus Christ, have recognized man's need of divine help and so have reverenced the traditions of those to whom God has revealed Himself.

And what of Fray Luis? Perhaps he does emphasize the Hebraic in his interpretations of Christian ideals, unlike many of his more nationalistic contemporaries. But, is this not what some Christians have always done? Indeed, his Hebraicism may seem more the mark of a very conservative theologian than of an innovator in the philosophical realm.

My own interpretation of Fray Luis depends upon a distinction between religious and rational forms of knowledge. I have supposed this is correct throughout this study. I do not claim that I can conclusively prove that it is a real one, but I do suppose that the issue is controversial and I am inclined personally to accept it. What is more to the point, it is a distinction Fray Luis himself made and it seems to apply in all his writings.

Both religion and reason are common to men. But, does reason adequately account for the sources of religious thought? In religion in general, whether that of the Jews or of the indigenous Mexicans, there may be an element of the human capacity to know manifested that is not identical with a solely rational understanding of his nature. Nevertheless, such elements would be universal as is religion itself.

Religion involves recognition, in thought and action, of man's relation with the divine. Reason may lead to natural religion, but may it not involve also an *a priori* union with the divine at some higher plane of understanding?

Everything depends upon human culture's being religious as different from its being rational. For Fray Luis the categories of religion can be more general than those of logic. It is in this light that one has to read him to see the significance of his interest in things Hebraic.

It was never unusual in Christian theology to insist that the Mosaic revelation really enlightened mankind benighted by sin. However, no orthodox thinker would see salvation as dependent upon knowing the Bible in Hebrew.

Nevertheless, Fray Luis does assume that the Hebrew religious culture is the most natural of all. In the same way, he assumes that Hebrew is the most natural of all languages. The reason for this is not only that the Old Testament is divine revelation. True religion, like speech, is something of which all men are capable with God's help. However, Fray Luis supposes, like the Old Testament itself, that reason alone is an insufficient basis for religion. In the same way not all languages are equally expressive of the truth. Hebraic spirituality is most esteemed by him not so much because of what it adds to man's natural capacities, but because of the way in which it perceives the natural limits of his rational ones.

Fray Luis was not unaquainted with the religions of the New World. His reverence for the religious element in all men is evidenced in his supposition that at least some of the native Americans may worship God worthily, even if they had not yet been evangelized by exterior preaching. Deeply impressed by the rapidity of the evangelization of Mexico, he saw that true observance of the divine law was already passing from Europe to America as it has passed to the Roman Empire from the Jewish evangelists. In a prophetic passage he wrote:

As the sun is ever sending forth its light which now illumines some part of the world and now fades away in other parts, so the doctrine of Christ is continually passing from one nation to another, illuminating some while others again sink into darkness.[1]

The analogy of Iberia's role in America and the Christian Jews' in ancient Rome is no accident. It rests upon his view that only Hebraic Christianity has adequately represented the message of Christ to non-Biblical peoples.

Christ came to unify men. His message was a spiritual one and among his gifts was supernatural grace. But, the oneness of man is by no means limited to the supernatural order. Indeed, the spiritual unity of man can be a natural phenomenon as well. No where was this more evident than in the rapid spread of Christianity in the Americas, certainly more so than in the evangelization of Rome. Moral unity can find its basis in man's asperations. And if these are expressed basically in religious categories, such conversions demonstrate the underlying humanity of the Christian faith.

It is the Hebrew-Christian tradition which best shows how the messiah overcomes the cultural differences of men. This is not done by force. As it is false that Jesus was a temporal ruler, it is no less false that techniques devised by man adequately explain the spread of the gospel and the apparent unification of men from diverse cultures that accompanies it.

I say the Hebrew-Christian tradition because the natural unity Fray Luis envisioned for men does not end at the spiritual level. Rather, he insisted that the hopes of Israel for a temporal, this worldly, reign of universal justice and peace can and must be satisfied. The spiritual and material hopes of man are focused in a universal religion, and in no other

[1] This is from Edward Schuster's abridged translation, Louis of León, O.S.A., *The Names of Christ*, (St. Louis: Herder, 1955), p. 161.

according to Fray Luis, because he saw they were needful of being satis-fied on a world-wide scale in a way never before imagined.

His longing is an Hebraic longing, but it is for him also the longing of the isles across the sea. Spiritual unity alone inadequately responds to the fullness of scope and depth in human expectations. So scientific logic fails to grasp the symbol of their natural authenticity, Fray Luis' Christ.

I will not account for the significance the discovery and evange-lization of Mexico held for Fray Luis in any detail. With this study as a basis, I hope to do so in the future. So one must not expect me to defend all I have just outlined.

Many other features of Fray Luis' thought are left undeveloped. Among the most suggestive are his concept of Church reform, his ideas about spirituality for women, especially married women, his innovations in language theory, and his notion of physical science and technology.

A word has to be said about my treatment of Domingo Soto. Of course I stand by what I say about his ideas in relation to those of Fray Luis. But, it would be wrong if one were to suppose that there was any personal bitterness or resentment between them. Besides the fact of Soto's seniority in age and experience, and his vast personal prestige, it is entirely likely that Fray Luis admired the liberality of the man who favored the Indians at Valladolid.

This works owes much to the efforts of Mmes. Fran Newman and Chris Scott and the resources of the libraries of the University of California, to Miss Suzanne Enos and Dr. Simon Cohen and to their respective libraries at Villanova University, Villanova, Pennsylvania, and the Hebrew Union College-Jewish Institute of Religion, Cincinnati, Ohio.

I offer my gratitude to Father Robert Welsh, O.S.A., President of Villanova University, Professor Raimundo Lida and Mr. Yosef H. Yerushalmi, Harvard University, Father Ernest J. Burrus, S.J., Pontifical Gregorian University, Professors Carlos Noreña, Stanley Moore, and Carlos Blanco, University of California, for their suggestions and valuable advise. Professors Claudio Guillén, Joaquin Casalduero, James Monroe, Paul Saltman and Avrum Stroll, University of California, all bolstered flagging spirits by the example of their personal standards.

I want to thank Professor Paul Dibon for his generous consideration of this book and Professor Richard H. Popkin who not only interested me in Fray Luis, but suggested what developed into a satisfying viewpoint from which to study him. I feel very much in his debt in many ways.

Finally, thanks to my wife, Mary Kottman, for her love and patience during the writing, and her talents in typing, *sine qua non*.

San Diego, California   K. K.

CHAPTER I

INTRODUCTION

This study will deal with interpreting the moral, social and spiritual views of the famous Spanish theologian and poet, Luis de León.

Luis de León was born in 1527 or 1528, in a town called Belmonte, probably in Cuenca, Spain. He was the son of Lope de León and Inéz de Varela. Originally planning a career in law like his father's, he was, however, professed in the Order of St. Augustine in 1544, at Salamanca. He studied law and theology there, and Bible at Alcalá, graduating in 1560. After 1561, he gained in turn various theological chairs at Salamanca. In 1572, he was arrested and imprisoned on charges of Judaizing and heresy and, though he was sentenced to torture five years later, a higher court annulled this. He was ordered restored to his post at the University. In 1579, he won the Chair of Bible which he held until his death. He was again denounced in 1582, for his views on predestination against the Dominican Bañez. This time he was admonished without sentence by the Inquisitor, Cardinal Quiroga, in 1584.

Fray Luis' problems with the Inquisition stemmed partly from the fact that he was discriminated against by Spanish law. His great-grandmother on his father's side, Leonor de Villanova, was condemned as a relapsed Jewess and this fact made him subject to statues which would ordinarily have barred him from the important and influential post he held. Pedro de Lorenzo, a recent biographer of Fray Luis, continues to doubt he was of Jewish descent, but one is compelled to accept the documentation offered by Coster and Father La Pinta.

The Augustinian Order did not accept members of Jewish descent through the male line, hence obviating the intent of Spanish law which required that those having Jews among the previous four generations of one's forebearers be excluded from positions of influence. Jews count their members through female descent, and Fray Luis was not a Jew by Jewish standards. Yet, he was thought to have been one for purposes of the Inquisition and he was forced to ignore his great-grandmother with his own denial of Jewish parentage at his trial.[1]

Aside from such incomparable works in poetry as Fray Luis' *"Oda a Salinas,"* a well known work is the prose devotional piece, *De los nombres de Cristo,* published in 1583, 1585, and 1603, each time with additions, and over twenty times since, into the 20th Century. His important works in latin include the *In Canticum Canticorum Expositio,* especially the 1589 edition, and other Biblical commentaries, some of which have been published posthumously and some of which remain in manuscript. He was the author of other theological works also in various degress of availability. Fray Luis was still planning further publications when he died on August 23, 1591, just after having been elected Augustinian provincial of Castile.

As an author of diverse interests and profound originality, a list of his own friends and admirers is an inventory of the important names in all the fields of human endeavor in his own day. He was a Biblical exegete, profound moralist, dogmatic theologian, poet of the highest genius, prose writer and co-creator of modern Spanish, philologist, mathematician, astronomer, politician, religious reformer and natural philosopher. He was a teacher of geniuses like Francisco Suárez and San Juan de la Cruz, friends of saints in the reform of Carmel, and a lifelong enemy of ignorance. He was a universal man. So universal was his appeal that scholars of many disciplines have commented upon his greatness and his contribution to their own studies.[2]

Theologians have found him to be central for the understanding of Catholic thought after the Council of Trent. Some have tried to see him only as a disciple of the most respected medieval Christian writers and strictly following such men as Aquinas and Scotus. These wish to see him as an orthodox thinker of the Counter-Reformation. Other theologians,

---

[1] Miguel Salvá and Pedro Sainz de Baranda, eds., *Documentos inéditos para la historia de España,* (Madrid: Calero, 1847), Vols. X and XI of this collection reproduce the documents of Fray Luis' trail of 1572-1577. Hereafter this title will be abbreviated as *Doc. ined.* Fray Luis is famous for having resumed his lectures in 1577 with the words: "As we were saying yesterday." On these matters one should see: A. Coster, "Luis de León," *Revue Hispanique,* LIII (1921), pp. 5 ff. Antonio Domínquez Ortiz, *La clase social de los conversos en Castilla en la Edad Moderna,* (Madrid: Consejo Superior de Investigaciones Cientificas [abbr. CSIC], 1955), p. 166. Pedro de Lorenzo, Fray Luis de León, (Madrid: Nuevas Editoriales Unidas, 1963), pp. 25-27. *Doc. ined.,* X, p. 386. Miguel de la Pinta Llorente, O.S.A., "Fr. Luis de León y los hebraístas de Salamanca," *Archivo Agustiniano,* XLV (1952), p. 348. Hubert Jedin, *Papal Legate at the Council of Trent, Cardinal Seripando,* (St. Louis: Herder, 1947), p. 208.

[2] See the plaudits accorded him in *Retratos de los Españoles ilustres con un epítome de sus vidas,* (Madrid: Imprenta Real, 1791, Unpaginated.)

like the Dominican Thomists of his University in his own day, have seen him as a heretic, Judaizer and corrupter of the faith, and some still view him with suspicion.[3] Recently, there is renewed interest with regard to Fray Luis' position on the great theological questions of his day, especially the problem of grace. This is true with respect to both the problem of its relation to human freedom and Fray Luis' position as an exegete of St. Paul.

Another class of theologians has been interested in Fray Luis. These are specialists in mystical theology and many authors have looked in his writings for a mystical doctrine based on his own experience. The topic of Fray Luis' mysticism has been under discussion in the circles of literary criticism as well.

Fray Luis is universally acclaimed a classic writer of Spanish and his works in that language are standards of unmatched greatness. One has only to look at Antonio de Capmany to find mentioned the laudatory opinions of such classical masters as Malón de Chaide, Quevedo, Nicolas Antonio and Gregorio Mayáns. Recent historians of literature such as Bataillon single him out as exemplifying the essence of the true spirit of the Counter-Reformation. Others compare him with El Escorial, the monastic capital of Philip II.[4]

Among Spanish historians, Americo Castro sees him as heir to an Hebraic tradition that is fundamentally Spanish. Others, like Sánchez-Albornoz, are anxious to reject this opinion. However, one must read such authors as Bell and La Pinta and an endless list of articles and books to see the wide range interests that are excited by Fray Luis. Most his-

---

[3] For an account of the controversy Fray Luis occasioned in his own lifetime see his biography: Aubry F. G. Bell, *Luis de León,* (Barcelona, Araluce, 1927). The question of his status as a model of orthodoxy is still in dispute. See: Miguel de la Pinta Llorente, O.S.A., *Estudios y polémicos sobre Fray Luis de León,* (Madrid: CSIC, 1956). The suggestion that Fray Luis used rabbinical exegesis made by the Jesuit Father Nober has provoked the recent denial of this in David Gutiérrez, O.S.A., "Fray Luis de León y la exegesis rabínica," *Augustinianum* (Rome), I (1961), pp. 533-550, every argument of which article seems to be unfounded, though the intent of the author may be correct. Any serious study of Fray Luis would be impossible without Salvador Muñoz Iglesias, *Fray Luis de León, teólogo,* (Madrid, CSIC, 1950). For an evaluation of this excellent work and the problems involved in studying Fray Luis' theology, see: Ursino Domínguez del Val, O.S.A., "La teología de Fr. Luis de León," *La Ciudad de Dios* (El Escorial), CLXIV (1952), pp. 163-178. See also: José M. Bover, "Fray Luis de León, traductor de San Pablo," *Estudios Eclesiasticos* (Madrid), VII (1928), pp. 417-431; and, David Gutiérrez, O.S.A., "Un comentario inédito de Fray Luis de León," *Augustinianum,* I (1961), pp. 273-309.

[4] Antonio de Capmany y de Mantpalau, *Teatro histórico-critico de la elocuencia Española,* (Barcelona, Gaspar, 1848), III, pp. 251 ff. Marcel Bataillon, *Erasmo y España,* (Mexico, Fondo de Cultura Economica, 1950), Two Vols., II, pp. 382, 390-391. Felix García, O.S.A., ed., *Obras completas de Fr. Luis de León,* 4th edition, (Madrid: Biblioteca de Autores Cristianos, 1957), Two Vols., I, p. 362.

torians agree that he was a model of the Spanish Renaissance, character-
istically Catholic, and fiercely loyal to his own country.[5]

Few philosophers have taken serious interest in Fray Luis in recent
centuries.[6] Those who have note that he was primarily a theologian. Some,
like Guy, have made him out to be a Platonist and Pythagorean, others
like Quintana have seen him as holding some kind of Thomist meta-
physics. Both of these have noted the unusual stress upon the role of
language in his philosophy. The classic work of Father Marcelino Gutiérrez, O.S.A., places him amid the various philosophical currents of his
day, and does not fail to note Fray Luis' importance as a natural philosopher. Some, like Guy, have stressed his significance as a philologist,
a realist for whom words have metaphysical import. Other students treat
the philological explanation of his philosophy as insufficient as the
scholastic explanation offered by Gutiérrez.

Assessments of Fray Luis as a moral philosopher are varied. Bell thinks
of Fray Luis as an Aristotelian, a believer in the justice of inequality.
Castro says he was a libertarian. Gutiérrez says he has a Stoic quality. As
to his social theory, there is nearly universal agreement that the issue that
concerns him most is the question of Spanish colonial policy, what does
and does not justify the conquest, what Spain's rights in America are
based upon, etc. This problem is generally thought to have been para-
mount in Spanish social and legal thought after Vitoria.[7] A more exact
study of his moral and political thought has been made possible by the
publication of Fray Luis' *Treatise on Law,* of which the first part has
appeared already but the second part does not seem to be forthcoming.
In his introduction to his edition, Luciano Pereña has drawn upon his

---

[5] Américo Castro, *La realidad histórica de España,* (México: Porrua, 1966).
Claudio Sánchez-Albornoz, *España, un enigma histórico,* (Buenos Aires, Sudamericana, 1956), Two Vols.

[6] Alain Guy, *El pensamiento filosófico de Fr. Luis de León,* (Madrid: Rialp, 1960).
Guillermo Quintana Fernández, "Los bases filosóficas de la teología de Fr. Luis de
León," *Revista de la Universidad de Madrid,* XII (1963), pp. 746-747. This is an
abstract of his thesis of which I have been unable to obtain a reproduction. J. García
Alvarez, O.S.A., *Fray Luis de León: La paz como perfection ontológica del hombre,*
(Paris: Institut Catholique, Faculty of Philosophy, 1962). The Institut Catholique
has not responded to my request of a copy of this. Marcelino Gutiérrez, O.S.A., *Fr.
Luis de León y la filosofía Española del siglo XVI,* (Madrid: Gregorio del Amo,
1891). S. Alvarez Turienzo, "Sobre Fray Luis de León, filólogo," *La Ciudad de Dios,*
CLXIX (1956), pp. 112-136. I agree that the categories of "scholastic" and "phi-
logist" are both much too simplistic to be of service and very misleading with respect
to Fray Luis' true stature as a philosopher as Alvarez seems to sense.

[7] Bell, *Luis de León,* p. 295. Castro, *Realidad histórica,* p. 282. Gutiérrez, *Fray
Luis,* p. 238 ff. Luciano Pereña Vicente, ed., *Fray Luis de León, De Legibus o Tratado
de las Leyes, 1571,* (Madrid: CSIC, 1963). I am informed by the Chief of Distribution
of Publications of the CSIC, that the remainder of the *Treatise* of 1571 will not be
published. Letter of Ángel Cabetas L. to Karl Kottman, Madrid, May 24, 1969.

very great erudition in the field of the history of legal theory in 16th Century Spain and Portugal. He places Fray Luis in the complex history of legal thought of those days, pointing out his significant original contributions. Like most authors, Pereña sees Fray Luis' contributions as connected with the Vitoria school, which though unquestionably influential in modern thought, is not yet clear as to its exact significance.

These preliminary observations raise anew the problem of the precise nature of his moral doctrine. Fray Luis, like other thinkers, found the highest embodiment of the moral life in the mystical life. He never wrote a formal treatise on moral or spiritual theology and all opinions on what it was are based upon assemblages of texts dedicated to other purposes. Two questions are involved here. First, of interest to both theologians and literary critics, is whether Fray Luis was a mystic himself. Did he have an original doctrine like St. Bernard of Sta. Teresa de Jesús? Or, was he merely an ascetic writer or commentator on the mystical experiences of others? The second question, unrelated to the first, and of special interest in this thesis, is a philosophical one. What seem to be the essential characteristics of Fray Luis' theory of morality? [8]

The best of recent studies of what is assumed to be the mystical doctrine of Fray Luis that touch upon this second question is that of Father Robert Welsh, O.S.A. This author stresses the role of Christ in the theology of Fray Luis as the final cause of nature as well as of grace. But, he does not discuss the actual reasons for this belief beyond saying that they were clearly Scriptural.[9] He insists that Fray Luis' moral doctrine is essentially

[8] Marcelino Menéndez y Pelayo, who regarded Fray Luis as a mystic poet, recognized the presence of Hebraic traditions in Spanish mystic poetry, but regarded Fray Luis' mysticism to have been modeled along Platonic and Pythagorean lines. Dámaso Alonso is much more sceptical about the supposed mystical elements in Fray Luis' poetry. Yet, such critics as Menéndez y Pelayo, Alonso and Valbuena Prat agree on the presence of Platonic elements. See: Marcelino Menéndez y Pelayo, *La mística española*, (Madrid: Aguado, 1956), pp. 143-144. Felipe Mellizo, "Fray Luis de León en Menendez Pelayo," *La Ciudad de Dios*, CLXX (1957), pp. 461-471. Dámaso Alonso, *Poesía española*, (Madrid: Gredos, 1962), p. 191. Ángel Valbuena Prat, *Historia de la literatura española*, 7th edition, (Barcelona: Gili, 1964), Two Vols., I, p. 589. Marcelino Menéndez y Pelayo, *Discurso leído en la Universidad Central*, (Madrid: Estrada, 1889), pp. 29, 70, 49.

[9] Robert J. Welsh, O.S.A., *Introduction to the Scriptural Doctrine of Fray Luis de León, O.S.A.*, (Washington: Augustinian Press, 1951), p. 23. In his final chapter, Welsh attempts to locate Fray Luis in the Platonic tradition of mysticism, but not on the basis of his own study. Father Welsh has expressed his own difficulty in understanding Fray Luis in the light of classic Christian authors. Letter of Rev. R. J. Welsh, O.S.A., to Karl Kottman, Villanova, Pennsylvania, May 22, 1969. Welsh considers the main texts of Fray Luis' spiritual doctrine to be: *In Canticum Canticorum Expositio, El Cantar de los Cantares, De los nombres de Cristo, In III Parte Divi Thomae (De Incarnatione)*, and *In Epistolam ad Galatas*. Crisógono de Jesús, O.C.D., "El misticismo de Fr. Luis de León," *Revista de Espiritualidad*, I (1942), p. 32, says "La médula de su doctrina espiritual es ajena a sus preferencias neo-platónicas y a

one of "Christian perfection," but he admits in criticism of Father David
Gutiérrez, that the latter neglects the fact that for Fray Luis the Mystical
Body of Christ extends "not only to the visible Church, but to all the just
who lived before Christ and . . . to the angels as well."

Another opinion is that of the late distinguished spiritual writer, Father
Crisógono de Jesús, O.C.D. He regards Fray Luis as an authentic mystic
of inspired originality. This writer's implication is that there is no philosophical moral doctrine at all in Fray Luis, only moral theology.

Francisco Marcos del Río, O.S.A., not only follows Menéndez y Pelayo's
view that Fray Luis was a mystic, but that his moral philosophy is rooted,
like that of the Church Fathers, in the Greeks.[10] So does Alain Guy. The
Carmelite author, Gustavo Vallejo, qualifies a like view by emphasizing
the eclectic and independent mind of Fray Luis and by showing with
much documentation and insight, that Fray Luis' spiritual doctrine was
clearly influenced by that of Sta. Teresa de Jesús.

In the face of all these opinions, one aims to study anew the problem
of determining the philosophical bases of Fray Luis' moral theory in
terms of its historical background. The philosophical concepts that will
be involved in this analysis are not difficult. According to the legal theory
held by all the authors examined and relevant to this work, the ultimate
basis of morality is the fulfillment of the divine will. God's will, as it is in
Himself, is called the eternal law. All things are dependent upon God's
creative power, and operate according to the divine plan. The laws of the
physical universe are laws insofar as they manifest the eternal law and
insofar as they are appropriate to the physical world that they govern.
In human society, civil laws are laws as they manifest the providential
care of God's eternal law in man's political life. The law upon which
civil positive laws depend, insofar as they are properly called laws, is the
natural law of reason. Reason directs man to social life and ought to
regulate his relations in a political context. Morality is the manifestation
of the divine will in individual conduct, and so forth.

The eternal law is not known to us directly. One infers its contents
indirectly. Its operation is seen in diverse forms. These include the laws
of physical nature, the laws of political society and God's revelation of it
in the Bible. We do not see it in individual conduct unless this is in conformity with its more obvious manifestations. The basic assumption of

sus aficiones renacentistas, como lo es el licor respecto del ánfora que lo contiene."
   [10] Francisco Marcos del Río, O.S.A., "La doctrina mística de Fray Luis de León,"
Religión y Cultura, II, III, IV (1928), pp. 531-543, 205-220, 223-236, respectively.
Gustavo Vallejo, O.C.D., *Fray Luis de León: su ambiente, su doctrina espiritual,
huellas de Santa Teresa,* (Rome: Colegio Internacional de Santa Teresa, 1959), p. 75.

this view is that all law of diverse types is unified and coordinated in God and this, like the Unity of God Himself, is something we do not understand.

In this study the mode of unifying only two kinds of law will be relevant for consideration. The two laws are the moral part of divine positive law revealed as to Moses and forming part of God's covenant with the Jews, the Decalog, which also forms part of the law of the gospel. And, secondly, there is the natural law of reason.

It is generally agreed, at least by Thomists, that the content of the natural law and the Decalog is the same. All men, it is supposed, could come to a knowledge of these precepts by means of their natural reason. All good societies observe these few laws, and, of course, many others. But these are seen to be basic. The question we find raised in Fray Luis and others is whether these two laws are formally the same, and therefore not really different laws; or, whether they are materially the same, but different formally and hence really distinct. All Thomists, for example, agree that the Decalog can be known by reason, but must it also be known by revelation?

Fray Luis' moral theory is philosophically dependent in some way on that of the Thomistic tradition of law. However, his interpretation of St. Thomas was conditioned by a special problem that existed in Spain. There, by the end of the 15th Century, a very large and important part of the population was made up of converted Jews and their descendents. It is in connection with this assertion that one must deal with the interpretation given by representative Thomists and others concerning the relation of the Decalog as divine positive law and the natural law. The purpose of this is to indicate that many Jewish converts of the 13th – 16th Centuries related Christianity to Judaism by seeing their conversion, not as the adoption of an entirely new set of moral practices, but as the fulfillment of the Mosaic Law in its spiritual and Christian form. These thinkers, it will be suggested, saw themselves as observing the fulfillment of the Law of Moses in its moral precepts as they also form part of the Christian moral observance. The Decalog was, for them, obliging Christians not only as natural law, but also as divine positive law, as the Old Law bound the Jews.

Fray Luis de León is to be seen as an exponent of this tradition. His work forms part of a development of the viewpoint of these convert Thomists into a position quite different than that of St. Thomas himself. This is that Fray Luis not only held that the Decalog was a divine positive law for Christians, as well as a command of reason, but also that Jewish mystical practice could be interpreted in a Christian sense, and, in fact, was seen by him as the authentic basis of that tradition in Christianity. It is in this vein that the coming chapter will note the presence of certain themes of Jewish mysticism, especially cabalism, its most important form, in the works of Fray Luis. It will be suggested that these may have been drawn from even rather early Christian Hebraists and polemicists in Spain, as well as the works of later Renaissance Christian cabalists of Italian or German origin.

An effort must also be made to show that the question of the relation of the Decalog to divine positive law and natural law was one under thorough examination in Spain in the 16th Century. Fray Luis' formal doctrine on this point in his academic treatise on St. Thomas' doctrine on law will be contrasted with the interpretation given St. Thomas by Domingo Soto whose views were very widely accepted in the latter part of the 16th Century. It is this comparison that will make apparent the relevance of the foregoing. The question that will be raised will be which author interprets St. Thomas correctly on the matter of the type of law the Decalog is for Christians, a matter not to be resolved in this study. Also, and this is what will be resolved, there will be the question of the exact basis of Fray Luis' moral doctrine, i.e. how is his supposed dependence upon Thomistic legal theory to be understood?

In attempting to determine this, this work will undertake a review of the Biblical commentary of Fray Luis to show that the Jews play a central role in his understanding of history and society. Christian history will be shown to be, for him, an extension of Jewish history. This, it will be argued, is in conformity with his belief that Christian moral practice is an extension of Mosaic moral practice. It is in terms of the observance of these laws that Fray Luis understood both world political history as well as the basic characteristics of Christian society at the end of time. For him the society of the end of history will be characterized by God's fulfilling His promise of temporal rewards to the Jews, after they have become Christians. It is in conformity with this belief that one is led to expect that Christian and Jewish moral practice may be seen as identified in the last days of history.

Characteristic features of Fray Luis' spiritual doctrine fit patterns one finds in Hebraic literature and cabalism, perhaps as drawn directly from Jewish books, but especially as perhaps found in the writings of Christian Hebraicism and Christian cabalism. In this manner, one can show, first, that previous interpretations of Fray Luis' moral theory have either overlooked or have been unable to understand important features of his writings on Christian morality. Second, it was entirely possible, and even probable, that Fray Luis was himself a Christian cabalist since certain historical influences might normally have been expected to be discovered in his thought. Having established these points, and by excluding all other likely interpretations, the object of this book will be attained by asserting that it is cabalism which is the basis of his moral thought. Thus, the philosophical basis of his moral doctrine will not be the same as St. Thomas' and any attempt to relate his doctrine of law to that of St. Thomas will have to account for this fact.

It is important to show how Fray Luis' moral theory is related to his personal position in Spanish society and how it is related to a longstanding problem of the religious history of Spain. Fray Luis was a New Christian under Spanish law and it is the development of this class of people that is of central importance in putting the issues debated by the theologians of Spain, and those relating to the Spanish situation, into perspective. Many of the converts to Christianity from Judaism in Spain, saw themselves in terms of their Jewish past even after their conversion. Thus, aspects of their interpretation of Christian theology were introduced which were perhaps unfamiliar to the traditional understanding of Catholicism of the Old Christians.

In order to understand this, one should recall that the Iberian peninsula, which had been under the control of Visigothic Christians, was invaded in 711 by Islamic forces which established control of the area except for the upper northern sector. These Moslems established a flourishing culture centered at Cordova, Granada and other great cities, which was unrivaled in the Occident at least until the 13th Century. At that time, it was Islamic Spain which began to inspire the emergence of Christian Europe from the difficult ages of transition following the collapse of ancient Rome.

Iberia was divided and the Moslems whose advanced culture thrived in the south far outshone the Christians in their rather rustic dominions of the north. In the midst of the Islamic population there also was a large Jewish population. Some of these Jews had been in Spain since they were exiled there by Rome, and, probably, others had lived there before the Christian era. It is said that the Apostle James, or Santiago, went there to tell them of Jesus. The Jews enjoyed the benefits of life in the cities of the Califate and shared the freedom of partners in its development. Occasional changes in Moslem administration, however, and consequent restraints on their liberties, caused Jews to flee to Christian controlled areas which began to expand in size as the crusade to expel Islam advanced. At times, the Jews were invited into the service of Christian kings as diplomats with Islamic rulers, as physicians and as advisers of various sorts. With additional pressures in the Islamic kingdoms, the financially and culturally advantaged Jewish population of Christian Spain expanded, and this growth was welcomed by the Christian princes who were anxious to develop their own domains with its much needed help.

This situation is best typified by the reign of King Alfonso X of Castile (1252-1284) who employed Jews especially in an attempt to make available to Christians the advanced civilization of Islamic Spain. His reign was characterized by the political freedom he allowed for Christian, Jew and Moslem in his kingdom. The legal status of the Jews of Castile and Aragon was secured by the kings' adopting them as their own possessions, and allowing them to be governed by their own laws and customs, independently of Christian, especially canon law.

All this began to change in the last quarter of the 13th Century. The social position of the Jews in Spain had been entirely unique. Nowhere had they ever been so influential in Christian society as then in Spain. But, it was the general spirit of Christian renewal of life in France and Italy, stemming from the Cluniac reform and the founding of the mendicant orders that came into direct conflict with the tolerant laws and ways of Christian kingdoms of Spain.

Apocalyptic movements were characteristic of Church reforms in the late middle ages in Europe as a whole. Nicolas of Lyra (d. 1340) declared that the foundation of the mendicant orders signaled the introduction of the third or spiritual age of the Church. This conception of the ages of the Church was introduced by an enormously influential gloss on Apocalypse or Revelation by Joachim of Flore (d. 1201).

In connection with these interpretations, a general apocalyptic fervor accompanied the renewal of Christian life in Europe and in Spain this fact, coupled with the unusual status of the Spanish Jews, led to an entirely unprecedented religious crisis. Pressure was applied by reforming influences in the Church to limit the traditional freedoms of the Jews whose continuing exercise of great political influence in the Christian kingdoms seemed to put the lie to French, Italian and German expectation of the apocalypse. Pressure increased to convert the Jews. One of the most famous and important figures of this effort was Vicente Ferrer (1350-1419) who was moved to his campaign to convert the Jews by a vision of Sts. Francis and Dominic. He was probably a Joachimite and was surely convinced of the impending apocalypse. He was not alone in seeing the schism of the Church as further evidence of this and he vigorously supported the claims of his friend, Pedro de Luna, as Pope Benedict XIII because, no doubt, he regarded the claimant at Rome as the antichrist. Unquestionably it was his fame as a theologian which helped the kings of Spain and France to support Benedict until the election of Martin V (1417) made even Vicente Ferrer see this as impossible.

This situation developed into violence and in 1391, the political power of the Jews of Spain was broken by incessant ecclesiastical attacks and an extremely large number of Jews was converted, by force or otherwise, that year and thereafter. The moving spirit behind the attacks on the Jews of these years was Vicente Ferrer.

A Jewish tradition holds that the family of David, from which the messiah is to be born, was exiled by the Romans to Spain. The degree to which messianic hopes were also excited among the Jews of this period is indicated by the development of cabala, the major form of Jewish mysticism, in 13th Century Spain. Cabala is connected with Jewish messianism and it gives a method by which the time of the end of the world can be indicated. Baer says that it was related also to an attack by poorer Jews upon those Jews who held great power in the Moorish and Christian courts. It was part of a call for moral reform in Spanish Jewry which grew with increasing messianic fervor as its plight worsened in Spain, culminating in the expulsion of 1492. Baer has associated the Jewish messianic movements of 1295 with similar movements such as that of the Franciscan Spirituals who were Joachimites. If this is correct, the connection of cabala, social reform, and apocalyptic fervor, has its roots in very old Spanish traditions, both Hebrew and Christian.

The most eminent of the converts of Vicente Ferrer, and typical of the new class of Christians that was being created, was the former chief rabbi of Burgos, Salomon ha-Levi. He was baptized in 1390 as Pablo de Santa María (1352?-1435), became a Paris graduate in theology, annotated Lyra's *Postillae* and was made bishop of Burgos and chancellor of the kingdom of Castile. Many other former Jews retained as Christians the influence at court and in Spanish affairs that Pablo attained and that they had had as Jews.[11]

[11] See the following on these matters: Joachim de Flore, *Expositio in Apocalypsim*, (Venice, 1527). Nicolas de Lyra, *Biblia Sacra cum Glossa Ordinaria*, (Antwerp: J. Keerbergium, 1617), pp. 1671-1672. This work contains Pablo de Santa María's additions. For an account of medieval, especially German apocalyptic fervor see: Norman Cohn, *The Pursuit of the Millennium*, (Fairlawn, N.J.: Essential Books, 1957). See page 146 of this work on Vicente Ferrer as well as the articles on him in: *The New Catholic Encyclopedia*, (New York: McGraw-Hill, 1967), XIV, pp. 680-681, and the *Enciclopedia Universal Ilustrada*, (Madrid: Espasa-Calpe, 1958), LXVII, p.

This situation not only led to continued jealousy on the part of the Old Christians who began to raise doubts about the orthodoxy and sincerity of the New Christians, but it led to a strict refusal to admit those who remained Jews to any high position in the state. Pablo de Santa María instigated laws separating Jews and Christians altogether. Part of his reasoning was apparently that to permit Jews political influence would be to permit them to argue that their own messianic hopes might yet be fulfilled in Spain.

Pablo did not deny the truth of apocalyptic expectations, but as a Christian, he could not permit them to be expounded by Jews. This would have prejudiced his own claim that his conversion was a sign that the Christian apocalyptic beliefs were true, not the Jewish ones. It was imperative for him that the unconverted Jews not be allowed to make their messianic claims in public. These could have been tolerated by the Old Christian nobility whose apocalyptic fervor, if any, stemmed in large part from non-Spanish sources such as Joachimism, or, at most, from Jewish ones introduced indirectly from abroad. But, the conversions of Vicente Ferrer's campaign changed this forever.

Hence, political issues were certainly involved in the religious debate between Spanish Christians and Jews and the reasons are two. The more basic one is concerned with the fulfillment of the prophecy of temporal dominion at the end of time. Both the Jews and the Christians believed it would be fulfilled in their respective religious communities.

Christians were required to attack Jewish messianic doctrine, and convince the Jews of the messiahship of Jesus, and the Jews' religion required them to resist this precisely because Jesus did not institute a political kingdom. An excellent example of this in the reign of Benedict in Spain was the Dispute of Tortosa (1413). This proselytizing effort was staged in the anti-pope's presence at the instigation of a former rabbi, Jerónimo de la Santa Fé, then Benedict's physician. The most important rabbis of Spain were forced to debate with Jerónimo who centered his attack on the Jews around the question of the messiahship of Jesus. The

---

532 ff. Also see: M.-M. Gorce, *Saint Vincent Ferrier (1350-1419)*. (Paris: Plon, 1924), especially pp. 195-198: Sigismund Brettle, *San Vicente Ferrer und sein literarischer Nachlass,* (Münster in Westf.: Aschendorffeschen Verlagsbuchhandlung, 1924), pp. 157 ff.; Le Roy E. Froom, *The Prophetic Faith of Our Fathers*, (Washington: Review and Herald, 1948), Four Vols., I, pp. 683 ff., and II, p. 67. Froom also treats Joachim of Flore and Lyra. Two works for the history of the Jews in Spain: Y. F. Baer, *A History of the Jews in Christian Spain,* (Philadelphia: The Jewish Publications Society of America [abbr. JPS], 1966), Two Vols., and, José Amador de los Ríos, *Historia social, política y religiosa de los Judíos de España y Portugal,* (Madrid, 1960). See also: Joaquín Carreras y Artau, "Arnaldo de Vilanova, apologista antijudaico," *Sefarad* (Madrid), VII (1947), pp. 49-62.

Jews regarded the central difference with Christianity as the problem of the temporal rewards due the Jews at the coming of the messiah. Jesus did not restore the Kingdom of Israel and this was, they said, sufficient evidence against Christianity. The messiah may have come, but if he did, he did not restore Israel and the rabbis could not accept anyone as messiah who did not.

Jewish history from the beginning is one of expectation of deliverance and for a long time one of expectation of a Liberator who will institute a political reign of peace for all men. The major exponent of this view in the late 15th and early 16th Centuries was Isaac Abravanel, the Sephardic or Spanish Jews' exiled leader, who proclaimed anew the proximity of the messianic coming in his own time. In a new exposition of the prophetic texts of Scripture, he refuted the Christian claims of the messiahship of Jesus and declared that far from this, the Christian age was only an extension of the fourth or Roman kingdom prophesied by Daniel. Christendom and Islam have been merely continuations of pagan Rome and the "little horn" of the fourth beast (Dan. 7) is the papacy, he said. Christianity is not the fifth or messianic kingdom precisely because it does not rule the whole world, according to him. This was also the general argument of Nachmanides against the ex-Jew Christiani at Barcelona in 1263, and the rabbis of Spain at Tortosa in the 15th Century, and it remains as a basis of the Jewish claim against Christianity to practice the true worship of God.[12]

This dispute between the Christians and Jews goes back in fact to the New Testament itself where the messiahship of Jesus is asserted without his having founded a temporal kingdom. Yet, one is promised in the future, and Jewish birth is not placed as a condition of participation in it. The rewards God promised the Jews were conditional upon observance of His commandments. St. Paul observed, however, that justification is by way of faith, for it was Abraham's faith that caused God to promise the world to his heirs (Rom. 4 : 13). But, though St. Paul stressed that in Christ there is no distinction between gentile and Jew, he did not deny that the Jewish Christians and gentile ones were indeed different. He insisted that the gentiles be humble, for at length, after the conversion of the pagans, Israel would be saved (Rom. 11: 25-26). The differences of the Jews and Christians on the nature of the apocalypse were and are theological, not political. But, during the close of the middle ages the

---

[12] Abba Hillel Silver, *A History of Messianic Speculation in Israel*, (New York: Macmillan, 1927), p. 116. B. Netanyahu, *Don Isaac Abravanel, Statesman and Philosopher*, (Philadelphia, JPS, 1953), pp. 213-215, 229.

Spanish Christian kings yielded to the temptation to settle the religious question by political means and destroyed Spanish Jewry.

This remarkable and very sad situation shows us that there were aspects of this religious debate that were much more political in nature than this Jewish-Christian debate which extends back to the New Testament. In fact, the religious question between the Christians and Jews of Spain was settled in a political way by the expulsion and destruction of Spanish Jewry in 1492. However, this and other events of that extraordinary year seemed to indicate that a new age was about to open for Christendom and it seemed a confirmation of her apocalyptic hopes. In 1492, Islam was driven from Iberia, America was discovered and a Spaniard, Alexander VI, was elected Pope.

The religious significance of these events depended in large part upon the expectations of the Spanish Jews, whether Christian or not. Since the apocalypse had been expected, many New Christians regarded themselves as the special reason for Spain's success in view of the fact that the temporal rewards Christians were to enjoy were conditional upon their conversion. Their participation in the events leading up to 1492 was not minimal. It was Jews and New Christians who encouraged the marriage of Fernando and Isabel. They paid for the fabulous pearl necklace that was Fernando's bethrothal gift in the hope that a strong monarchy would calm the violence over religious matters. It was they who financed Columbus' voyage the apocalyptic significance of which was clear even before he sailed. His sailing coincided with the sailing of the exiles and the admiral himself thought his windfall a providential happening of the last days. Fray Luis believed that the discovery of America was known to have to happen by the Jews and by Pablo de Santa María.[13]

A second religious aspect of the Spanish political situation has to do with the problem of the relation of the Decalog and natural law. This is so because of the variety of explanations that were offered for the events that were taking place. There were the traditional messianic hopes of Jews like Abravanel. There were the traditional apocalyptic expectations of the Old Christians, on the other hand, which, though they became cool in the 16th Century, were not necessarily connected with those of the

---

[13] Cecil Roth, *A History of the Marranos*, (New York: Meridian Books, 1959), p. 271. Froom, *Prophetic Faith*, II, pp. 159 ff. An early example of apocalyptic vision under Abravanel's influence is Samuel Usque's *Consolation for the Tribulations of Israel*, trans. by M. A. Cohen, (Philadelphia, JPS, 1965). *Magistri Luysii Legionensis Augustiniani Divinorum Librorum Primi apud Salmanticenses Interpretis Opera nunc primo ex Mss. ejusdem omnibus P.P. Augustiniensium studio edita*, (Salamanca: Episcopali Calatravae Collegio, 1891-1895), Seven Vols., III, pp. 153-158. This work will hereafter be referenced as Fray Luis, *Opera*.

Jews at all. In Spain, however, the confluence of these two traditions created an entirely new class of people among the New Christians, large numbers of whom were very cultivated, whose position vis-a-vis the other two groups was ambivalent.

Those people who saw the conversion of the Spanish Jews as significant in the apocalyptic process saw them as the remnant of the Jews referred to by St. Paul who would be the ones to be ultimately saved, and they saw in their conversion the manifestation of the divine plan in history. Those who did not see the conversion as essential in this process, e.g. the Jews and some Old Christians, were not committed to this view. It is in this context that we shall see that one of the characteritsic differences between Fray Luis and Domingo Soto is over the question of whether the law is promulgated.

Divine positive laws are, of course, promulgated in the Bible, civil and ecclesiastical laws are found in statute books. And, according to Thomists, the natural law is proclaimed in good civil laws and in political history. But, New Christians such as Fray Luis claimed that since the course of historical events was related to the conversion of the Spanish Jews, and would be influenced by the conversion of the rest of the Jews, then the moral law of the Jews and Christians must be identical as divine positive law, not just in pre-Christian Judaism, but even afterwards. Further, the basis of Christian morality could not just be reason's law, for this would obliterate the distinction of Jews and gentiles one finds insisted upon by St. Paul. It is here that the point of the dual formality of the Decalog is crucial. And, it is this problem of the relation of natural law and divine positive law in the Decalog which divides Soto and Fray Luis. This question is not a formally theological one for it divided Catholics, not Christians and Jews. Yet, it is religious in the material sense that it involves the philosophical interpretation of Catholic belief.

These two aspects of the religious-political problems of late medieval Spain must be kept separate from a third overtly political and possibly pseudo-religious problem of Spain which was developing in this period, that of racism.

Despite St. Paul's teaching of humility for the gentiles, it is a fact that the 15th Century and 16th Century in Spain were characterized by an increase of national pride, especially with the advent of the Hapsburg monarchy and the discovery of America. Pride of nobility became pride of race and religion and this was the source of much difficulty for the New Christians. By the 16th Century, *"limpieza,"* or proof of freedom from "taint" of Moorish, Jewish or heretical blood was required not only by the knightly orders, but the universities, the Inquisition, even by associations of artisans, some religious orders and like societies. Sánchez-Albornoz agrees with Castro that perhaps the origin of this racism is to be found among the convert Jews themselves. The one perhaps most responsible for it in the late 15th Century, Alfonso de Espina, was of Jewish descent. False documents of *"limpieza"* must have been rather easily obtained as evidenced by the fact that many of the most distinguished Spaniards of the era were of Jewish blood. In 1532, a law was sought to limit the proof of *"limpieza"* at four generations, and a book of that time tried to prove that most noblemen had Jewish and Moorish ancestors.[14] It has been asserted that the king had Jewish forebearers *via* the parentage of King Fernando.

It is important to note the pervasive character of the Inquisition and the extreme importance of the issues involved in it, whatever they were, for its contemporaries. One has only to read any of the works of H. C. Lea which document the significance of this institution in the daily life of those times. The Primate of Spain, Archbishop Carranza, was imprisoned for years for heresy. The Pope could not secure his release. Scandal after scandal was uncovered by the Inquisition which did not hesitate to find heresy in the highest places. The stigma attaching to anyone who had a Jew among any of the previous four generations of forebearers was suspicion of heresy. This indicates the enormous measure of civil liberties that were threatened by the Inquisition which could, by simple arrest, disappropriate, disinherit and financially ruin anyone, to say nothing of the social blemish incurred by himself and his family. Probably, nearly ten percent of the whole Spanish population of a number approaching ten million persons in the 16th Century was liable to this threat.

Descent from Jews was enough to have made one a political inferior in Spain at that time. One will have no trouble imagining the suspicion that practices associated with Mosaic Law would arouse, such as circumcision, special diet or celebration of Jewish holidays. However, it does not follow that theologians of the calibre of Domingo Soto, who denied the divine positive character of the Decalog and that promulgation is of the essence

---

[14] Ludwig Pfandl, *Introducción al siglo de oro,* (Barcelona: Araluce, 1959), p. 135. Sánchez-Albornoz, *Enigma histórico,* II, pp. 288, 135. Castro, *Realidad histórica,* pp. 48 ff. It might be of interest to point out that Pablo de Santa María composed a discourse on the *Origin and Nobility of His Lineage.* His prestige stemmed, as he claimed, not from any natural right, but from a divine right. To this day, Castro says, Sephardic Jews of Holland hold themselves superior to those of German families. In 1434, Alonso de Cartagena, Pablo's son, in a discourse before the Council of Basle, justified the preeminence of the King of Castile with respect to the King of England on grounds that the former's nobles were related to Christ.

of law, were racists or even necessarily partisans of the Inquisitorial policies. It is certain that the laws of Spain were racially discriminatory. The problem in evaluating the Inquisition, however, involves the religious justification for these laws. Supporters of the Inquisition and many of its critics hold that the Jewish converts were, in fact, insincere Christians and that the preservation of Catholicism demanded the persecution of those of Jewish origin. Baer sees no reason to believe that Catholicism should justify racism in its behalf. A recent scholar of the problem, B. Netanyahu, has good evidence to show that only a small percentage of the New Christians were secret Jews and that the lengths to which the Inquisition went could not be justified on religious grounds no matter what one's attitude to Catholicism. To him it was a case of anti-Semitic racism.[15]

Perhaps there is another alternative. The justifiability of the Inquisition may have been pseudo-religious for another reason besides the racist one. Soto's characteristic position which separates him from that of Fray Luis, was not one of race or religion. Their differences lay in their conceptions of Christian culture. This is a problem of expressing Catholic belief, not a difference of belief as such. For Fray Luis, the New Christian, all true Christian morality is based on a divine law given alike to Jews and gentiles, and for Soto, thought to have been an Old Christian, there was no necessity to ally gentile and Jewish culture in Christianity. In fact, he supposed the Jewish nation lost all its significance after the death of Jesus. This seemed to him the clear teaching of Aquinas. But, if Fray Luis' view was defensible theologically, and Soto's view was at all typical as we have reason to believe it was, then one could locate the reason for the Inquisition in cultural conflict, and not in race or in theology.

One of the lessons of this thesis is that, although Soto's theology may not have been racist, it did prejudice the New Christians' claims, also seemingly well founded in Aquinas, to the place of equals in Spanish society. Soto did not, on Thomistic grounds as he saw them, reconcile Jewish culture and past Christian practice. But, the prejudice was perhaps a cultural prejudice, not a theological or racial one. The problem of

[15] B. Netanyahu, *The Marranos of Spain,* (New York, American Academy for Jewish Research, 1966), pp. 3, 4, 235-245. Henry Charles Lea, *Chapters from the Religious History of Spain,* (New York: Burt Franklin, 1967). Salazar de Miranda, *Vida y subcesos del Illmo, y Rmo. Sr. Dn. Bartholmé Carranza y Miranda,* Romero Collection MSS, Library of the University of California, San Diego, 18th Century. For an account of the trial of Fray Luis' fellow defendent see: Miguel de la Pinta Llorente, O.S.A., *Proceso criminal contra el hebraísta salmantino Martín Martínez de Cantalapiedra,* (Madrid: CSIC, 1946). Albert A. Sicroff, *Les Controverses des Status de "Pureté de Sang" en Espagne du XVe au XVIIe Siècle,* (Paris: Didier, 1960).

the relation of morality and culture was, after 1492, a new one for moral philosophy. I believe Fray Luis, with Montaigne perhaps, was one of the first to offer a formal solution with the new understanding of human affairs.

Let us begin an examination of Fray Luis' theory of morality by briefly outlining the double heritage utilized by Fray Luis. On the one hand there was the Thomistic tradition that the Decalog is divine positive law. On the other, there was a Christian tradition of relying upon Hebraic literature in expressing the content of Christian moral doctrine to the Jews. These two traditions became unified in the Renaissance and appear to be proper reference points for interpreting the contribution of Fray Luis de León in the history of moral thought.

CHAPTER II

CHRISTIAN HEBRAISM:
ITS THOMISTIC BASES AND ITS PRESENCE IN LUIS DE LEÓN

There is a basis for the assertion that Fray Luis' moral doctrine is Hebraic in character. It was a part of Thomistic tradition in legal theory that the Decalog is divine positive law, as well as perhaps being St. Thomas' own belief. Fray Luis' position on this point will be developed in the next chapter.

In fact, there was an historical basis in Christian thought in general, and Thomistic thought in particular, for the relation of Hebraic, even cabalistical, themes and those of traditional Christian moral doctrine. Sections of Fray Luis' writings do suggest the presence of such Hebraisms and these may well be in line with previous Christian practice. Further examples of this will occur in Chapters Four and Five. With this background in mind, it will be possible to determine to what extent Fray Luis' own moral thought differs from that of traditional Thomism.

Although his dependence upon Aristotle is well known, it may not be necessary to insist that St. Thomas Aquinas espoused Aristotle's theory of the natural law as it applies to morals and politics. There are apparent internal discrepancies in St. Thomas which incline me to suppose that his theory of law grants the religious significance of the Decalog. There is such a discrepancy between *Summa Theologiae* (abbr. S.T.) I-II, 94, 2, (see also *Summa Contra Gentiles* III, 129) and I-II, 94, 4, as to whether the natural law is known intuitively without reasoning only in the first moral principle, or in certain derived propositions as well, such as the commands of the Decalog. Aquinas holds that the natural law is the same for all peoples only in the first principles, not in their detailed knowledge of it. Yet, he also says that the precepts of the Decalog can be derived by reason. He notes (S.T. I, 1, 1) that the rational creature needs revelation to know divine things, and (S.T. I-II, 98, 5) that the observance of the Mosaic sanctified the Jews who were bound to the moral law of the Decalog like all other men, but who knew it by revelation. This suggests that he does not intend to deny the need of a religious law in addition to what he calls the natural moral law. If so, this may help solve the problems of S.T. I-II, 94, since, though all can know the natural law, and are obliged to observe it, it is not through principles of reason only that men came to know it in fact, but that a religious context was, and is, required.

In addition to indications arising from the writings of Aquinas themselves, it is quite clear that early Thomists accepted the Decalog as divine positive law. It was Ramón de Peñafort, Master General of the Dominicans (1238-1240), who ordered both the composition of the *Summa Contra Gentiles* and the launching of an intellectual apostolate to the Jews and Moslems of Spain. The Dominicans opened schools to train missionaries in Tunis in 1250, and in Barcelona in 1281. Ramón Martín, O.P., whose book *Pugio Fidei* appeared in various forms in the Renaissance, labored in both these houses of study. The evidence that he composed it as a parallel to the effort of Aquinas is ample.[1]

Martín's approach to the Jews was direct. He was the source of the arguments used by Pablo Christiani in the celebrated debate with the great rabbi and cabalist, Moses ben Nachman (1194-c. 1270), held in Barcelona in 1263, before the king of Aragon. In an attempt to demonstrate that Jesus was the messiah of the Jews, he was forced to argue from Hebrew Scripture and rabbinical commentators exclusively. The *Pugio Fidei* represents, in part, the result of a minute scrutiny of the Talmuds, the Talmudic commentators, and the midrashim. Since the Jews considered untranslatable details of their language as theologically significant, the Dominicans were not loath to regard even rather late Jewish commentators as authoritative. Such were the medieval rabbis Moses ha-Darsan of Narbonne (fl. 1050), and Moses ben Nachman. The plan of the *Pugio Fidei* is scholastic and the main theses of Christian belief are stated and defended by an interpretation of the Jewish literature deemed appropriate.

The exact historical relation of Ramón Martín's *Pugio Fidei*, written in 1278, and Aquinas' *Summa Contra Gentiles* has been disputed. The best recent assessment of the problem of the obvious correspondence of the latter and the *"Pars Prima"* of the former is that of Tomás and Joaquín

---

[1] Raymundi Martini, O.P., *Pugio Fidei adversus Mauros et Judeos*, (Lipsiae, Lanckisi, 1687). This book has been reprinted by the Gregg Press, Farnsborough, Hants., England, 1967. A. Berthier, "Un Maître Orientaliste du XIIIe Siècle: Raymond Martin, O.P., *"Archivum Fratrum Praedicatorum* (Rome), VI (1936), pp. 267-311. Paul Vulliaud, *La Kabbale Juive*, (Paris: Nourry, 1923), Two Vols., II, pp. 147 ff. See also Father Eschmann's notes on the circumstances of the composition of the *Summa Contra Gentiles* in Etienne Gilson, *The Christian Philosophy of St. Thomas Aquinas*, (New York: Random House, 1956), pp. 385-388.

Carreras y Artau. In their book they carefully weigh the evidence proffered over the years since 1904, when the Arabist Miguel Asín Palacios asserted that St. Thomas had drawn upon Martín. They conclude that though Martín studied in Paris under Albert the Great, and was writing before Aquinas, there is better reason to suppose that Martín copied the work of the younger Aquinas who had already died by the date the *Pugio* itself sets as that of its composition.[2]

However, I think these authors are mistaken in their estimation of the doctrinal value of Martín's work and its possible relation with that of Aquinas on the divine positive character of the Decalog. All but the first part of the *Pugio Fidei* is omitted from consideration by them on the grounds that it argues almost exclusively in terms of Scriptural exegesis and is not of philosophic value, whereas the first part is directed against pagan philosophers with philosophical arguments taken from other authors. A close reading reveals, however, that Martín actually says that the arguments of the *"Pars Prima"* are addressed against pagans who do not have the natural law.[3] They are not directed against those who claim to observe the law, and these he lists as the Jews, Christians and Saracens. Martín does attack certain Aristotelians with regard to such issues as the ability to rationally prove that God can know singulars and the immortality of the individual soul as the Carreras' say.[4] But they are obviously wrong in their assumption that Martín was writing as a Christian against Moslems and Jews on rational grounds alone.

In fact, Martín does not claim to oppose Judaism or Islam, but rather he claims to represent their positions insofar as they claim to be observers of the natural law. Therefore, this first part is definitely connected philosophically with the others.

[2] Tomás y Joaquin Carreras y Artau, *Historia de la filosofía española.* (Madrid: Real Academia de Ciencias Exactas, Fisicas y Naturales, 1943), Two Vols, I, pp. 164 ff. Father Luis Getino replied to Asín in 1905, maintaining the priority of Aquinas. Getino's position seems to be secured by parts of an unpublished lecture of 1929, of Canon José M. Llovera printed by the Carreras' noting that the *Pugio* has a pronoun referring to the author of the texts in question, obviously Aquinas. One can read Asín's assertion in: Miguel Asín Palacios, *Huellas del Islam,* (Madrid: Espasa-Calpe, 1941), p. 67. None of this answers Asín Palacios' most important point, that Aquinas took from Averroes the thesis of the harmony of faith and reason which remain formally distinct. One can find support for the position that in St. Thomas the Decalog binds as divine positive law as well as natural law, in the work of this distinguished scholar.

[3] Martín, *Pugio Fidei,* I, 1, 1-3., "Viam verae fidei et veritatis errantium turba, licet quodammodo fit incomprehensibilis, et infinita, potest tamen quodammodo sub duplici distinctione concludi. Quicunque enim a fidei veritate exorbitant, vel sunt habentes legem, vel minime legem nisi naturalem habentes. . . . qui non habent legem . . . vel temporales, vel naturales, vel philosophi, . . . Denique legem habentes, vel sibi legis vocabulum arrogantes, aut sunt Judei, aut Christiani, aut Saraceni.

[4] Carreras, *Historia de la filosofía,* I, pp. 159-160.

This is so because the natural law as it is understood in this first part is not something to be found in "gentile" (i.e. non-Christian) philosophy, but only in revealed religion which accepts the Decalog as divine law. This is what the Jews, Christians and Saracens have in common, Martín thinks. The *Pugio Fidei,* as a whole, is directed to them with the assumption that they will agree on the matter of the basic precepts of the natural law against those who will not accept the necessity of any divine revelation beyond reason. This provides a starting point for religious discussion in which only members of the three religions can participate, certainly not pagans. He concedes to the Jews, throughout the book, that only Scriptural and Hebrew exegetical works can be adduced to convince them of Christian belief, though he expects them to allow, without question, that belief and reason are not mutually exclusive sources of truth. As Aquinas himself supposes, I believe, the minimum which Martín expects is that the Jews will concede that the contents of the moral part of the divine positive law are the same as those of the natural law and are not reason's law alone.

This being the case, the whole of the *Pugio Fidei* is philosophically consistent on the point of its concession to the special role of a religious basis for moral practice in Christianity. Since the Christians claim to be the true observers of the divine law, it is not out of line for Martín to try to convince the Jews that this is so from their own religious authorities. The assertion that the *Pugio Fidei* is inconsistent is also belied by the use it had by men of superior philosophical ability, like Pascal and Bossuet, for over 500 years. The Carreras's class it with polemical literature like that of Pablo de Santa María and Alfonso de Espina. I object that it cannot be compared with the latter's *Fortalium Fidei* which expressly denies what the *Pugio Fidei* supposes, the indispensable nature of revealed law in its moral precepts.[5]

---

[5] The history of the *Pugio Fidei* is a long one. It was used for polemical purposes for centuries, by Victor Porchetus de Salvaticis in his *Victoria contra Judeos* (1303), by Jerónimo de Santa Fé and by Alfonso de Zamora at Alcalá, perhaps not more than 30 years before Fray Luis studied there. It was drawn upon by Pietro Galatino, O.F.M. (1460-1520), confessor to Leo X, in his *De Arcanis* written to defend Reuchlin, a work used by Fray Luis, Cardinal Seripando, Alfonso de Mendoza and others. Scaliger found in 1603 that Galatino's work was composed in part of large sections of the *Pugio Fidei* mixed with cabalistical and pseudo-cabalistical literature in an effort to prove Jesus was the Messiah from Jewish texts. Fray Luis may have also known of the forgery since he seems to have used portions of the *Pugio Fidei* not found in Galatino or Alfonso de Zamora. He may not have used it himself for it might well have been copied in other works. Alonso de Orozco may have used it in the 1560's as the appendix indicates. The *Pugio Fidei* was very rare until published in 1651 by Joseph Voysin. The best known edition is Carpzov's 1687 reprint. Portions of it were used by Pascal in the *Pensées* around 1658-1659. Voysin made public the Galatino forgery. Moore has shown that the pronunciation of the word "Jehova" stems from a variant

There are indications that other Spanish Thomists accepted the Decalog as divine positive law. The most influential Spanish theologian of the late 14th and early 15th Centuries was, perhaps, Fray Vicente Ferrer who, as was mentioned, inspired the campaign to convert the Jews of his time, an event which altered the course of Spanish history, as did his support of the anti-pope Benedict XIII. By far the most notable convert of Fray Vicente was Salomon ha-Levi, rabbi of Burgos. Baer and Amador de los Ríos believe the story that he was converted while listening to Fray Vicente preach in 1390, upon the Old Law according to the doctrine of St. Thomas.[6]

We do not know what was said, but we do know that the rabbi, baptized as Pablo de Santa María, regarded Christianity as the true Judaism and never abandoned his belief in the political significance of the conversion of the Spanish Jews. Hence, he probably interpreted St. Thomas as meaning that the moral law of the Decalog was not only natural law, but also divine positive law given to gentiles and Jews equally.

On these grounds he seems to have defended the political importance

---

of one of the manuscripts of the *Pugio Fidei* and the very general use of this word in the 16th Century indicates its influence as a source of knowledge of Jewish lore among both Catholics and Protestants. On these matters one should see: Federico Pérez Castro, *El manuscrito apologético de Alfonso de Zamora,* (Madrid: CSIC, 1950). José Llamas, "Documental inedito de exégesis rabinica en antiguas universidades españolas," *Sefarad,* VI (1946), pp. 289-311. George Moore, "Notes on the Name IHWH," *American Journal of Theology,* XII (1908), pp. 34-52. François Secret, "Notes pour une Histoire du *Pugio Fidei* à la Renaissance," *Sefarad,* XX (1960), pp. 401-407, and "Girolamo Seripando et la Kabbale," *Rinascimento* (Florence), XIV (1963), pp. 254 ff. Eusebio Cuevas, O.S.A., "Fr. Alfonso de Mendoza, agustino, primer tratadista de Cristo-Rey," *La Ciudad de Dios,* XLIV (1942), p. 349. Pietro Galatino, *De Arcanis Catholicae Veritatis,* (Frankfort, 1612). The first edition was at Ortona, 1518.

[6] Johann Christoph Wolfll, *Bibliotheca Hebraea,* (Hamburg: Liebezeit, 1715), Four Vols., I, p. 963, refers to the episode of Pablo de Santa María's conversion. It is not without interest to note that a writing of Vicente Ferrer of 1414, gives some indication of his position. In his *Tractatus contra Perfidiam Judaeorum,* written at Tortosa, he gives as one of the signs that Christ has come the fact that the Jews no longer have a priesthood and sacrifice, temple, feasts, etc. This he says is a sign that the Old Law is no longer in effect since a priest is a minister of the law. With the cessation of the law, there is a cessation of its function, in this case the priesthood of the Old Law. The termination of the Kingdom of Juda and prophecy are also such signs against the Old Law being in effect. These institutions were the agencies of the administration of the divine positive law of the Jews, and *a fortiori* must have been regarded by Fray Vicente as having their counterparts in the New Law. Thus, the moral law of Christianity must also be a religious law insofar as it accords with the functions of Christian kingship and priesthood. See: Le Père Fages, O.P., ed. *Oeuvres de Saint Vincent Ferrier,* (Paris: Picard, 1909), Two Vols., I, pp. 16-23; See also: Manuel García Miralles, O.P., "San Vicente Ferrer, Anotador de Sto. Tomás," *Revista Española de Teología,* XV, (1955), pp. 452-453, where Ferrer states that the Decalog binds as divine positive law.

of the Jews' conversion. Whereas the "unfaithful Jews" as he called them, believed that the power of Spain was connected with their presence, Pablo replied that he considered his conversion as providential for Spain, for the destiny of the Jews would be fulfilled in them as Christians. In the special case of Christian law, law and the morality of the gentiles and Jews were joined. Contrary to Aristotle's teaching (*Nic. Eth. V, 7, 1134b*), this was a case of two laws with a single justice. Legal justice and moral justice had to be the same for gentile and Jewish Christians.[7]

This concept of equality under a single Christian law was developed by Alonso de Cartagena (1385-1456), son of Pablo de Santa María, also bishop of Burgos and notable at the Council of Basle. He wrote a treatise in favor of the convert Jews whose position in society was being weakened by increasing suspicion of their orthodoxy and anti-Semitic violence. He did not hesitate to quote St. Thomas (S.T. I-II, 98, 5) in favor of the views of his father on the special role of the Jews in history.

According to Alonso, the Old Law and the New do not differ as to their purposes. The moral commands of the Old Law are not, as Soto would later have it, mere deductions from the law of nature. But, they have special significance in that their observance sanctified the people in expectation of Christ. The Old and New Laws differ, not as natural law and divine positive law in their moral commands, but only as the New Law more directly confers sanctity. The Old Law did so only by way of expectation, or as he says, as a "teacher of children."

The Jews, then, had a special destiny in history and their law was the same as that of Christ in this regard, though not in the manner of its promulgation. There can be no Christian history without Jewish history. This was Alonso's point, there can be no difference between Christians, whether Hebrew or not.[8]

When did this interpretation of the relation of natural law and divine positive law in the Decalog change? Perhaps it was under the influence of Latin Averroism. Seemingly, it was not generally altered in Spain until at least two hundred years after Aquinas. There appeared in 1459, the work which was the proximate source of much woe for Jews, both Christian

---

[7] Pablo de Santa María, *Scrutinium Scripturarum*, (Mantua, 1475). Francisco Cantera Burgos, *Alvar Garcia de Santa María y su familia de conversos*, (Madrid: CSIC, 1952). Luciano Serrano, O.S.B., *Los conversos D. Pablo de Santa María y D. Alfonso de Cartagena*, (Madrid, CSIC, 1942).

[8] Alonso de Cartagena, *Defensorium Unitatis Christianae*, ed. by Manuel Alonso, S.J., (Madrid: CSIC, 1943), pp. 72-77. Aeneas Silvius, later Pope Pius II, said that Alonso was "... the splendor of prelates, ... delight of Spain, ... mirror of science." Martin Grabmann, *Historia de teología católica*, additions by David Gutiérrez, O.S.A., (Madrid: Espasa-Calpe, 1946), p. 152.

and non-Christian. This was the *Fortalium Fidei* of Alfonso de Espina (d. c. 1491), a converted Jew and Franciscan who had risen to high places in the state, Church, and University. He inspired in the name of orthodoxy a persecution of Jews that was to last for centuries. He changed the nomenclature of Jews introduced by Pablo de Santa María and drawn from the teaching of Vicente Ferrer and of Aquinas. Whereas Jews had been called "faithful" and "unfaithful" they were now called "public" and "secret." As Baer says, his purpose was very clear, the establishment of the Inquisition and the expulsion of those retaining Jewish cultural identity from Spain.[9]

The change of attitude generally provoked by Alfonso de Espina was not necessarily a change in the Thomistic tradition, at least not at that time, for he could well have based his own ideas in Occamism in which theory the Decalog is dispensable, and, incapable of being distinguished from reason's law.

Espina proposed that Spain suffered under Jewish subversion as had England, insinuating that the solution was expulsion. By comparing Christian practice in Spain, with its many ex-Jews, to that of the rest of Europe, he insinuated that these New Christians were heretics and needed control. At his instigation, an inquisition was established for this purpose.[10]

The key part of his intellectual attack was his denial that the moral part of the Law of Moses endured as divine positive law in Christianity.[11] It is this proposition that we find under discussion in the 16th Century.

Fray Luis agreed with Ramón Martín and the Santa Marías on the matter of the Thomistic interpretation of the relation of the divine positive law of the Decalog and natural law. The problem here is not to discuss this issue in itself, but to show that it is related historically to another similarity that exists between the writings of Martín and Luis de León. The exact mode of Fray Luis' knowledge of the *Pugio Fidei* is not known, but that he knew it seems likely if one is to judge from a parallel reading of their works.[12] As for Martín, Jewish literature seems to afford Fray

[9] Baer, *History of the Jews*, II, p. 284.

[10] Baer supposes that Espina's accusations that the Jews committed dreadful crimes against Christians were false, but he seems to take as true the view that Espina's evidence of Judaic practices among New Christians implies that they were "secret" Jews. Expecting Christ to soon reappear, even among Jews, and the practice of circumcision were not considered as evidence of heresy by such authorities as Cajetan, Vitoria, or Egidio da Viterbo.

[11] Alfonso de Espina, *Fortalium Fidei contra Judeos, Saracenos, aliosque Christianae fidei inimicos,* (Nuremberg: A. Koberger, 1494), pp. 11, 15, 83.

[12] See Appendix I.

Luis a means of expressing central features of Christian doctrine. Like Martín he seems to wish to indicate the spiritual and non-racial character of Christianity by showing the appropriateness of the use of Hebraic literary themes in Christian dogmatic expression as well as by indicating that the observance of the natural law by Christians is related to divine positive law as the Jews claim their law is.

To judge from the texts presented in the appendix, Fray Luis' interpretation of Canticles has elements seemingly drawn from the *Pugio Fidei*. But their similarity in using Hebrew literature does not end with similarity of texts, but goes beyond this to a difference which shows them to be men of different ages, though of similar interests.

Many of his similarities with Fray Luis' commentary on Canticles stem from Martín's having used the Hebrew midrash, or ancient rabbinical commentary, on Canticles, called *Sir ha Sirim Rabba*. Fray Luis, however, seems to draw also upon cabalistical themes in his treatment of Canticles which are not present in the *Pugio Fidei* either because they were not developed yet, or because they were introduced into the Christian world at a much later time.

Cabalism is the most important form of Jewish mysticism. Though its roots are very ancient, its most significant development occurred in the Spanish Hebrew communities of the 13th Century. It became generally known in the world of Christian scholarship through the efforts of such figures as Giovanni Pico and the Swabian Hebraists Johannes Reuchlin in the late 15th Century. It is embodied in a literature that is distinct from Jewish literature of earlier times such as the Talmudic and midrashic writings, and, of course, the Bible itself. However, after its appearance in medieval Spain, it was taken by many to represent a tradition of great antiquity and of comparable authority with other post-Mosaic Hebrew literature. Christian reaction to cabalism was, notably, quite varied.

Father Ricard Simon, the founder of what came to be known as higher criticism of the Bible, though he was not a cabalist, declared in the 1680's that it was impossible to understand Christian religion and its foundations without a knowledge of that of the Jews, including cabala. A century earlier in Spain, Juan de Mariana (1535-1624) had declared its value in exegesis as had Sixtus of Sienna, O.P. (1520-1569), in Italy. Francisco de Ribera, S.J., Fray Luis' contemporary rejected it as useless and, at the turn of the century, Martín del Rio, S.J., was suspicious of it. Whether it should be used by Catholics was a question dividing Catholic Biblical exegetes in the 16th and 17th Centuries.[13]

[13] Secret, *Kabbalistes Chrétiens,* p. 126. D. F. Walker, *Spiritual and Demonic*

Perhaps a general description of cabalism's main features will be helpful in pointing out their appearance in Fray Luis' works. Jewish mysticism is speculation on the essence of the Torah or Law of Moses in the first books of the Bible. This is just as Christian mysticism is about the Bible or Moslem mysticism is about the Koran. The essential part of cabalism, Jewish mysticism's most important form, is, according to Gershom Scholem, that it takes as the object of its study the world of divine emanations or Sephiroth in which the creative power of God is deployed. These ten emanations are identified with ten names for God in Hebrew and so the hidden world of God is also a world of language. The letters of that language are in those of Scripture, but they are not ordinary modes of communication. Nor are they simply configurations of divine power. Rather, there is a parallelism between the world of creation and the world of language.[14] Creation is reflected in two worlds, that of the Sephiroth and the letters of Scripture, and that of nature.

The magical character of the Torah and the importance of the name of God is a very old idea in Judaism and is supposed in the midrashim, one of which declares that God created the world on the model of the Torah. This idea was developed in a new way in 13th Century cabalism. The Torah was called the "primordial Torah" and was identified with the wisdom of God, called *Hokhmah,* the second emanation of the hidden being that is God. According to the 13th Century cabalist, Joseph Gikatila, the Torah is really an explication of the name YHWH which is like God, hidden in that it cannot be pronounced. The Torah's deepest meaning, then, is as a weaving of this name, or its letters. The Torah or Law

Magic from Ficino to Campanella, (London: Warburg Institute, 1958), has a survey of authors on cabala. Christian cabalistic interpretations were still acceptable in Fray Luis' day if one is to judge by several such works dedicated to Pope Gregory XIII (1572-1585). François Secret, "Le *Tractatus de Ano Jubilaei* de Lazaro de Viterbo. Grégoire XIII et la Kabbale Chrétienne," *Rinascimento,* XVI (1966), pp. 305-333. For cabalism's influence on contemporary music see: E. E. Lowinsky, *Secret Chromatic Art in the Netherlands Motet,* (New York: Russell and Russell, 1946), pp. 137 ff. It was Jewish historians of the 19th Century who discovered that cabalism's main books date only from the 13th Century, though the books themselves, such as the *Zohar,* claim to contain a Mosaic oral revelation or tradition (hence the word "cabala") handed down among the leaders of the Jews over the centuries. See: Vuillard, *Kabbale Juive,* I, pp. 7 ff. E. Amann, ed. *Dictionnaire de Théologie Catholique,* (Paris: Letouzey, 1941), XIV, cols. 703-707.

[14] It is to Scholem's works that I owe my knowledge of Jewish cabalism. Scholem does not write on Christian cabalism. I hope I adequately express some of his ideas. Edward J. Schuster, "Fray Luis de León and the Linguistic Approach to Epistemology," *The Kentucky Foreign Language Quarterly,* VI, (1959), pp. 195-200, notes this theory of parallelism in Fray Luis, but I do not think he entertains the possibility of its cabalistic significance. Gershom G. Scholem, "La Signification de la Loi dans la Mystique Juive," *Diogène* (Paris), XIV (1956), pp. 45-60, and XV (1957), pp. 76-114.

is a web of divine names or attributes. Furthermore, the cabalistic mystic sees the Torah as alive and active as God is. It is an organism with the name YHWH as its fundamental structure. The Law, then, is the living name of God.

Scholem says that the idea that the Law is a structure with life is older than Spanish cabalism. The idea that the Torah is a name and that the name is like a living organism was later established by the rabbis of Gerona (near Barcelona, Spain). In the *Zohar* of Moses of Leon (d. 1305), the main cabalistic text, the Torah is called a tree with branches, roots, trunk, etc. From this idea, another cabalist of the time declared that the Torah is a body with head, heart, mouth, and other members. These were made to parallel a mystic conception of the community of Israel. So the cabalists considered the mystical organism of the Torah, which materializes the Name of God as parallel to the mystical body of the people of Israel which is thereby not only considered as the historical organism of the Jewish nation, but, as Scholem says, as an esoteric symbol of the *Shekinah* or presence of God itself. Jews of the historical nation are members of the divine presence to man.

Analogous themes are found in Fray Luis. His special regard for the Hebrew Scriptures as well as his theory of the special naming qualities of Hebrew have been noted by Schuster and others. But it is also the historical aspect of cabalism he makes central to his interpretation of Canticles. Here the Jewish people are identified mystically with the Church. They are one stage of the Church's historical growth. We find him relating passages in Canticles which either describe the body of the bride or have to do with the body of the lover or bridegroom as connected with the Jews or the Christian Church.[15] We find him explaining that the litter of Solomon (Cant. 3:7) is the disposition of the camp of the Israelites in the desert. The Midrash on Canticles does not detail the correspondence of the various portions of the camp as Fray Luis does, but rather associates it with the priestly blessing of Num. 6: 24-26, which mentions the all important Name. Fray Luis says that the litter, standing for the Jews, is Solomon's becaue the king is really Christ who will lie there. The same imagery is used in when Fray Luis has the bridegroom praising the camp of the Israelites as though it were a woman, comparing the various parts of the camp to the four groups of the Twelve Tribes as though they were features of the female body. Moses and Aaron are the breasts as the midrash quoted in the *Pugio Fidei* indicates. But the other

[15] See Appendix I-II for details and texts.

features such as the eyes, the hair, the lips, and neck are also cabalistic features of the kind described by Scholem.

That the divine presence is to be found in the Jews is said by Fray Luis to be symbolized by the ark being in the center of the camp of the Israelites. The ark is in the interior part of the Tabernacle and it is where God, who burns with love of the Jews, resides. According to Fray Luis, the presence of God is manifested in Christian charity now, just as God was present in the Jews because of His presence in the ark. Christ himself is said to be described in Canticles (Cant. 5: 10-16) and the Zoharic derivation of this exegesis seems quite clear. The aroma of the spice garden (Cant. 6: 2) is that of the ways of Christ's love, says Fray Luis.

The attributes of the camp are transferred to the Church in the commentary on another description of the bride (Cant. 7: 1-9). Here Peter and Paul are the breasts, the Doctors are the neck, the feet are missionaries, the belly is spiritual richness, and so forth.

What seems to be implied is that the Jews know, by cabala perhaps, that the Law is spiritual, and that the Christian Church is the authentic Israel and that the love of God showed to the Jews in the Old Law is the same love he continues to show them in Christ and the Church. This is evidenced by the extraordinary explanation of another text (Cant. 7: 5), where Christ is the head of the body, but also a mountain of infinite goodness. This idea is, perhaps, from the *Pugio Fidei* and is developed in the *Nombre de Cristo: "Monte."* The purple hairs of the head are the images of the charity of the early Church. As the king is bound in channels, as those of a palace through which water runs, so Christ and the Church are tolerant of adversity. The influence of cabalism on this imagery may be further indicated by the fact that Christ's body is presented as that of an androgyn, for the Church is but the female part or one aspect of the body of Christ who is the head.[16]

Would there have been precedents for Fray Luis' use of Hebraic rabbinical and cabalistical imagery? Elements of cabalism and Jewish

---

[16] The idea that the names of God and the parts of the body and the description of the Israelites' camp are related is found in H. C. Agrippa von Nettesheim, though the account of the correspondence of the bodily parts, the points of the compass and the Tribes is not quite the same as Fray Luis'. The historical significance of the Name of God, with a letter added to make it correspond to the name of Jesus, is found in Reuchlin's *De Verbo Mirifico,* reproduced in Pistorius' anthology. See fn. 22. It is also in Michael Aitsinger's *Pentaplus Regnorum Mundi,* (Antwerp: Cris. Plantin, 1579), which supposes the identity of the body of the Church and the body of Israel and charts with elaborate graphs how cabalistical prophecies correspond with world history. Henricus Cornelius Agrippa ab Nettesheym, *De Occulta Philosophiae,* (Graz: Akademischer Druck, 1967), pp. 122, 123, 144, 145. This is a reprint of the 1533 edition with explanatory material and photographs of Renaissance cabalistical artifacts.

exegesis were known to Christians and used for apologetic purposes long before the Renaissance, though it was then that the classic cabalistic books became generally known and studied. One finds an interpretation of Scripture based on the significance of letters, which are also numbers in Hebrew, in Jerome and Rabanus Maurus. Aquinas, though he was not a philologist, was aware of the usefulness of exegesis based on Hebrew letters.

Ramón Martín had used rabbinical commentaries in an attempt to show that the main beliefs of Christianity can be verified in them and implied that the Jews were guilty not only of denying the truth of their own Scriptures, but also of their own exegesis. He did this, for example, by trying to show that the Jews of early times expected spiritual as well as temporal rewards for observance of the Law. The Christians who used his work hoped this would provide a basis upon which the Jews would accept the gospel.

Pedro Alfonso, a rabbi who converted in 1106, used such devices as letters with spiritual meaning against Jews in Spain. Joachim of Flore used them and there are many examples of this kind of argument in the *Pugio Fidei,* in Martín's pupil, Arnold of Villanova (1235?-1313?), in Nicolas of Cusa (1401-1464) and Lyra. The cabalist, Abraham ben Samuel Abulafia (1240-1284), set off to convert Pope Nicolas III to Judaism by using them. King Alfonso the Wise (d. 1284) wished to translate the cabalistic books as well as the Koran and the Talmud, an indication of the level of importance they had in those times.

The study of Hebrew and Jewish mysticism and cabala later made more headway among Christians right into the 16th Century. Secret notes the German Dominican who studied in Spain, Peter Schwarz (Nigri) who published his cabalistic *Stella Messiae* in Cologne in 1475. The most fascinating evidence that cabala was very fashionable indeed is the *Sermo de Passione Domini* preached before the court of Pope Sixtus IV on Good Friday, 1481. The preacher was one Flavius Guillelmus Ramundus Mithridates, a Jewish convert, cabalist and teacher of the famous humanist, Giovanni Pico della Mirandola (1463-1494). His spirit is that of Martín whom he follows in Christological interpretation of Jewish literature. The study of Hebrew and cabala did not go unopposed. Although as early as 1312, the Council of Vienne had decreed that Hebrew was to be taught at Paris, Oxford, Salamanca, and Bologna, this was not implemented. One of the first of these teachers, in the late 15th and early 16th Centuries was the cabalist Johannes Reuchlin (1455-1522) who was most responsible for the spread of Hebrew culture in

Christian Europe. He defended the use of the books of the Talmud and cabala for Christian purposes and was often instrumental in preserving them from the fires. His efforts earned him the emnity of the Dominicans of Cologne who, having failed to have his works condemned in Germany because of the favorable intervention of Pope Leo X, obtained such a condemnation from the University of Paris in 1514. Nevertheless, the Paris theological faculty was not agreed in this matter and Reuchlin continued to have many supporters. The Roman Curia took no judicial action against him.[17]

Insofar as he was a Thomist, the case of Peter Schwarz is evidence that perhaps cabalism and Thomism were not inconsistent in those days. But, surely few Renaissance Thomists were cabalists. Peter Ciruelo published in 1538, at Salamanca, a detailed criticism of the use of cabala by Christians. This man was a collaborator of Alfonso de Zamora (d. 1531) in the production of the Alcalá Polyglot Bible and perhaps he was attempting to resist cabalism among such New Christians as Alfonso. He evidenced a knowledge of the major works on the subject written in Germany and Italy, and the significance of this work is not only what works were known to him, but such a response constitutes an indication of the prevalence of the influence of Italian and German Christian cabalists in Spain.

The possibility of cabalism returning to Spain in a Christianized form *via* Italian sources is further suggested by Egidio da Viterbo's visit there as papal legate (1518-1519), the year after the composition of his first cabalistic work. Perhaps one of the first to link cabalism and the teaching of Aquinas was the Dalmatian Giorgio Benigno de Salviatis (d. 1520), the teacher of the Florentine Pope Leo X's brother, Pietro de Medici.[18]

[17] François Secret, "Les Débuts du Kabbalisme Chrétien en Espagne et son Histoire à la Renaissance," *Sefarad*, XVII (1957), pp. 36-48. Chaim Wirszubski, ed., *Flavius Mithridates Sermo de Passione Domini*, (Jerusalem: Israel Academy of Sciences and Humanities, 1963). François Secret, "L'Interpretazione della Kabbala nel Rinascimento," *Convivium* (Turin), XXIV (1956), pp. 551 ff. S. A. Hirsch, "Johann Reuchlin: The Father of the Study of Hebrew among the Christians," *The Jewish Quarterly Review*, VIII (1896), pp. 445-470. Augustin Renaudet, *Préréforme et Humanisme à Paris*, (Paris: D'Argences, 1953), pp. 645 ff. François Secret, "Pedro Ciruelo: Critique de la Kabbale et de Son Usage par les Chrétiens," *Sefarad*, XIX (1959), pp. 48-77.

[18] Another celebrated cabalist of the day was Galatino. See: Arduinus Kleinhans, O.F.M., "De Vita et Operibus Petri Galatini, O.F.M.," *Antonianum* (Rome), I (1926), pp. 145-197, 327-356. Francis X. Martin, O.S.A., "The Problem of Egidio da Viterbo, a Historical Survey," *Augustiniana* (Heverlee, Belgium), IX, X (1960), pp. 357-379, 43-60. On Benigno see: S. Gliubich, *Dizionario Biografico degli Uomini Illustri della Dalmazia*, (Vienna: Rod. Lechner, 1856), p. 28. Giovanni B. Picotti, *La Giovinezza di Leone X*, (Milan: Hoepli, 1927), pp. 22, 23, 55. Giorgio Benigno de Salviatis, *Dialectica nova secundum mentem Doctoris subtilis; et beati Thomae Aquinatis aliorumque realistorum*, (Florence, 1488). These men were predicting the

Another important student of cabala of this period was Cardinal Girolamo Seripando. He seems to have been at once a cabalist and a Thomist. Yet, because of his possible significance in the development of Fray Luis' moral thought, a more complete discussion of him will be reserved for Chapter Five, though he should be at least mentioned here.

The earlier Christian usage of cabala, and Jewish materials in general, seems to have been of a polemical nature, at least primarily. It was an attempt to develop an interpretation of Scripture upon which both Christians and Jews could agree. Giovanni Pico della Mirandola, at least by his own claim, first expanded the established principles of Christian exegesis to include cabala. He listed the four Augustinian types of interpretation and explained that the three Jewish ones, including cabala, were sub-classes of these. In his *Apology for Thirteen Questions* he wrote on the question of natural magic and cabala and expressed this idea clearly. One of his primary interests in this work was to show that the best proof of Jesus' claim to divinity was his excellent knowledge of cabala, especially the physical interpretation of Scripture by which Pico thought the cabalist could gain control over physical nature.[19]

apocalypse and reform. Perhaps these interests were connected in the visit of the great authority of the time on cabala, H. C. Agrippa von Nettesheim (1486-1535) to the Council of Pisa (1511-1512) at the request of Cardinal Bernardino Caravajal, whose Jewish descent and interest in occultism are known. He attempted, with the blessing of the French king and the Emperor, to hold a Council anticipating the death of Julius II, who was gravely ill, for the purpose of Church reform. Julius recovered called his own Council at the Lateran for 1512, which opened with an appeal for reform by Egidio da Viterbo. Caravajal was degraded by Julius, but one of the first acts of Leo X was to restore him in 1513, and he died as Dean of the Sacred College in 1523. L. Sandret, "Le Concile de Pise (1511)," *Revue des Questions Historiques,* XXXIV (1883), pp. 425-456. It is interesting that Caravajal, as legate to Rome, delivered a discourse in 1492, calling for reform of the Church. After the election of Alexander VI, he delivered another pledging the loyalty of the Spanish monarchs to the Church. This address, another reform appeal, is one of the earliest references to Columbus' discoveries which are mentioned to the Pope in connection with the messianic prophecy of Isaiah 11, with reference to which he said that the Spanish lion is not only charged with evangelizing the Indians but also is made to lie at the feet of the Pope by the inspiration of the Infant Jesus with whose aid he wishes the Pope to obtain eternal glory. Bernardini Carvjal, "Oratio de Eligendo Summo Pontifice," *Thesaurus Novus Anecdotorum,* ed. by E. Martène and U. Durand, (Paris, 1717), Tome II, pp. 1775-1787. H. Harrisse, "Un Rarissme Americanum," *Bulletin du Bibliophile et du Bibliothécaire,* (1897), pp. 71-76.

[19] Picus Mirandulanus (J.), *Opera,* (Bologna: B. Hectores, 1496), unpaginated. Est autem ulterius sciendum quod ista expositio bibliae proportionatur modo exponendi bibliam qui apud nos dictus anagogicus. Sicut enim apud nos sive allegoricus, tropologicus, et anagogicus. Ita est et apud hebreos litteralis apud eos dicitur Pesat quem modum tenet apud eos Rabi Salomon, Chemoy et similes. Allegoricus Midras unde sepe apud eos audies Midras ruth Midrastillym Midras coaleth, . . . et sic de aliis. Et istum modum sequuntur maxime doctores Talmutici. Tropologicus dicitur sehel, quem sequuntur Abraam abnazara, ubi litteraliter non exponit et Levibengerson et multi alii et ante omnes Rabi Moyses egypticus. Anagogicus dicitur cabala, et hoc quia illa expositio quae dicitur ore dei tradita Moysi et accepta per aeccessionem

As Scholem has observed, there was good reason for such a supposition. The similarity between traditional Christian and Jewish interpretive methods is striking. An early midrash, says Scholem, compares the Torah to a nut because it has layers of meaning like the layers of a nut, the shell and the meat: and, one finds precisely the same metaphor in Joachim of Flore.[20]

The expression of this notion in the *Zohar* is contained in a section very suggestive of themes in Fray Luis and Santa Teresa.

She the Torah is like unto a beautiful and stately damsel, who is hidden in a secluded chamber of a palace and who has a lover of whom no one knows but she. . . . She opens a little door in her hidden palace, discloses for a moment her face to her lover, then swiftly hides it again. . . . She knows that he who is wise of heart daily haunts the gates of her house. . . . No one understands her message save he alone, and he is drawn to her with heart and soul and all his being. . . . When he comes to her she begins to speak to him, first from behind the curtain which she has spread for him about her words suitable to his mode of understanding, so that he may progress little by little. This is called "Derasha" [Talmudic casuistry]. Then she speaks to him from behind a thin veil of finger mesh, discoursing riddles and parables which go by the name *Haggadah*. When at last he is familiar with her she shows herself to him face to face and converses with him concerning all her hidden mysteries and all the mysterious ways which have been secreted in her heart from time immemorial. Then such a man is a true adept in the Torah, a "master of the house," since she has revealed to him all her mysteries, withholding and hiding nothing.[21]

According to Scholem, the term *"Haggadah"* of this text designates

modo praedicto quasi semper sensum sequitur anagogicum qui etiam inter omnes est sublimior et divinior sursum nos ducens a terrenis ad coelestia a sensibilibus ad intelligibilia . . . Et hinc enim quod validissima inde argumenta habentur contra judeos quia descordia quae est inter eos et nos ut maxime patet ex epistolis Pauli hinc tota praecipue dependet quod ipsi sequuntur litteram occidentem nos autem spiritum vivificantem . . . Magia et cabala certificat nos de divinitate Christi. . . . At hoc enim est miracula Christi nobis suam testentur divinitatem, . . . Cum ergo talia maxime cognoscat illa pars cabalae quae est de virtutibus corporum coelestium et illa pars scientiae naturalis quam ego nunc voco magiam naturalem et plures etiam catholici velint. Ideo non heretice non superstitiose sed scientifice sed verissme sed catholice dixi per talem magiam et cabalam adjuvari nos in cognoscenda divinitate Christi.

[20] Scholem, "La Loi," p. 80, quotes Joachim's 12th Century *Enchiridion in Apocalypsim*: "Si ad nucis dulcedinem parvenire volumus, primo necesse est ut amoveretur exterior cortex, secunda testa, et ita tertio loco perveniatur ad nucleam."

[21] *The Zohar,* trans. by H. Sperling *et al.*, (London: Soncino Press, 1933), Five Vols., III, pp. 301-302. The source of the image of the soul as a palace in Sta. Teresa has never been conclusively identified in Christian literature. It does occur in Fray Luis. I believe that cabalistic books are probably the source of Fray Luis' image and, since many authors have noted a similarity in their doctrines, perhaps one can be allowed to suggest that Teresa of Avila was a cabalist too. See: Robert Ricard, "Le Symbolisme de 'Château Intérieur' chez Saint-Thérèse," *Bulletin Hispanique* (Bordeaux), LXVII (1965), pp. 25-41. Sta. Teresa de Jesús, *Obras Completas,* (Madrid: Biblioteca de Autores Christianos, 1954), II, p. 341.

an allegorical meaning of the Torah such as used in the midrashim which the cabalist sees as having been composed by the "masters of the palace." This allegory is a prophetic allegory and is distinguished by the cabalists from another kind of allegory, a mystical one of spiritual morality. This is the one which characterized the adept or "master." Another mode of interpretation is the *"Derasha"* or legalistic one. These, with the literal reading and a method of number equivalence called *gematria,* give five possible exegetical tools. The first four roughly correspond to the Augustinian methods of exegesis. These would be the literal reading, the historical allegory of words or prophetic, the tropological or moral-legal, and the anagogical and mystical allegory.

In the course of the development of cabalism the Torah is also compared to the Garden of Paradise, wherein the four rivers of Gen. 2: 10-14, are identified with the four ways of interpreting Scripture. This allusion is later developed in a more interesting way when Eden is compared with the "nut garden" of Cant. 6: 11. Solomon's descending into the garden is taken to mean that the *Shekinah,* or divine presence, is in exile. The tenth Sephirothic name of God, *Tikkunim,* is identified with the *Shekinah.* The significance of this is that insofar as the mystic manifests the action of God in the soul, he also represents a link between earthly creation and the divine names which are its pattern in God from Whom creation comes forth. Thus, the prevalence of mysticism is a sign of the proximity of God to man in that the *Shekinah* is returning from exile which is what will occur when the messiah comes, along with wonderous changes on earth that will accompany this. All this becomes more fascinating when one sees that the mystic or pseudo-anagogical sense of Scripture is called a "fountain" because the Hebrew words for them are similar. This idea is developed in Gikatila whose *Portae Lucis* was translated by Rici into latin early in the 16th Century.

As important as the presence of Hebraic imagery in Fray Luis is understanding of its significance. Scripture was interpreted by both Jews and Christians in several ways. Of interest especially is Scripture read as a prophecy of future events, and read as a basis for a spiritual type of morality. The use of cabala by Christians, like Pico, was justified by their claim that the methods of the Jews were essentially the ones used by the Fathers of the Church. One would expect that the Christian cabalist would assign the high point in spiritual history to the time of Jesus. He would agree with the Jews about the general signs of the end of history, but the Jews would also expect the end of history and the high point of moral interpretation by way of cabala to coincide because they do not recognize Jesus as the messiah, but look for one who will be the leader of a temporal kingdom.

The adaptation of cabala to Christian moral theory was made by Paul Rici (fl. early 16th Century) who presented Jesus' teachings and Christian mysticism as one and the same as proper Jewish moral practice. This idea is found later in Agrippa who, like Rici, identified the angelic doctrine of cabala and the pseudo-Dionysius, the Christian mystic, insofar as angels were seen in both systems as having charge of the mystical life.

This identity does not, in fact, seem to be real as Scholem has indicated. However, this was the assumption of such influential exegetes as Sixtus of Sienna as we shall note further in Chapter IV. Although a similar four-fold system of interpretation had long been in use by Christians, Scholem thinks that it was possible that the Jewish and Christian systems developed independently. Nevertheless, these systems were identified by Christian cabalists. That this was widely accepted is evidenced by the high praise Rici's *De Coelesti Agricultura* won in 1540, from important Catholic theological faculties.

Rici also clearly related Aquinas' writings on law and cabalism. His argument about the divine positive character of the Decalog was the same as that of Alonso de Cartagena. But, for Rici, not only is the historical destiny of the Jews and Christians the same, but the practical cabala is asserted to be a valid form of Christian morality. Here the conversion of the Jews is linked with their mystical practices and Thomism is featured as a program of ecclesiastical reform in connection with this. Rici cited St. Thomas' statement that the natural law and the Decalog are the same as his basis for identifying Jewish and Christian mysticism.[22] Rici, with other reformers of the time, pointed out that the source of the Church's

---

[22] Johannes Pistorius, *Artis Cabalisticae: hoc est Reconditae Theologiae et Philosophiae Scriptorum Tomus,* (Basel: S. Henricpetri, 1587), pp. 97-98, 102. He writes "Compertum siquidem habemus quicquid continet Legis observantia quadripartite conducibile fuisse ad salutem, prout literalis sensus (ex quo solo efficax trahere licet argumentum) declarat. Mysticus vero et figurarum intellectus pii et spiritualis exercitii potius, quam certitudinis gratia probatur: Si enim singula mandata rectae rationis examine inspicias, omnium veram, et Lege naturae solidatam dari causam plane intelliges: quae si expuisitius scire desideras: divi Aquinatis (S.T. I-II, 103) praeclara de his scripta et monumenta evolve: ... divus Aquinas: qui amplissime de singulis horum mandatorum differendo rationem, et causam, Legi naturae consonam, et inde roboratam ostendit." This book is an anthology half dedicated to Rici and includes works of Reuchlin, Leone Hebraeo and Burgonovo. In this passage it is obvious from the context that the "Mysticus ... et figurarum intellectus" refers to a cabalistic interpretation of the Law of Moses wherein the mystic takes only the figures of the letters in Hebrew as significant, and not their meaning as parts of words, or the literal sense, which Rici, like Fray Luis, says is the only efficatious method of theological argument. But, as he says, right action is more important than scientific certitude: See: pp. 193-194, for the approbation of the theological faculties bestowed upon Rici's *De Coelesti Agricultura.*

degradation and her many miseries was contamination with paganism and he draws upon Aquinas to show that it could be purged by association with Jewish practices.

Rici said the moral part of the Law of Moses is the only part to which any Jew is obliged outside of Palestine. This corresponds to the moral obligations of the Christians. The Decalog is, however, also the indispensable part of the Law of Moses and it cannot be abrogated. The special significance of this is that, according to Rici, what is essential for Jews is that idolatry be avoided at all costs and he quoted the Talmud to the effect that to worship idols is to deny the whole Law whereas not to worship them is to observe the Law. The rest of the Law of Moses, about circumcision, diet, etc., is not necessary.[23] Accordingly, for him, the Christian Jew continued to have a special moral mission, the avoidance of idolatry. Rici proposed that the Jews, converted to the true observance of God's Law, Christianity, are the ones who manifest the reforming spirit of the Church.

Furthermore, Rici concluded that the essence of Christian mysticism must include cabala, since it, like the Decalog, is based on divine law, as must be all Christian moral practice. Rici, before he became professor of Hebrew at Pavia in 1521, had explicitly identified the mystical doctrine of the cabala and that of Dionysius the Areopagite whose works are classics of Christian mysticism.[24] He declared that the moral laws of the Christians and the Jews were identical and as Blau says, he made of cabala a "possible itinerary of the mind to God."

However, there is also an historical dimension as well as a moral or mystical one in cabalistic interpretation of Scripture. According to Scholem, a later motif of cabalism was the notion that the body of the Torah is enveloped in vestments which are the events of profane history. Prophetic speculation is to be found, for example, in the work of Isaac Abravanel, and the fundamental assumption of this type of prophetic speculation is the year-day principle. The six days of creation correspond to the six supposed millenia of the world's history. The cabalist looks in the Torah for the plan of historical events. In the *Zohar*, the *Shekinah* or *Matrona*, or feminine aspect of the cabalistical deity, is identified with the Torah as revealed to man through mystical interpretation. The color of the vestments of the Torah corresponds to the historical periods of the Jews. For example, black refers to the period of exile which was not char-

---

[23] *Ibid.*, p. 74.
[24] Joseph L. Blau, *The Christian Interpretation of the Cabala in the Renaissance,* (New York: Columbia University Press, 1944), p. 74.

acterized by mystic observance of the Law, but by observance of the literal reading of the Law. However, the presence of God in the good works of the mystics at the time of the messiah's coming is symbolized by varied and splendid colors. The mystic then puts off the drab colors of legal interpretation and sees the Torah as wearing lighter ones, that is, those symbolizing the mystic interpretation of the Torah.

This doctrine is found, it seems, in Fray Luis where Christ is character-ized by the red and white and the golden yellow of Cant. 5: 10-16.[25] This is as much as to tell the Jews that what they were looking for at that time, i.e. the messianic age, had already happened in the past when Jesus lived. For Fray Luis, this color imagery is seemingly essential to his doctrine of the mystical life.

One finds in Fray Luis the suggestion of the importance of cabalistic mysticism in his view of history. Fray Luis apparently rejected the mes-sianic calculations that Abravanel had based on the book of Daniel. Rather, he regarded, seemingly, his own theory of future history as Christian and he followed Joachim of Flore in making the Apoca-lypse the central text for this purpose. This does not necessarily mean that his interpretation was any the less cabalistic. When he discussed the mysticism of his own time, he compared it to that of the early Christians who were Jewish. His continued use of cabalistic metaphors suggests that he rejected the Jew's messianic doctrine, not cabalism as such. He even indicated that grace in the soul of the mystic is like the waters of the mystical river or fountain coursing in the souls of the Jews and said with Rici that God's working in the souls is like a celestial agriculture.[26]

---

[25] Cf. Appendix III. This type of speculation is still characteristic of the mystic school of Safed, Israel, which was founded by Sephardic exiles after 1492. One finds Abravanel's theory about the Christian and Islamic branches of the Roman empire partially accepted in Benito Arias Montano, *Commentaria in Duodecim Prophetas,* (Antwerp, 1571), pp. 811-813. It is flatly rejected in Fray Luis' *Nombre: "Rey de Dios"* which prefers to base its interpretation of events in Apocalypse, which allows for a fifth beast identified by Fray Luis with the Turks. García, ed. *Obras completas,* I, pp. 601-603. For a more complete treatment of the mutual influence of Christian exegetes and Abravanel see: Froom, *Prophetic Faith,* II, pp. 223 ff. On Safed mystic-ism see: Gershom Scholem, *Major Trends in Jewish Mysticism.* (New York: Schocken Books, 1961), pp. 244 ff.

[26] What is quite remarkable about Fray Luis' mystical theory, however unlike Jewish cabalism, is that the mystic can be female. Postel saw this as an important sign of the superiority of Christian mysticism in the last days. See Fray Luis' "Carta-Dedicatoria a las Madres Priora Ana de Jesús," where he says: "Y no solamente en su Orden son luces de guía sino tambien son honra de nuestra nación y gloria de aquesta edad, flores hermosas que embellecen la esterilidad de estos siglos y cierta-mente partes de la Iglesia de las más escogidas, y vivos testimonios de la eficacia de Cristo y pruebas manifestas de su soberana virtud, y expresos dechados en que hacemos casi experiencia de lo que la fe nos promete." García, ed., *Obras completas,* I, p. 907. On Postel see: William J. Bouwsma, *Concordia Mundi: The Career and Thought of*

Also suggestive of cabalism are Fray Luis' poetic longings for the true fields and hidden valleys full of a thousand good things mentioned in his poem to Oloarte.[27] There is a cabalistic doctrine in connection with the idea that the consummation of history will restore mankind to a state of bodily perfection and delight, just as union with God in the mystic's soul is attributed to the union of God's verbal and physical manifestations. It is the mystic as part of physical creation and social reality who becomes a "master of the palace." Fray Luis seems to have expected that this union is not merely private between God and the soul, but is to be realized in the world as a whole in the last days. The idea that such would be the case is present in the writings of Abravanel, though it is explicit in those of Isaac of Luria of Safed. Such predictions of the coming of the last days with similar characteristics are to be found in the writings of Cusa and Savanarola (1452-1498). But, the significance of Jewish mysticism in the apocalyptic process does not seem to have been recognized in any general way at all until the next century when the work of Christian cabalists like Reuchlin produced such a result.[28]

As a final note, in connection with the moral and historical aspects of cabalism, one will notice in Fray Luis an element of difference with Rici. Rici's view was that Jews and Christians will be saved at the end of time inspite of differences of religion.[29] Perhaps it was this doctrine that accounts for the banning of the works of "Paulus Ricius, Israelita" in 1570. The proscription may well account for Fray Luis' never quoting such an eminent cabalist. His reputation was surely known to Fray Luis for he is referred to in Sixtus of Sienna, whose work Fray Luis knew, and, as we shall continue to see, it seems likely that Fray Luis owed him an intellectual debt.

In sum, the fact that Fray Luis may insist upon a peculiarly Jewish character in Christian moral observance is not surprising when one recalls that this is a position maintained by Martín and others of the 13th-16th Centuries. One of the key points in this position for Thomists is the proposition that in Christianity the Decalog now obliges gentiles as religious law, just as it obliges the Jews. The other point, one stemming from this, is that implied in much of the polemical literature that it is legitimate to defend and express Christian dogma by recourse to Jewish exegetical

---

Guillaume Postel (1518-1581), (Cambridge: Harvard University Press, 1957), pp. 151 ff.

[27] García, ed., *Obras completas,* II, p. 260.

[28] Froom, *Prophetic Faith,* II, pp. 24, 158.

[29] Blau, *Christian Cabala,* p. 67. *Index Librorum Prohibitorum,* (Antwerp: Chris. Plantin, 1570), p. 47.

material dealing with the mystical and moral life. Just as Jews and gentiles are equally bound by the divine positive law of the Decalog, so also is Jewish and gentile religious expression of Christian morality equally significant.

The usage of cabala by Christians seems to have been built upon this polemical tradition and seems to have spread to other countries than Spain. However, in Reuchlin and particularly in Rici, Egidio da Viterbo and Seripando, cabalism seems to have been part of a theory of ecclesiastical or moral reform, a point to be developed in connection with Fray Luis in Chapter Five. What is important to note here as well as later is that at least Rici and Seripando also claimed to be Thomists, as did Fray Luis.

What will be of interest in the next chapter will be comparing the theories of two Thomists of the latter half of the 16th Century. What will be shown are seemingly new positions on the question of the basis of Christian morality. Ramón Martín and the other Thomists discussed here apparently assumed that Christianity is a spiritual religion not based on race. Nevertheless, they allowed putting moral beliefs of Christians in Jewish terms by maintaining that the Decalog, the basis of Christian moral law, is a religious law. Christian cabalists like Rici presented the mystical beliefs of Christians as well in Jewish terms. But, the Renaissance Hebraist Thomists asserted nothing that the older Thomist had not. They all seem, insofar as they were orthodox, to have presented Christianity as a trans-cultural religion whose moral tenents are equally capable of being expressed in Greek or Hebraic terms since they are based on divine command and not the moral superiority of one or the other racial or cultural group.

But, as we shall see in the next chapter, perhaps it was the propriety of this that was at issue late in the 16th Century. All Catholics agree that their religion is spiritual and not based on race or nationality. But, they have not always agreed upon the mode of expression to be employed in expressing their moral beliefs. Some, like Martín or even Rici, were not loath to express Christian moral ideals in Hebraic terms as well as in traditional Thomistic ones which seem to have a neo-Platonic and Aristotelian cast. Others, like Alfonso de Espina, saw heresy latent in Jewish culture, and even though he was racially a Jew, he completely spurned the Hebrew moral law in favor of that of the gentiles.

The point that divides Fray Luis and Soto, as the next chapter will show, seems to have been novel in the Thomistic tradition in that Soto not only followed Aquinas in putting his view of Christian morality in

Greek terms, but followed, like Alfonso de Espina, the opinion excluding the possibility of Christian morality being based in the religious law of the Decalog. While Fray Luis seems to have agreed with interpreters of St. Thomas like Martín, Alonso de Cartagena and Rici about the nature of the Decalog against the opinion of Soto, it is not clear that he agrees with them that neo-Platonic-Aristotelian and Jewish mystical and moral practices are identical regardless of apparent differences. This is something St. Thomas never considered as far as we know, and certainly his works evidence no real interest in the terms of this debate of the 16th Century. Soto clearly must have rejected cabalism which was regarded as a spiritual, and more than rational, observance of the divine law of the Decalog.

Exactly what Fray Luis' position was is the question that this study aims to answer, and it will be discussed in Chapter Five, after his thought and that of Soto are more adequately contrasted. But, the problem they were raising is clear enough when contrasted with the views of earlier Thomists. It asked whether the human race was morally one as well as biologically one on grounds of natural reason alone or on account of the common religious aspirations of man.

Many Christian Hebraists, like some of the earlier Thomists mentioned, did not raise this question for they saw no fundamental difference between Jewish and gentile Christian moral expression. Even Rici and Martín would have had no answer, though they clearly distinguished between those who observe the Decalog and those who do not. This was, notably in Martín's case, a theological distinction, for it supposes there is already a certain moral unity among Christians, Jews and Saracens insofar as they all claim to be observant of God's positive commands, which are actually given by Christ.

But, Soto's emphatic denial of the divine positive character of the Decalog will make him, in the next chapter, unclear as to whether human moral unity is possible on religious grounds. He seems to have made the moral righteousness proper to man's nature the exclusive result of natural reason. He does not seem to have allowed that a truly human morality could only characterize those whose righteousness had a religious identity as well as a rational one. Examples of such men would include Hebrews as well as some in yet to be evangelized parts of the world, perhaps.

Accordingly, Fray Luis' response to Soto must have gone well beyond the medieval Thomistic position if it was to meet this problem. It may be expected that it stated that what constitues proper moral unity among men is not only the same as Christian observance in a theological sense as earlier Thomists did, but also that the moral unification of man is not something accomplished merely by reason, but is the special and unique characteristic of the fulfillment of what are in fact the religious hopes of all men whether presently evangelized or not. This he thought was accomplished by Christianity which he saw as representing the truth in the religions of mankind.

> I am, for my part, persuaded, and I hold it as self-evident, that only this conversion of the world, considered as it ought to be, puts the truth of our religion beyond all doubt and question . . .[30]

---

[30] García, ed., *Obras completas,* I, p. 571. "Yo persuadido estoy para mi, y téngolo por cosa evidente, que sola esta conversión del mundo, considerada como se debe, pone la verdad de nuestra religión fuera de toda duda y cuestión, . . ."

CHAPTER III

DOMINGO SOTO'S DEFINITION OF *JUS GENTIUM*, FRAY LUIS DE LEÓN'S *DE LEGIBUS*, AND THE LAW OF THE DECALOG

It is sometimes asserted that the development of the theory of *jus gentium* credited to the Salamanca school of Francisco Vitoria marks the beginning of international law. But, as Bernice Hamilton remarks, such a claim is absurd.[1] There was no clear understanding of the application and interpretation of treaties between sovereign states then as there is now. Rather, she says correctly, these thinkers were the first to raise the modern questions of the need for such a law and to inquire into what the nature and content of laws that would control the relationships of countries with one another should be. Such laws have long been believed to exist. The concept of *jus gentium* or law of nations goes back to Roman times. But, Hamilton sees the impetus of bringing them under renewed discussion is to be attributed to the discoveries of the New World and the expansion that followed them. There is much justification for this view. Vitoria wrote extensively on the political theory of colonization and his treatise *De Indiis* is one of many discussing these problems. Luis de León and Soto saw their theories as applying to imperial policy.

Whatever the merits of this opinion, we have delineated our perspective to establishing the positions of two representative Thomists on the question whether the Decalog continues to be religious law as well as natural law. It is in this connection that a reconsideration of their teaching about *jus gentium* becomes relevant. It is in their discussion of this matter,

---

[1] Bernice Hamilton, *Political Thought in Sixteenth-Century Spain,* (Oxford: Clarendon Press, 1963), p. 98. Fernando de los Ríos, *Religión y estado en la España del siglo XVI,* (Mexico: Fondo de Cultura Economica, 1957), pp. 120-125. Lewis Hanke, "Mas polémica y un poco de verdad acerca de la lucha española por la justicia en la conquista de América," *Revista Chilena de Historia y Geografía* (Santiago), (1967), pp. 5-66. Luciano Pereña Vicente, "El descubrimiento de América en las obras de Fray Luis de León," *Revista Española de Derecho Internacional* (Madrid), VIII (1955), pp. 587-604. Vicente Beltrán de Heredia, O.P., *Domingo de Soto,* (Madrid: Ediciones Cultura Hispánica, 1961), pp. 262-265.

usually thought to have to do only with America, that we find their opinions dividing on the character of the Decalog.

Domingo de Soto (1495-1560), whose pupil Fray Luis was most probably, heard Vitoria lecture on Aquinas in Paris before Vitoria's return to Spain and was one of his early converts to the Thomist cause. Later they were members of the Dominican convent of San Esteban at Salamanca at the same time. Occasionally Soto substituted for the older man in his university lectures. When Vitoria, who had been chosen imperial theologian at Trent, proved too ill to attend, it was Soto who was sent in his place.[2]

Soto clearly agrees with the tradition that *jus gentium* characterizes man alone and is not to be simply identified with the necessary commands of natural law. However, he distinguishes the *jus gentium* from natural law because it depends on premises and conclusions and not because it depends on human will for enactment.[3] It is, therefore, not of a different kind than natural law, because it is no less evident than it.

[2] A little background on the revival of Thomism may be useful. Francisco Vitoria (1483-1546) studied at the Paris Dominican college of S. Jacques where he was influenced by the pupils of John Major and the varied intellectual currents of the French capital. He studied under Peter Crockaert who, in 1507, together with his contemporary, Thomas de Vio Cajetan (1468-1534), revived the study of the *Summa Theologiae*. They used this work to replace the *Sentences* of Peter Lombard as the standard teaching text of theology. Because of their influence, numerous editions of Aquinas with lengthy commentaries began to appear throughout Europe. The works of Soto and Fray Luis are but two of these. Vitoria was elected to the Prime Chair of Theology (lectures at 6 a.m.) at Salamanca in 1526. Until his death he continued to teach from the text of Aquinas, though this practice was forbidden in Salamanca until 1550, by correlating the *Sentences'* order of questions to that of the *Summa* and by lecturing on both. Vitoria published nothing, but his lectures were avidly copied from dictation, a Paris mode he introduced in Salamanca. His ideas were surely known to Fray Luis who had at least some of these student notes in his care. The texts of Aquinas that were Vitoria's favorites were the parts of the *Summa*, II-II, dedicated to moral topics, and the part of most interest to us, I-II, QQ. 90-108, where the doctrine of law is expounded. See: Muñoz, *Fray Luis, teólogo*, p. 10. Ricardo G. Villaslada, S.J., *La Universidad de Paris durante los estudios de Francisco de Vitoria, O.P., (1507-1522)*, (Rome: Universitas Gregoriana, 1938). Renaudet, *Préréforme*. Avelino Folgado, O.S.A., "Los Tratados *De Legibus* y *De Justitia et Jure* en los autores españoles del siglo XVI y primera mitad del XVII," *La Ciudad de Dios*, CLXXII (1959), pp. 275-276. Pereña, ed., *De Legibus*, pp. xv-xvi. Doc. ined., X, p. 236. Teofilo Urdanoz, ed., *Obras de Francisco de Vitoria*, (Madrid: Biblioteca de Autores Cristianos, 1960). Luciano Pereña, "El concepto del derecho de gentes en Francisco de Vitoria," *Revista Española de Derecho Internacional*, V (1952), pp. 603-628.

[3] Domingo Soto, O.P., *De Justitia et Jure libri X*, (Antwerp: apud P. Nutium, 1567), Lib. I, Q. 5, art. 4. Some remarks may be helpful in establishing Soto's importance with regard to Fray Luis. Even before his appointment as mediator in the celebrated Las Casas-Sepulveda dispute of 1550-1551, Soto had enjoyed a distinguished career as a theologian. He had served as Charles V's confessor. In 1552, he succeeded Vitoria's own successor in the Prime Chair, Melchor Cano, O.P. Soto was Fray Luis' sponsor at his academic promotion in 1560. This may account for his delivering Soto's eulogy later that same year. Soto's main work on law, the *De Justitia*

St. Thomas, Soto notes, follows Isidore of Seville in positing in human law a distinction into two kinds, first *jus gentium,* and second civil law.[4] Soto presents his own position saying that it is obvious that man differs from animals in that he is governed by the use of reason. The laws flowing from this use of reason are the *jus gentium* and civil law. Soto says, on Aquinas' authority, that *jus gentium* is elicited from general natural principles of the things under consideration as ordered to the same end by way of conclusions. For example: "Fields are to be cultivated, and men are more negligent about things held in common than about their own property, therefore fields should be privately held." Civil law, on the other hand, is elicited from only one general natural premise, the other premises being set by man, and looks to some special law. Soto cites the division of the Law of Moses into moral (Decalog), ceremonial and judicial parts. The first is natural law, but the others are of civil law as would be, for example, the just price of wheat at a particular time and place being five sickles. The minor premise of this moral reasoning is not from natural law. The same would be the case in the reasoning that evildoers are to be punished, and so therefore are to be hanged. This is the first differences between the two laws.[5]

The second difference follows from this. *Jus gentium* does not require some sovereign authority or assembly, council or prince, in order that it be constituted as does civil law.

Third, it seems that *jus gentium* is common to all peoples whereas civil law is particular to each people or state. Soto accepts the division of Isidore and develops what he thinks is St. Thomas' position on the matter.

After a brief discussion of Aristotle's view, Soto illustrates his point with some additional questions.[6] Are the laws of religion toward God and the

---

et Jure, first published at Salamanca in 1553-1554, was revised by the author in 1556, and was published as many as twenty times before 1600. It was said of Soto, "Qui scit Sotum scit totum." The material it treats was first lectured upon by him before Fray Luis' profession in 1544. At that time Soto must have held the Vespers Chair (1540-1541). But, he taught it again in 1552-1553 and it is possible that Fray Luis heard him then. Nevertheless, Fray Luis quotes his book which was revised and in wide use eleven years before his own lectures on law in 1570-1571. By that time Soto must have been the major Thomistic legal authority in print, Canonists of Salamanca had published on law. Two are considered with Vitoria to be creators of Spanish political thought. These are Diego de Covarrubias (1512-1577) and Martín de Azpilcueta (1492-1586) whose *Enquiridion* of 1550 saw fifty editions. See: Bell, *Luis de León,* pp. 118-119. Folgado, "Tratados *De Legibus*," pp. 285-286. Muñoz, *Fray Luis, teólogo,* pp. 9-10. Luciano Pereña Vicente, *La Universidad de Salamanca forja del pensamiento político español en el siglo XVI,* (Salamanca: Universidad de Salamanca, 1954), pp. 24, 34, 41, 58-92.

[4] Thomas Aquinas, St., *Summa Theologiae,* (Turin: Marietti, 1952), I-II, 95, 4.
[5] Soto, *De Justitia et Jure,* Lib. III, Q. 1, art. 3, headed: "Utrum jus gentium sit idem cum jure naturale."
[6] *Ibid.,* III, 1, 3. Nam praeceptum religionis et honorandi parentes in decalogo

honor of parents and the state of *jus gentium?* How about the law of self defense? Soto's opinion is that both these cases belong to the law of nature. To those who, like Vitoria, say that the jurists have made *jus gentium* too broad, Soto replies that religion, etc., are part of natural law and therefore the traditional inclusion of these in *jus gentium* is correct. Vitoria opposed this view, as did Cano and others.

Soto continues to elucidate his position by saying that just because *jus gentium* is elicited by rational inference from natural principles, it does not follow that such a inference is altogether necessary. In fact *jus gentium* falls far short of being a complete law in the sense of commanding all the things that the natural law might in fact demand of all peoples. All that is required is that it be fitting with a view to the ordering of the nature of a thing to its end. That one ought not kill follows fittingly from the principle "Do unto to others," etc.[7]

A final point completes Soto's arguments on this question. This is whether the *jus gentium* admits of any dispensation. The answer is that in some matters it does not because to do so would lead to social breakdown and so be inconsistent with the purpose of law. One cannot cancel property rights, except among religious, without such a result. Other precepts of the *jus gentium* are dispensable. Slavery was a matter of *jus gentium,* but is no longer.

What stands out about Soto's view on the matter of the definition of *jus gentium* is the importance he sees in its consequences for the interpretation of religious laws with respect to the natural law. This matter is, of course, important for Aquinas who considers the question of the Old Law (S.T. I-II, 98-108). Soto insists that the Mosaic Law can be divided into three parts and that the moral part, or Decalog, obliges *only* because of its being contained in the natural law discovered by reason. Ceremonial

sunt; qui, ut supra satis demonstravimus, germen est naturalis juris. Et propulare injurias conclusio est illius principii. Unaquaeque res appetit se conservare, ergo jus gentium idem est, quod naturale. ... Et secundo id ipsum arguitur. Libro proximo hunc saepe repetivimus differentiam inter moralia praecepta ex una parte, et ceremonialia, atque iudicialia, et jus civile ex altera, quod moralia interferuntur ex principiis naturae per modum conclusionibus: nam autem reliqua, ut modo declarabamus. Quo de causa diximus decalogum esse de jure naturae. Si ergo jus gentium infertur ex eisdem principiis per modum conclusionis fit ut fit pariter de jure naturale. ... Consent namque tali appellatione comprehendi quidquid cunctis mortalibus est commune: et jus naturale id dumtaxat esse, quo etiam bruta cum hominibus conveniunt: cum tamen multa sint naturalia juria, quae peculiariter conveniunt humanae naturae et non brutae: ut est decalogues, quam nos posuimus, scilicet quod ea quae inferuntur ex absoluta rerum natura, et consequentia necessaria, pertineant ad jus naturale; illa vero quae non ex absoluta consideratione sed modo exposito in ordine ad certum finem, sint de jure gentium. Quare Decalogus non de jure gentium set de jure naturae est.

[7] *Ibid.,* II, 3, 1.

and judicial precepts are mutable human laws. The Mosaic Law of the Ten Commandments enjoys great prestige not because of a religious obligation, but simply as a codification of the law of natural reason.

Soto distinguished three degrees of dependency on natural principles. First, are those directly arrived at by reason for anybody, e.g. honor parents, do not kill, steal or commit adultery. These, he says, obviously follow from the precept "Do unto others." A second class is made up of those rules not so easily arrived at and are known only to those who are wise because of long meditation on the general principles. Such would be the commands like "honor the old," or "call no man a fool." He includes in this class the prohibition of simple fornication for he says that though the Decalog forbids it, it is not so obviously wrong as adultery is.[8]

A third class of laws discovered by reason are known only to those whose minds have been specially enlightened by God to see them. Such are the imperatives not to make idols or to use the name of God in vain. The precepts of the First Table are arrived at only after much reasoning from the simple principle that good is to be done. Aside from Moses, of course, Soto mentions that among the gentiles we find some such as Job, the Sibyls and Hermes Trismegistus also so favored by God.

The Mosaic Law, for Soto, still is law in its moral commandments only, because it is substantially the same as the law of natural reason. For this reason, the moral precepts oblige, whereas the ceremonial and judicial ones do not any longer. All the moral precepts of the Old Law are reduced to the Decalog and these are reduced to natural law. The obligatory character of the ceremonial and judicial laws ended with the death of Christ. Furthermore, Soto says, not only did these laws cease, but so did any obligation to obey them and it is sinful to observe them.[9]

Soto's discussion of this point is of extraordinary length, over five full pages. It parallels St. Thomas' in *S.T.*, I-II, 103, 3 and 4. Soto discusses with great care the position of Scotus which he says must be "most urgently" opposed. According to Scotus, the Law of Moses was not abrogated at the death of Jesus. He held that the reception of baptism was not obligatory from the time of the Crucifixion, prior to which time it was only an intention of Christ, not a law. Rather, against Aquinas, Scotus taught that the law of the gospel remained in intention until it

---

[8] *Ibid.*, I, 4, 3 and 4; II, 5, 3.

[9] *Ibid.*, II, 3, 3. Nam illa generalia principia continentur in Decalogo, sicut principia in proximis conclusionibus. . . . Lex Moysi per legem Christi cessare debuit, atque adeo omnino cessavit.

Ibid., II, 5, 4. Ceremonias legis veteris nullatenus iam modo licet post evangelii promulgationem observare: sed esset mortale peccatum atque adeo haeresis contra facere.

was promulgated. Scotus held that Mosaic circumcision was legitimately practiced as was baptism from the time of the latter's institution until its promulgation. Therefore, the Old Law was not completed at the death of Jesus, but was of obligation among the Jews until the gospel was sufficiently promulgated. This promulgation began on Pentecost and lasted for some time. A Jew, Scotus said, upon hearing the gospel on Pentecost could either have his child circumcised or baptized. The preceptive character of the gospel depended upon sufficient promulgation.

Soto's answer is that with the death of Jesus, the Old Law, whose entire function was to prefigure that of the gospel, was finished. The fact that a Jew did not know the gospel saved him from fault, not obligation. But, even if Scotus was right that the Mosaic Law lasted until the destruction of Jerusalem, Soto feels the need to note that in any case it ended before the time of Augustine. He remarks that it is wicked to continue to observe these ceremonies and criticizes Cajetan who saw no wrong in baptized Indians being also circumcised in imitation of Jesus.[10]

For Soto, the Mosaic Law has no prescriptive character aside from what it derives from reason's law. He treats the Decalog as deductions from natural principles and the ceremonial and judicial laws as though they were like civil law. The latter two ceased with the death of Jesus, the former continues because its basis is unchanged by Christ.

Clearly, for Soto, the relation of the Decalog and natural law determines the definition of *jus gentium*. Soto refuses to accept the Scotist position, not because it is necessarily different from his own on this point. Rather, he does so because if its principles were to be extended, as Soto obviously thinks some to have done, then it would be impossible to affirm, as he does, the formal identity of the Decalog and natural law. If the gospel were not sufficiently promulgated, then, on Scotist principles, the moral part of the Law of Moses would still have to be thought of as properly in force as divine law since there would be no other grounds for distinguishing it as divine positive law and as the law of nature. Its material content would be the same, but also, and this is where the problem rests, one could not tell if the Decalog obliged as being inferred

---

[10] *Ibid.,* II, 5, 4. "Neque excusari potest quin habeat speciem mali. Neque vero ad haec abunde Cajetanus respondet."

Some natives of Mexico practised circumcision as a pagan rite when the Spaniards arrived. These people were not thought to be lost Jews as is sometimes asserted. See: Lee E. Huddleston, *Origins of the American Indians, European Concepts, 1492-1729,* (Austin: University of Texas Press, 1967). Vitoria earlier pointed out the obvious, that one can receive circumcision without observing Mosaic ceremonial practice. Francisco de Vitoria, O.P., *Comentario al tratado de la ley, (I-II, QQ 90-108),* ed. by Vicente Beltrán de Heredia, O.P., (Madrid: CSIC, 1952), p. 42.

from natural law, or still also as a divine positive law which he is obliged to observe. Thus, the consequence of Scotus' view would be to nullify Soto's definition of *jus gentium* as merely the deductions of natural reason for if such were the case, it could, on principle, command none of those things commanded by Moses' Law. The range of *jus gentium's* possible imperatives would have to be considerably narrowed because the laws of the Decalog would have to be understood as standing independently of natural law and so of *jus gentium*. They would still be undifferentiated from divine positive law and Soto's inclusion of them in a law subject to human dispensation would be improper. Soto solves this by denying that promulgation is of the essence of law and by asserting that the obligation imposed by the divine positive law of the gospel is imposed upon the Jews even without their knowing it.

Soto, it should be observed, did not deny that *jus gentium* is positive human law. Nevertheless, his definition of it makes it clear that it is not the same as human law. For Soto, the commands of the Decalog are everywhere obliging, even though the Law of Moses is in effect no longer, precisely because of their formal identity with the natural law.

Soto was followed in this by Miguel de Palacios whose commentaries on law date from 1554, though they were published in 1585, and 1588. Palacios, who held the Durandus Chair while Fray Luis was a student, advanced the thesis that, since the ruler legislates in the name of the people, the people retain the right to change forms of government and create new leaders.

Vitoria, on the other hand, seems to have held that *jus gentium* is distinguished by human legislation. *Jus gentium* is like civil law, but just not limited to one nation.[11] This view was adopted by Vitoria's student and successor, Melchor Cano, who lectured on Aquinas from the Prime Chair from 1546 until 1551, when he went to Trent. According to the list of texts given by Muñoz, the portions of the *Summa* on law were not lectured upon during the period of Fray Luis' studies.[12]

It is known that in addition to Cano, Diego de Chavez, Domingo de

---

[11] Palacios, with the Franciscan canonist, Alfonso de Castro (1495-1558) is named as the probable source of the concept of the synthesis of separate acts of the intellect and will in law which characterizes Fray Luis. Pereña, ed., *De Legibus,* pp. lxxix, lxxiv. Muñoz, *Fray Luis, teólogo,* p. 10. Pereña, ed., *Ibid.,* lxxix, lxxx. Muñoz, pp. 7, 8.

[12] Fray Luis, as a student, had copied his lectures, as was customary, and had them in his library. But, it is not unlikely that he also possessed Cano's *De Justitia et Jure* which dates from 1545. He testified at his trial that he had in his possession lectures of Vitoria, Cano, Vega, Pedro de Sotomayor, Juan de la Peña, Gallo, Guevara, Cipriano, Villalobos, and there were others he said he had borrowed the titles of which he could not remember. Among these could have been Cano on law. *Doc. Ined.,* X, pp. 239, 236-237. Pereña, ed., *ibid.,* p. lxxxiii.

las Cuevas, Gil de Nava, and Vicente Barron sided with Vitoria on the matter of the definition of the *jus gentium* against St. Thomas and Soto.[13]

To begin a discussion of Fray Luis on these same questions, one should note first his extraordinary emphasis on the positivity of law. Law is a product of mind and will. Pereña indicates that Juan de la Peña, whose manuscript on justice dates from 1559, influenced him in his stress on the positive character of *jus gentium*. Apparently the Augustinian, Juan de Guevara, who had been Fray Luis' teacher in his art courses, held much the same view.[14] Soto, while he admitted *jus gentium* was positive law, defined it as natural law.[15]

Even though law is positive, Fray Luis is careful to note the consistency that must obtain between the general good and the particular goods of the citizenry and the interests of the civil ruler. Kings may not reduce the

---

[13] Fray Luis, no doubt, heard Chavez when he substituted for Cano in 1549, and Barron when he did so in 1550. But, neither lectured on law at those times. Perhaps, he did hear Chavez substitute for Soto in 1549, when he lectured on justice. Also, he may have heard Nava who substituted for Soto in 1546-1547, when he may possibly have lectured on law. See: Pereña, ed., *ibid.,* pp. lxxviii, lxxix. Muñoz, *ibid.,* pp. 7, 10.

[14] *Doc Ined.,* XI, p. 269. Pereña, ed., *Ibid.,* pp. lxxii, lxxv. Muñoz, *Ibid.,* p. 8. Pereña reports a treatise on justice and law of Mancio de Corpus Christi, onetime teacher of Fray Luis, dating from 1566. He said *jus gentium* is customary law. He mentions also a treatise *De Legibus* of Juan Gallo in Fray Luis' possession in 1572. This work is now lost and the one attributed to Gallo in the Vatican Library seemingly accords with that of Fray Luis himself, leading to Pereña's speculation that unless one supposes that Gallo pirated that of Fray Luis, the Roman manuscript must be Fray Luis' mistakenly attributed to Gallo. The following seem to be the only extant manuscripts of Fray Luis' *De Legibus*: Fray Luis de León, *De Legibus,* Coimbra MSS, 1843 (434 folios), complete; Juan Gallo, *De Legibus,* Vatican Library MSS, Ottob. Lat. 1.004, complete; Fray Luis de León, *De Legibus,* Real Academia de la Historia MSS (Madrid), 9-9-8/2081 (fols. 176r-187v), partial, but certainly owned by Fray Luis himself with a note in his own hand. Apparently Fray Luis was going to publish the treatise, but died before accomplishing this.

[15] It may be helpful to note what treatments of St. Thomas on law were available to Fray Luis in 1570-1571. Soto's exhaustive work of 942 pages in folio in the 1562 edition had been published already seven times at Salamanca, twice at Lyon, and once each at Venice and Antwerp by 1571. Gil de Nava (d. 1551), Melchor Cano (1509-1560), Diego Chavez (1507-1592), Domingo de las Cuevas (d. 1559), Juan de Guevara (1504-1600), and others, some teachers of Fray Luis had lectured on St. Thomas' *De Legibus* by then. But, so far as I have been able to determine no Spanish theologian except Soto appeared in print on the subject prior to 1571, except the following: Antonio Agustín (1517-1586) whose *De Legibus et Senatusconsultis Liber* touches upon Aquinas incidentally and appeared in Lucca in 1567; Juan de Medina's (1490-1546) *Codex de Restitutione et Contractibus* draws upon Aquinas and appeared in Alcalá in 1546; the Mexican Dominican Tomás de Mercado (d. 1575) follows Soto in his *Suma de Tratos y Contratos,* published in Salamanca in 1569. It is very interesting to note that Robles' contrast of Fray Alonso de la Vera Cruz, O.S.A., (1504-1584), a founder of the University of Mexico, and his fellow Mexican missionary, Mercado, seems to be consistent with the contrast made in this chapter between Soto and Fray Luis. See: Oswaldo Robles, *Filósofos Mexicanos del Siglo XVI,* (Mexico: Porrua, 1950), pp. 61 ff. Folgado, "Tratados De Legibus," pp. 281-285. Muñoz, *Fray Luis, Teólogo,* pp. 7-12. Pereña, ed. *De Legibus,* pp. lxxxiii, lxxxiv.

common good to their own utility. They have no right from nature to rule over others. Their right derives from the express or tacit consent of their people and this right cannot confer on him any absolute dominion over the particular goods of each of his subjects.[16]

In making laws, the king must use the advice of wise men (I, 28). In commanding them to be observed, a king represents, not himself, but the entire community which has this power by immediate concession from God (I, 29, 30). The laws of a community oblige in conscience and violators in capital cases may be put to death by the power of God. On the other hand, it is not necessary that the people consent to laws given by a civil or ecclesiastical authority for them to have force. Canon law does not depend upon the community. In the civil community, once people have given power to the king, they give it over until he misuses it, and they must obey him (I, 33).

However great his emphasis on the rights of the ruler, it is very interesting to note that Fray Luis dedicates over a third of the first chapter to the question of the promulgation of law. Aquinas handles the matter with dispatch. But, Fray Luis seems to be forging a novel view and is apparently anxious to make it clear. The relation of Fray Luis' to Soto's view will be obvious. Fray Luis urges the Scotist thesis without citing Scotus by insisting that promulgation is an essential condition of the imposition of obligation.

It was a common and certain opinion, he says, that law has no force before it has been sufficiently promulgated. God promulgated the Old Law with thunder and lightning (Ex. 20: 18) and the New Law with the sound of a wind. This is a reference, no doubt, to the Scotist view that the gospel law dates from Pentecost. There can be no law and no obligation before it is known (I, 34). But it is no small matter to determine when one ought to believe a law is sufficiently promulgated and when, therefore, it obliges. Surely the natural law is known to all by the light of reason. It is not promulgated sufficiently by reason, however (I, 35). Just because a king promulgates his law in his court, it is not law. For a law to be suf-

---

[16] Pereña, ed. De Legibus, I, 22. The section numbers will be included in the text hereafter. It is of interest that he justifies this point by reference to the election of Don Pelayo whose mandate to power was limited to driving out the Moors. Mariana describes Pelayo's election in exactly the same way although his work was not published until 1595. See: Joannis Marianae, S.J., Historiae de Rebus Hispaniae Libri Triginta, (Hague-Comitum: Petrus de Hondt, 1733), Tom. I, Lib. 8, cap. I, p. 258. One will note a similarity between the thought of Fray Luis and Mariana if one also reads: Guenter Lewy, A Study of the Political Philosophy of Juan de Mariana, S.J., (Geneva: Droz, 1960). What is significant in Fray Luis' use of this example is the fact that Don Pelayo was elected king for a religious purpose. It is the religion of the people which is a source of the king's mandate to rule in Spain.

ficiently promulgated, it is not necessary that it be made known to all to whom it is directed. But, laws are to be considered sufficiently promulgated only after they are published in a manner which, morally speaking, they would be able to be known by all. This is particularly important, he observes, in spiritual matters.

Once a law has been sufficiently promulgated in the opinion of prudent persons, it obliges all, even those invincibly ignorant of it, though these latter remain free from fault if they do not observe it. (I, 46). With Aquinas, Fray Luis defines law as an ordinance of reason for the common good made by him who has care of the community, promulgated.

If natural law may not be sufficiently promulgated, then what is his concept of it? All those things he says appropriate to man as man, pertain to natural law (V, 8). But, many actions to be done are so only because of the disposition of human law. These acts do not belong to the natural law. The natural law embraces all those things which are self evidently necessary and those which, though not so readily understood, can be shown to be so by reasoning and by way of premises and conclusions. The natural law does not embrace those things, which, though they tend to the same end, are able to change with time and place. Things Soto said were once part of *jus gentium,* like slavery, are not part of natural law. Positive command determines law in changing situations and these oblige only after the intervention of the will of the ruler (V, 20). But, human law is not of its essence good and just because it has been commanded. It must seek the same end as natural law, but human law is not the same as natural law, or is so at most only in an indirect manner since it requires the command of the ruler (V, 10). Not everything that pertains to natural law is ordered by it. Nature also may be perfected by supernatural laws. In fulfilling the evangelical law, one might more perfectly fulfill that which the natural law intends.

Is the natural law variable? Do all men know the same natural principles? Fray Luis observes that an action is determined as appropriate not only by the objects intended by it, but also by the circumstances in which it is done. So practical reason is subject to error since it is difficult to know all relevant circumstances. Furthermore, our sensual desires often make clear reasoning difficult. Even though the principles of natural law may be clear to all people and oblige all in the same way, nevertheless, conclusions deduced from them by much reasoning, although necessary, may not be just (V, 14, 15). Therefore, the natural law is not clear for all in these particular conclusions (V, 16).

Here is his difference with Soto and the basis of his own version of the relation of natural law and the Decalog. St. Thomas says that the law of nature cannot be changed in its principles because these are fixed, but the application of principles may vary with the circumstances. Fray Luis agrees with this saying that it is one thing to change the law, but another to perfect it. To change law is to make it different by way of annulling it or when what was just becomes unjust. But, the law may be perfected when circumstances give it a greater goodness. The supernatural and human laws do this, the former by adding the dimension of grace, and the latter by establishing penalties adding greater force (V, 17).

It is interesting to observe the implications of this view with regard to the Mosaic Law. For Soto, the moral part of the Law of Moses simply reflects the law of natural reason. For Fray Luis, however, this moral law obliges men not only as rational dictate, but as a religious law as well. The Mosaic Law, in its moral commands, is superior to a mere law of reason for it brings about a natural perfection in it. The understanding and observance of the natural law is, then, not a mere matter of deduction from rational principles. It is special circumstances surrounding its promulgation that require men to observe the natural law, not only know-ledge of its contents. Thus, the Old Law and the natural law justify be-cause they are obeyed in the hope of the future Christ. This does not derive from reason alone, yet it is for Fray Luis the common expectation of nature as we shall see in the *Nombre*: *"Pimpollo."*

Fray Luis then applies the principle of how man's understanding of the natural law needs to be improved to the relation of natural law and human law. It is useful that there be human laws in addition to the eternal and natural laws. Transgressors of the natural law need to be punished. The natural law is too abstract. Although it commands that God be worshipped, for example, it is necessary that human law deter-mine the manner in particular (VI, 1).

In this connection, Fray Luis makes such of a point mentioned only in passing by Aquinas.[17] Is the state better ruled by a good prince without

---

[17] S.T. I-II, 105, 1, Obj. and Rep. 1. Here St. Thomas is answering an objection that the Mosaic Law could have had no judicial precepts since the Hebrews had no king at the time it was imposed. St. Thomas' own view is that the best state has a mixed constitution wherein a king is chosen by the people from an aristocracy on account of his exceptional qualities of soul. In the case of the Hebrews only, God reserved to Himself the choice of a king. However, other forms of government, specifi-cally the rule of the aristocracy of the seventy-two elders, were still possible. Like any human laws, the judicial precepts of the Mosaic Law ceased to bind with the Jewish state. Fray Luis seems to be pointing out here that although the judicial precepts of the Old Law no longer oblige, neither do the Jews have any king except Jesus. He interprets Aquinas as holding that a king may not be sovereign in a Christian political state for this reason. What is taken by Father Gilby to have been a constitution only recommended by Aquinas, is taken by Fray Luis to have been the only possible one

laws, or by good laws without a prince? His answer is that if it were possible to find a single man whose qualities were greater than those of the rest of men so that he could be a standard for others, then it would be better to have him as ruler than laws. Jesus Christ, even if he had not been God, says Fray Luis, reasonably could be king of all men. The qualities of the reign of Christ, then, are human qualities within the reach of men if they could improve themselves. On the other hand, taking into account the condition of men, where nothing is perfect, two things follow: a good king needs laws, and to have good laws, a good king is necessary (VI, 4).

Laws are needed because it is through them that men cooperate harmoniously and written laws are needed because this could not be done by mere customs or friendship alone. Some principle of unity must be added. Written law also serves to extend the burdens of the law to all; no one would wish to be treated more harshly by it than another (VI,4). As few things as possible, then, ought to be left to the discretion of the king and most things ought to be determined by laws.

Further, regarding the matter to the relation of human law and natural law, Fray Luis follows St. Thomas (S.T. I-II, 95, 2) in saying that one law can derive from another: first, as a conclusion from principles; and second, an ordering in particular what the other orders in general (VI, 5). All such laws, as law, are derived from natural law (VI, 6), but some laws are derived by way of determining in detail its general precepts. In the first way, for example, natural law indicates outlaws are to be punished. The manner of punishment is a determination of this general precept. If human laws derive from natural law, is human law any different from it? While it is true that the justice of any human law comes from the natural law, nevertheless, human law is what makes specific actions of obligation. We are not obliged to do everything that is reasonable, but we are obliged to do what has been commanded by human law (VI, 8). Just because all laws derive from the natural law, it does not follow that there cannot be something which is good because it is made so by law, though the natural law itself is law because it is good.

for him to have adopted insofar as Aquinas himself observes that God has reserved the choice of a king for the Jews. No other king except Jesus, Fray Luis thinks, can be shown to have been appointed by God. Surely this is an assertion of Spanish spirit when one recalls both what outlandish theological claims were being made then and would be made in the future for the House of Bourbon, and how influential Jewish Christians were in the government of Philip II. Fray Luis seems to find in Spain the very embodiment of the Thomistic ideal state. Cf. Thomas Gilby, *The Political Thought of Thomas Aquinas*, (Chicago: University of Chicago Press, 1958), pp. 284-300. Cf. St. Thomas Aquinas, *On Kingship*, trans. by G. B. Phelan and rev. by I. T. Eschmann, (Toronto: Pontifical Institute, 1949), pp. 61-62, #109-110.

Those human laws which were said to derive from natural law because they are conclusions deduced from it perhaps are not human laws at all? But, they are because the human law often orders what the natural law does in order to impose greater punishments or because they derive necessarily only after many intermediate conclusions and so are not entirely evident. So that no one may claim ignorance, the human law often orders the same things as natural law. Other human laws may derive from the principles of the natural law, though there may not be any necessary connection between them and natural justice they are useful nonetheless because they help one seek it. So, in a certain way, these are in accord with it. Such laws are human laws, and the obligation to observe them derives only from the authority of the human legislator (VI, 10, 11). It does not derive from strict deduction from natural principles.

It will be recalled that Soto made the same distinction between two kinds of human law. The former, laws necessarily deduced from natural law, he classed with Isidore and St. Thomas as *jus gentium*. The latter, not necessarily deduced from it, he called civil law. But is Aquinas' division of human positive law into *jus gentium* and civil law proper? About this matter, says Fray Luis, there is the greatest doubt. This is Aquinas' doctrine that we found Vitoria, Cano and others denying.

Fray Luis undertakes his own examination of Aquinas. He notes that St. Thomas approves Isidore's distinction (*S.T.* I-II, 95, 2 and 4). Aquinas also says (I-II, 95, 4) that *jus gentium* is distinct from natural law which is common to all animals, being distinctively human. In another part of the *Summa* (II-II, 57, 3), he says that they are distinct, *jus gentium* pertaining to human law. On the other hand, he says (I-II, 93, 2) that natural inclination is of natural law. Therefore, the Decalog is also of *jus gentium,* especially as it deals with relations with one neighbor to another. Therefore, *jus gentium* belongs to natural law (VI, 13). This is, of course, the position of Soto. The fact that natural law and *jus gentium* are distinct does not prevent the latter from pertaining to the former as a part of it, though it is also a part of human law. Human law and natural law overlap, as it were, in *jus gentium*. This is why it is called a natural inclination of man.

Fray Luis notes that the common opinion of Aristotle, Cicero and Isidore is that *jus gentium* is common to all men and is therefore natural law (VI, 14). Soto, he notes, agrees. But, Fray Luis is himself not satisfied with Soto's explanation how this is so, as apparently Cano was not. Fray Luis says:

This opinion is by no means able to stand: first, because thence it would follow that all the precepts of the Decalog would be of *jus gentium,* because they all would be conclusions deduced from the principles of the natural law through discourse by necessary consequence. This is necessarily false as I prove, because in those things which are of *jus gentium* there are those things which are able to be abrogated and deleted by some one commonwealth; but no commonwealth can delete the precepts of the Decalog nor any precept of the natural law at all.[18]

The reason for Fray Luis' disagreement, as we see, is his refusal to accept the mutability of the Decalog and his insistence upon the incorruptible quality of Mosaic Law. Laws deduced from natural law by necessary consequences are natural law, for without them there could be no natural justice. God, who demands that there be natural justice, commands the means to it and so the *only* way it can be had is by observance of all the laws conclusively deduced from natural law. Obviously, there is some natural justice in human law, e.g. the *jus gentium,* but just how it is to be seen as connected with natural law has to be explained in another way.

Fray Luis falls back on the distinction of the two kinds of human law. The first kind, he says, is deduced by way of absolute necessity from general natural principles. Such would be the Decalog, for example. Such things are also matter for human legislation. Other laws can be said to be derived from natural law, not absolutely, by way of deduction, but indirectly and conditionally after having made some material supposition. These would assume that there are some differing situations and conditions of man which would be circumstances in terms of which the general precepts derived necessarily from reason might be applied differently, depending upon the situations supposed. These would be precepts of natural justice, though in a conditional sense, since nature, in commanding the end of man to be sought for, also commands the means to that end. The *jus gentium* cannot have natural justice absolutely considered, but is of natural justice conditionally speaking, insofar as it seeks in particular the end sought for by natural law in general (VI, 16-18). It differs from civil law only in that it is common to all peoples and is not made by a pact among them.

By way of example, Fray Luis says that it follows from man's nature,

---

[18] Pereña, ed., *De Legibus,* p. 82. Et haec sententia stare nullo modo potest; primo, quia inde sequeretur quod omnia praecepta decalogi essent de jure gentium, quia omnia illa sunt conclusiones necessaria consequentia deductae ex principiis legis naturae per discursum. Hoc autem est manifeste falsum ut probo, quia in his quae sunt de jure gentium possunt ab una aliqua respublica abrogari et deleri, at vero nulla respublica potest delere praecepta decalogi nec ullum.

absolutely considered, that matrimony is indissoluble so that children might be educated, but man being what he is, it follows conditionally that matrimony be surrounded with church ceremonies, solemnity and admonitions to guarantee that the partners will not separate. Natural law commands that there be peace, but man, fickle as he is, is often embroiled in warfare. But since peace is the goal of all law, *jus gentium* requires that the inviolability of embassies be observed and that captives obey the captor so that his wrath will be soothed and will not make further war. Property rights are also of *jus gentium* because of man's natural general duty to cultivate the land and his fallen nature which inclines him to take what is common to all and so impede its fulfillment (VI, 18). These examples are very similar to the ones Soto uses. It ought to be observed that now the range of *jus gentium* accorded by Soto against Vitoria need not be curtailed. One would suppose that the worship of God or the honoring of parents would not be considered as obligations under *jus gentium,* but as following upon man's nature taken absolutely. If universally commanded also by human law, however, Fray Luis would say they were so because of man's proud or slothful nature and they would be obligations under *jus gentium.* Human law may also command what the natural law commands, but they formality of such laws in different in each case. This formal distinction will allow Fray Luis to preserve the formal distinction of natural law and the Decalog.

Jus gentium, then, enjoys a position intermediate between natural law and civil law. It has the characteristic universality of natural law, but the characteristic derivation from the consent of man of civil law (VI, 19). *Jus gentium,* properly speaking, belongs to positive law, and so the dictum of Isidore is to be preserved. But its formal definition is narrowed so it no longer includes among its instances religious laws which, like the Decalog, may not be changed, though its prohibitions, taken materially, remain the same. What it includes has to be able to be changed, yet it includes all universal positive laws. (VI, 20, 21).

Before going on to examine Fray Luis' treatment of revealed supernatural laws, it may be interesting to note his differences with Soto on the matter of customary law. When does a custom become law or when may it cancel a law? Does custom have the force of law? Soto (I, 7,1) says it does: 1) if it is a public custom and interprets laws, 2) if it has been established and approved it may cancel laws, and 3) custom may originate an unwritten law.[19] Fray Luis' criticism of these conditions is the follow-

---

[19] Mention should be made of the reforms of law that should follow from the principles that Fray Luis poses. Writing explicitly against Luther, Wyclif and Huss, he

ing. The first is so, Fray Luis says, only because the prince takes it into account when he interprets laws because it is so universally accepted that everybody knows it. But if, though practiced by many, a custom is not known to the legislator, it cannot interpret law. The second requires that the prince formally or interpretively approve the law custom introduces. Just because the prince does not punish those who observe a certain custom, it does not mean that the prince gives his consent to the custom (VIII, 2-6).

Custom may establish or cancel law after ten or twelve years. If a law explicitly states that it has force notwithstanding any custom, Soto says that the custom falls before the law. Fray Luis objects that custom is nothing but the tacit will of the legislator. Therefore, custom can annul law because the source of their authority is the same (VIII, 9).

With regard to Soto's third condition, Fray Luis admits custom can originate law provided four things: 1) that the thing in question is material for law, that it be in conformity with reason; 2) the custom has to be universal; 3) those who observe the custom do so because it is morally necessary; 4) the express or tacit approbation of the legislator is necessary for those who transgress this custom are to be punished (VIII, 10). Here we have a theory of law which admits of the intrinsic binding character of custom, but one that insists on its being based in positive command. Soto, on the other hand, is forced to admit that custom establishes no right which the king may not violate. Perhaps implicit in this is a constitutional theory of government but, surely, with the other reforms he suggests, it seems Fray Luis was not unaware of the right of a political minority to protest wrongs.

What does Fray Luis have to say when he treats the Old and New Laws formally?[20] The question is raised whether the Old Law promised

says that the power of human law is such that it is not merely an explication or deduction of natural or divine law, but is of itself constitutive of obligation. Therefore, human law whether civil or ecclesiastical binds in conscience whether or not it follows directly from reason because it nonetheless seeks the common good indirectly (VII, 6). In order that a law be just, Fray Luis writes against Luther, it must be given by legitimate authority and to be just in conscience does not exempt anyone from the obligation to obey positive law (VII, 45), although laws are given for the unjust, not the just (VII, 47). Also, he notes, though by law heretics lose ownership of their goods and their civil rights, *ipso facto,* they cannot lose their use of them until condemned by a judge. Furthermore, custom does not allow one to continue to charge more taxes than the legal amount and clergy have only the use, not ownership of their benefices and so must make restitution if they do not fulfill their obligations. Finally, he says that legislators are bound in conscience to obey their own laws which extend to all equally. If a pope or king breaks one of his own laws, he sins privately and is obliged before God, nature and his own will, though a sovereign, if he be pope, cannot be excommunicated, or if a king, infamous. (VIII, 41-53).

[20] Pereña, ed., *De Legibus,* pp. xxv, xxvi, xxvii, Fray Luis, *De Legibus,* Coimbra MSS, fols., 216v, 217, 217v, 218v.

only temporal rewards and punishments? Calvin asserted that it promised only the eternal and spiritual goods which the gospel promises. Fray Luis says that such eternal and spiritual rewards are nowhere promised in the Law of Moses or in the Old Testament whether interpreted spiritually or literally to those who observe the Mosaic Law as such; but only temporal goods were promised. However, the Mosaic Law was the type of the evangelical law and therefore it promises the rewards of the New Law by way of prefiguring. The fathers of the Old Testament did have faith in the eternal rewards of heaven. He says that the good and faithful, justified by faith and love of the future Christ, were understood to be given some eternal and spiritual rewards, not determinately, but confusedly, and this seems clearly enough to be expressed in the literal sense of the Old Testament. However, Fray Luis says the eternal reward of the just, that is, those who would become just, was not expressed in the literal sense of the Old Testament to be the vision of God, but in the New Testament only. However, he says that some of the fathers of the Old Testament knew of it.

Of the statements on the New Testament, we find the following. First, Christ is truly and properly the legislator in the New Testament. Second, Christ, in the New Law, besides the counsels which he imposed, also confirmed the natural principles in the Decalog and explained certain parts of it obscured by the customs of the Pharasees. Also, he brought the new laws and new precepts of the sacraments and other things. Third, these precepts, whether natural and confirmed and explained by Christ, or, supernatural and newly explicated by him in a public way, were given to men by Christ in two ways. He and his apostles gave them exteriorly in themselves, propounding them by word or by writing. And, he gave them interiorly, by moving our propensities and inclinations through the infusion of grace and charismas into our hearts and will. These impel men to do those things which he propounded exteriorly. Fourth, Fray Luis says, each of these impositions of precepts, exterior or interior, constitutes and makes up and establishes the New and evangelical Law. But, the proposition of precepts by exterior teaching does not belong to the New Law, nor does it principally belong to it, but secondarily. This was already done in the Old Law. But, this imposition by the interior impression and infusion of grace does belong to the New Law, and is that which principally and properly constitutes the New Law in it.

The religious law of the Decalog of the Jews is not abrogated, according to Fray Luis. He does not say that the Mosaic Law is in force in all respects. He follows Aquinas in holding that the judical precepts of the Old Law no longer bind the Jews for they no longer form a unique political state (III, 21). He never holds that the ceremonial laws of Moses oblige any longer. On the contrary, it is his opinion that the New Law obliged the Jews as soon as it became known to them, enjoining new sacramental rites that were only prefigured in the old ones. However, the moral law imposed by Christ was not new in its precepts, but only confirmed that of Moses. Thus, its obligation as religious law after Christ does not differ from that after Moses. Pentecost is presented as the new Sinai precisely because both are external promulgations of *one* divine moral law. It is the Decalog's character as a religious law that accounts for Fray Luis' rejection of Soto's theory of *jus gentium*. Can there be any doubt that Fray Luis thinks the Decalog is in force as divine positive law? And, why was this propisition so desperately rejected by Soto? If it was not anti-Semitism, then it was perhaps his inability to accept another conception of the relation of religion and political philosophy than one based on rational categories.

For Fray Luis law can have a religious significance that it does not have in Soto. It is the religious aspect of the Decalog which seems to be one foundation of temporal rights for Fray Luis. For him the content of a law of human reason can be also a command of religion. Soto, on the other hand, sees no relation between *jus gentium* and the Decalog as religious law. He divorces religion and reason, making the similarity of *jus gentium* and the Decalog one attributable only to human reason and not religious aspirations as well. For Soto, commands of human civil law and *jus gentium* are never obligations of religion also, but of reason only. Thus political activity, for him, can never also be religious in character, but only rational.

The view that the Decalog no longer has a special character as religious law seems to be still propounded by Thomists and is the usual opinion one finds among Thomistic philosophers and Catholic theologians, even very distinguished ones. It is true that these do not wish to discriminate racially against Jews, whether Christian or not. But, it is equally apparent that they do so culturally since their spirit of political toleration is not rooted in the Bible or religious law.

A recent and excellent example is John U. Lewis' thesis, *Man's Natural Knowledge of the Eternal Law*. After a careful consideration of the perplexing texts of the *Summa Theologiae*, I-II, 94, about the state of man's knowledge of natural law, Lewis suggests that St. Thomas' doctrine is that natural law is not a true law at all. Rather, he thinks, it signifies, in a metaphorical way, that part of the eternal law which is promulgated to us in human positive law. Soto, for example, rejected the idea that there is a philosophical ground for natural law in the eternal law.[21] Lewis, correctly, I think, sees that St. Thomas takes the notion of the eternal law to be philosophically significant in that it serves to unify all the laws of our experience. The eternal law of God is promulgated to us in what Lewis natural law and in human law. Also, Lewis wants to add divine positive law is a law of the experience of religious people. It is to accommodate this law that the concept of the eternal law is philosophically significant. But the natural law, he reasons, is not a separate kind of law because it does not mediate divine and human positive laws. Rather, natural law is identified by him with human law. Since it is taken on religious faith as being founded in the eternal law there can be no opposition between natural law, i.e. human law, and divine positive commands, at least in principle.[22] If Lewis is correct, then, there is no warrant in St. Thomas' theory of law for criticism of a theory of politics from specifically religious principles. The goodness of laws depends upon the natural reason of the lawmaker and not conformity to any religious standards.

Another and similar example is found in the writings of the late John Courtney Murray, S.J., where it seems to be argued that the natural law is something found out by the wise.[23] It is not to be equated with civil law, but is something that is a guiding principle according to which good laws ought to be made. The concept of natural law he espouses does not appear to claim a formality as religious law. The characterization of the wise as religious is not essential to his political theory.

The distinguished German theologian, Karl Rahner, S.J., argues, I think correctly, apparently against all Neo-Thomists of the Renaissance,

---

[21] Soto, *De Justitia et Jure*, I, 3, 2. . . . jus est, illud iustum debitum et aequum quod in rebus temporalibus et actionibus humanis reperitur, a quibus omnino alienum est quidquid habet rationi aeterni . . .

[22] John U. Lewis, *Man's Natural Knowledge of the Eternal Law*, (Milwaukee, Marquette University Doctoral Dissertation, 1966), pp. 139 ff., pp. 143-144. He writes, "Man discovered, or 'natural,' law is simply the eternal law naturally promulgated. It is the eternal law made naturally known through man's basic inclinations. And although it is necessary for a law to be promulgated if it is truly to be law, if that is, it is to be binding, nevertheless, promulgation is not a part of the essence of law. It is not a comprehensive note of the concept of law, a fact which can be seen simply by realizing that a law could not possibly be promulgated . . . unless it were already constituted in its essence.

"Because man discovered law is simply a promulgation of the eternal law, then, the conclusion here is that it is not, strictly speaking, a law at all, any more than the words entered into the statute books are human law. Each is merely the promulgation of a law."

[23] John Courtney Murray, S.J., "Natural Law and Public Consensus," *Natural Law and Modern Society* (contributions by John Cogley, Robert M. Hutchins, *et al.*), (Cleveland: Meridian Books, 1966), pp. 48-81.

that there is no existential separation implied between the orders of natural law and divine law, between nature and grace, in the writings of St. Thomas. According to Father Rahner, St. Thomas admits the possibility of a formal but non-existential distinction of these orders. Hence a Thomist need not accept some Neo-Thomists' claim (e.g. Soto) that these laws are formally and existentially distinct. Rahner rejects the consequences of such reasoning, i.e. that the world of grace is one removed from the world of of experience. However, Father Rahner perhaps analyzes insufficiently the reason for the distinction of these orders in St. Thomas and other Thomists. It is true that such Thomists as Fray Luis held that there is an existential difference between the observance of reason's law and divine positive law as it is found in different people, the saved and the damned. But followers of Giles of Rome's version of the real distinction of essence and existence could admit such an existential separation of these orders without denying the further possibility of the existential character of the order of grace as Rahner seems to imply that they do. For Giles, we have reality in virtue of two separate acts of existence.

Rahner is anxious to point out that grace is not without relevance to the world of individual experience.[24] However, the notion that the distinction of the orders of natural and divine positive law, of nature and grace, is not existential and only formal was taken by Fray Luis to mean that grace was operative not only in the individual but in political history as well. For him grace, i.e. observance of divine positive command, leads men to look for changes in world history. The divine law can be manifested in cultural change and social experience. Rahner seems to overlook the social significance that at least some 16th Century Thomists saw in the doctrine of Aquinas. For Fray Luis, the effect of Christian belief is, unlike for Rahner, not reconciliation of man with his secular reality, but of secular reality with the ideal humanity of Christ.

The question whether the Decalog is still divine positive law is un-

---

[24] Karl Rahner, S.J., *Nature and Grace,* (New York: Sheed and Ward, 1964), pp. 129-130. He writes, "Grace also penetrates our conscious life, not only our essence but our existence too. The teaching of St. Thomas on the specific object of the entitatively supernatural elevated act, an object which (*qua* formal) cannot be reached by any natural object, must be re-thought and made prevalent again. Here 'object' does not mean 'objectively given, distinguishable from others through reflection and seen together with others.' A formal object is neither an object of knowledge nor just the bringing together of what is common to many individual objects by abstracting it afterwards, it is the *a-priori* 'mental horizon,' which we are conscious of in being conscious of ourselves, which is, the context of all our knowing and recognizing of *a-posteriori* individual objects." This is from a translation by Dinah Wharton.

resolved in key writings of the late Augustin Cardinal Bea, whose role in the Papal Curia gave him responsibility for ecumenism. The Second Vatican Council (1962-1965) declared the following to govern the relations of the Church and the Jews:

The Church repudiates all persecutions against any man. Moreover, mindful of her common patrimony with the Jews, and motivated by the gospel's spiritual love and by no political considerations, she deplores the hatred, persecutions and displays of anti-Semitism directed against the Jews at any time and from any source.[25]

Cardinal Bea, in describing the relation of the Church and the Jews after the Passion wrote:

... that the Jewish people are no longer the people of God in the sense of an *institution for the salvation of mankind*. The reason for this, however, is not that it has been rejected, but simply that its function in preparing the kingdom of God finished with the advent of Christ and the founding of the Church. From then on, the nature of the people of God and the way of becoming incorporated in it changed completely: the "people of God" of the New Testament is no longer confined to a single nation and is no longer propagated by descent according to the flesh but by faith. All this, however, does not in fact imply the disavowal of the election of "Israel according to the flesh." On the contrary, "the gifts and the call of God are irrevocable" (Romans 11: 29). Israel remains most dear to God for the sake of its fathers (cf. Romans 11: 28).[26]

The question of the validity of the principle of the formal distinction of the Decalog as divine positive law and natural law in Christian moral observance is relevant for interpreting the Council's declaration and Cardinal Bea's statement. The Church declares herself to be resisting anti-Semitism for non-political reasons. If the Council's statement implies that the Christian moral law forbidding anti-Semitism is based upon a divine positive law, it seems to follow that the Church can say it is motivated by the "gospel's spiritual love." If, on the other hand, it implies that the rejection of anti-Semitism is based on a law of natural reason, contained in the Decalog, but not exclusively a part of the Christian law, then it is difficult to understand how purely political considerations in this matter are avoidable. Would not the ideal state of affairs be a political condition wherein anti-Semitism did not exist? How would the goal of tolerance enjoined upon Catholics differ from the goal of achieving this

---

[25] Walter M. Abbott, S.J., ed., *The Documents of Vatican II*, (New York: Guild Press, 1966), p. 116. This is from the decree *Nostra Aetate*, promulgated October 28, 1965.

[26] Augustin Cardinal Bea, S.J., *The Church and the Jewish People*, Philip Loretz, S.J., trans., (New York: Harper and Row, 1966), pp. 95-96.

political situation? However, if this political condition also has a religious formality in which the Church has an interest then it can excuse itself of acting from political motivation.

Without extending the consideration of contemporary theologians further, it may be wondered if the old theological principle of the formal distinction of the laws of the Decalog may indeed still obtain. If this is the case, then it is a point of Catholic belief that one is not morally obliged, and is forbidden, to recognize in principle that the laws of any particular secular state are, by the mere fact that they are civil law, or because they are in conformity with reason, necessarily deriving from natural law or are based in the eternal law of God.

Is it Vatican II's view that Christian morality, at least in the matter of anti-Semitism, is based upon a religious law as well as a natural law? If so, the Council also seems to reaffirm a medieval principle that the Church's differences with Judaism and Islam are also religious and not only moral as Soto, and perhaps Rahner and others, seem to imply. Any civil law that contradicts the religious character of moral law would then be unacceptable. A law enjoining general anti-Semitism would be a case in point for it would seem to preclude the possibility that there may be religious considerations in moral relationships with Semites which would also have a bearing on one's attitude toward them. Purely political grounds would be insufficient for justifying racial persecution. A Christian's moral position also involves religious differences with Jews and Moslems. Such a person can express his moral differences with them in religious terms, not only in political ones. Perhaps this is the point the Council insists upon when it says it finds its motivation for racial toleration only in the gospel.

The Thomism of Soto does not seem to require that men recognize the presence of religious considerations in the moral interpretation of their political acts. Soto supposes that the moral bases of society are to be grasped by natural reason without need of religion or revelation. The fact that the law of the Decalog and Christian morality do coincide in practice is attributed to the enlightened state of the Christian's natural reason not to his religion.

God's positive law, according to all Thomists, cannot be in opposition to natural law. For Soto social relationships among Christians are not different from those springing from what is to be found in an examination by man's own reason. For Soto, social relationships incumbent upon Christians are different than those imposed on non-Christians. What constitutes human social morality in a situation where there is no Christian revelation is only reason's law without religious considerations.

Fray Luis seems to think that the social morality of Christians also springs from what is natural for humanity. It is true that he maintains that those laws which characterize Christians differ from those imposed by God before Pentecost. Yet, in opposition to Soto, he seems to go further to say that the moral order of the Old Testament was also different than that where there was no revelation of any kind. No communication of divine law conflicts with the law of nature and all perfect it. Religion's laws do conform materially with the moral precepts of the natural law and they seem to be relevant to moral considerations of social relationships in general, whether natural, Mosaic or Christian.

In line with this the next chapter concerns Fray Luis' social theory. It is his view of ideal social relationships that will be examined. His attitude is not one which can precind from religious suppositions as one might expect from Aristotle or from such modern theorists as Hobbes and Rousseau. On the other hand, his is not a theory of society wherein only Christendom is considered to be of importance. Rather, it seems to be his view that religious law forms an essential part of human society. His analysis of social morality depends upon the relation of various religious laws, natural ones, as well as Mosaic and Christian. It is not only a philosophical theory of society, but a religious one as well. It is the former because different religious laws are subjected to rational evaluation. It is the latter because it involves an evaluation of various religious laws from a single religious perspective which he would say is the Christian one. Let us examine his view in some detail.

CHAPTER IV

FRAY LUIS' SOCIAL THEORY

This chapter will discuss a characteristic feature of Fray Luis de León's thought. His theory of society is expressed in religious terms. What is special for him is that the Jews, as a religious people, play a unique role in the shaping of society. Their conversion to Christianity has a profound effect upon the course of history and, in his view, the end of history will be marked by God fulfilling His ancient promise to His chosen people. They will enter the kingdom of the messiah as Jews and as Christians. Fray Luis' theory is not presented as an exclusively Christian view of society. While society is viewed in theological terms by him, he uses both Jewish and Christian religious writings to support his social interpretations. As a Christian, he does not see non-Biblical Jewish material as having theological authority. Nevertheless, he accords them importance insofar as he considers Judaism to have been a true and revealed religion.

Modern scholars of Fray Luis have noted that there are apocalyptic tendencies in his writings. They have also observed that he occasionally draws upon rabbinical authorities in his theological works. But, there is much difference of opinion as to whether this constitutes grounds for classifying Fray Luis as a Christian social theorist in any special sense. Such apocalyptic tendencies are not unknown among the Fathers of the Church, and occasional use of rabbinical or cabalistical material does not prove that his theology is based on any but the most traditional patristic interpretations of Scripture. However, if there is a relation of dependence between these factors, this might suggest that Fray Luis recognized the apocalyptic events as occurring in his own time. Specifically, this would involve the ultimate conversion of the Jews.

Catholic apocalyptic doctrine is based upon the belief that the Church is the New Israel, and that the theological-political claims of the Jews are transferred to a Church which is destined to enjoy primacy in the physical kingdom of Christ after the last days.

Augustinian authorities are generally agreed that there are traces of rabbinical material and occasional cabalistic arguments in him, but they generally regard Fray Luis' theology as basically patristic and his apocalyptic leanings as exaggerated, though doctrinally based only in the Fathers and the medieval scholastics. What Jewish influences they do admit are usually limited to Fray Luis' acceptance of the superiority of the Hebrew Scriptures over the Vulgate for exegetical purposes.[1]

A second view is shared by some Catholic and Jewish scholars. It is that Fray Luis was partial to Jewish Biblical exegesis, and was interpreting contemporary events as the apocalyptic ones. As for the Catholics, Dominicans of the Salamanca convent of San Esteban, men like Medina, regarded Fray Luis as a Judaizer and heretic and so were responsible for his denouncement and almost for his death. The great Jesuit exegete, Ribera, found his views unacceptable because they were too Jewish.

Some Jewish scholars have, in the course of their studies suggested, but never fully argued, that Fray Luis was a cabalist. Ariel Bension located Fray Luis in the Hebraic tradition of Spanish mysticism and compares him (and Juan de la Cruz and Santa Teresa as well) with such figures as Moses of Leon and Abraham Abulafia.[2] Francois Secret also suggests that Fray Luis was a Christian cabalist and was part of an authentic religious movement of the times and was not merely an anti-Jewish propagandist, but a man whose own deep personal beliefs were cabalistic. Furthermore, one has the impression that Baer, the distinguished historian of Spanish Judaism, regards at least some with apocalyptic tendencies among 16th Century New Christians as secret Jews.

A third view is that of recent Hispanists associated with the Instituto Arias Montano in Spain, who do find very considerable influences of rabbinical and cabalistic writers in Fray Luis and these are of the opinion that its significance from a critical point of view is greater than ever admitted by the Augustinian school. José Millás Vallicrosa is the author of an important article on this matter. An interesting book by his disciple, Alexander Habib Arkin, has investigated this viewpoint further and con-

[1] Gutiérrez, *Fray Luis,* p. 466. Mariano Revilla, O.S.A., "Fray Luis de León y Los estudios bíblicos en el siglo XVI," *Religion y Cultura,* II (1928), pp. 506, 508.

[2] Ariel Bension, *El Zohar en la España musulmana y christiana,* (Madrid: Ediciones Nuestra Raza, 1934), pp. 37, 68-69. This book has a preface by Miguel de Unamuno. Secret, *Kabbalistes Chrétiens,* p. 224. Baer, *History of the Jews,* II, Chapters 13-15. For a completely new approach to the problem of the Marranos' religion, see: B. Netanyahu, *The Marranos of Spain,* (New York: American Academy for Jewish Research, 1966).

cludes that there is a direct link between Jewish authors and Fray Luis' literary production.[3]

None of these aspects substantiates the position of this study. The Augustinian position admits the presence of both Jewish theology and apocalyptic consciousness. But, it rejects their relationship. Though the investigations of Millás and Arkin are not of a philosophic nature, Millás adds evidence that this position may be incorrect. Yet, he treats the Jewish influence as collateral with patristic exegesis and so not necessarily involving a dependency upon it. Arkin takes great pains to show that the Jewish sources are distinguished from Christian ones which he admits are the ones of dominant theological impact.

Bension's and Secret's positions lack not only desirable evidential support, but interpretive value. My own view is that their findings regarding Fray Luis' cabalism are correct. Neither presents an adequate textual analysis to establish this, however. They do not detail how cabalism can be consistent with Christian theology. The Dominican position has been opposed by the Augustinians for centuries and their public polemic seems to be carried on now more in terms of old Salamanca's academic personalities and politics.[4] The old Dominican position would deny that Fray Luis was an orthodox Catholic. The settlement of this matter may well be historical, not theological. But, the Dominicans were correct that there does exist a relation of dependence between rabbinical theology and apocalyptic consciousness in Fray Luis. However, this need not be evidence of Judaizing.

This fact can be best illustrated by showing that his opinion concerning a central item of Christian doctrine, purpose of the Incarnation of God and the divinity of Jesus, is argued from Jewish authorities. The divinity and messiahship of Jesus are according to Fray Luis integral to Christianity and so, in his view, to authentic Jewish belief. The messianic prophecies of temporal dominion concern the Jewish people and they still obtain if they are Christianized.

[3] José Millás Vallicrosa, "Probable influencia de la poesía sagrada Hebraico-española en la poesía de Fr. Luis de León," *Sefarad*, XV (1955), p. 283. Alexander Habib Arkin, *La influéncia de la exégesis hebre a en los comentários biblicos de Fray Luis de León,* (Madrid: CSIC, 1966), p. 4. Also pointing to the Hebraic character of Fray Luis' thought, though not to say the rabbinical and cabalistical side are: Michael Nerlich, *El Hombre Justo y Bueno: Inocencia bei Fray Luis de León,* (Frankfurt a/M: V. Klostermann, 1966); John B. Wang, *Estudio analitico-sintetico de las poesías originales de Fray Luis de León,* (Ann Arbor: University Microfilms, 1968), and "La poetica de Fray Luis de León," *Revista de Estudios Hispanicos* (University, Alabama), IV (1970), pp. 99-105.

[4] This is true at least on the Augustinian side of the dispute. See: La Pinta, *Estudios y polemicos,* pp. 185, 217 ff. The intensity of the dispute suggests the theological question is by no means settled.

If Fray Luis' messianism is based on Hebraic authorities it does not mean that he thereby denies patristic doctrines about the second coming, but only perhaps that he is arguing what could not be argued from the Fathers, namely that the prophecies are being fulfilled in his particular time in history. By citing Christianized versions of Hebrew authorities, he reveals his belief that the climax of spiritual history already took place in the Incarnation. Yet, in citing them he also suggests perhaps that the patristic doctrines of the second coming apply to his own time. This latter may have been suggested to him by his own improved exegetical techniques if he was a cabalist.

The central importance of Fray Luis' theology of the Incarnation was clearly seen by the greatest expositor of the Augustinian position, Marcelino Gutiérrez, O.S.A. The answer to the philosophical question of the purpose of creation, the final cause of man, his history and his laws, is, for Fray Luis, a question answered by theology. Nature has no purpose other than the humanization of Jesus Christ.[5] Gutiérrez, however, only associated Fray Luis with Abelard, Lull, Scotus, and the whole Franciscan school on this point. On the question of Jewish influences he wrote:

But it seems to us supposing somewhat to speak of rabbinical influence when one considers Fray Luis as a philosopher.... The famous Augustinian roundly denied that he had read, much less looked with desire to reproduce the opinions of any rabbi. And, he did not distinguish between expositors and philosophers. This justified his conduct, for the versions most in agreement with the Hebraic text and favorable to rabbinical opinion were by him as an act of toleration, and not always of sentiment. This affirmation gets rid of all possibility of his having been inspired by Jewish books with respect to the first part of his life. On this rests the evaluation we oppose.[6]

Fray Luis' own words do confirm this opinion that he was not introducing a new theological opinion into the Christian schools. He was, nonetheless, apparently the first to introduce a new mode of theological

---

[5] Gutiérrez, *Fray Luis,* pp. 151-152. "Y decimos una cuestión téológica, porque, si bien es cierto, como hemos notado antes, que algunos filósofos españoles traían á la doctrina católica de la creación ideas de tinte un tanto platónico ó rabínico, nuestro sabio muestra claramente haber bebida aquí sus pensamientos en las fuentes más puras de la tradición eclesiástica ... no tiene Fr. Luis el mérito de haber traído á la Escuela, antes que ningún otro, tan singular opinión." See also p. 449.

[6] *Ibid.,* p. 418. "Pero nos parece un tanto supositicio hablar de influencias rabínicas, cuando se considera á Fray Luis como filósofo.... El insigne Agustino negó redondamente [*Doc. Ined.* X, pp. 329-332] que hubiese leido, cuanto más buscado con deseo de reproducir sus opiniones, obras de rabino alguno, sin distinguir entre expositores y filósofos, justificando su conducta para con los versiones más ajustadas el texto hebreo y favorables á los opiniones rabínicas, como conducta de tolerancia y no siempre de asentimiento; afirmación que, respecto de esta primera parte de su vida, quita toda la posibilidad de haberse inspirado en libros judios, en que se apoya la apreciación que impugnamos."

expression at Salamanca. Also, contrary to Gutiérrez, it was not necessary for him to have read Jewish books to have known rabbinical authors rather well.

Gutiérrez considered various parts of Fray Luis' own testimony at his trial as evidence of his dependency upon the theology of Scotus. However, the opposition of the Dominicans was not on account of his maintaining the Scotist position, but his novel reasons for doing so. The point at issue was not the orthodoxy of Scotus, but the introduction of a new feature in the teaching of dogmatic theology. Let us read Fray Luis' own words:

And of this the fathers of the Society of Jesus of that place will be great witnesses. The opinion of Scotus which says that the Word should be incarnated because of the humanity of Our Lord Jesus Christ, although Adam did not sin, was sustained in the schools only by the Franciscans. This is an opinion much in honor of this most holy humanity. I, in my lecture, showed with reasons which no theologian had discovered, that it was the most probable and true opinion. Since then it has been sustained in Salamanca by all those who put forth conclusions on that matter. This is one of the reasons which inflamed the Dominicans against me. They complain of it in public and say I have deviated from St. Thomas' probable opinion in this. This is no more or less than to say that our Redeemer, Jesus Christ, merited for us not only the first grace, but also its disposition which precede it, which Driedon and Soto and other doctors deny. I was the first one in that school to sustain it and I taught and I demonstrated that they were mistaken, and that their opinion was dangerous, and so thence forward was sustained always what I said.[7]

What was this new feature of theological expression which moved Fray Luis, and after him, as he said, nearly all the other theologians, to accept his position on grace and justification? I think that this was not only the acceptance of the value of Hebrew versions of Scripture. It was also, perhaps, the importance of the use of Jewish exegetical methods in-

---

[7] *Doc. Ined.*, X, pp. 386-387. Y desto serán grandes testigos los padres de la Compañia de Jesus de aquel lugar, porque la opinion de Escoto que dice que fuera la humanidad de nuestro Señor Jesucristo, y que el Verbo encarnara, aunque, no pecare Adan; porque es opinión muy en honor desta sanctisima humanidad, no es sustentaba en las escuelas sino por los franciscanos; yo en mi lectura monstré con pasos de Escritura y con razones, las cuales ningun teologo habia descubierto, que era opinion probabilisima y verdadera; y desde entonces se sustenta en Salamanca por todos los que ponen conclusiones de aquella materia, que es una de las causas de encendió a los dominicos contra mi, porque publicamente se quejaron dello y de que había dejado en esto a Sancto Tomás siendo su opinión probable. Ni mas ni menos decir que nuestro Redemptor Jesucristo nos mereció no sola la primera gracia sino otros doctores; yo fuí el primero que en aquella escuela lo sustení y enseñé y monstré tambien los disposiciones della que le anteceden, lo cual niegan Driedon y Soto y otros doctores; y fuí el primero que en aquella escuela lo sustení y enseñe y monstré que se engañaban, y que su opinión era pelegrosa, y ansi se sustento de allí adelante siempre lo que yo decía.

terpreted in a Christian sense. The question may also have been whether what such use signified was a reality. For some in the 16th Century, to use Jewish material was to agree with the Jews that the end of history was at hand and that their destiny was about to be fulfilled. If this was the case, then this would be to reject as immoral the racial laws of Spain. If this was not the problem then the question of whether Christian theology was wedded to Aristotelian expression certainly was.

The case of Augustinian scholarship on this point rests on its contention that Fray Luis was at most guilty of opposing the canons of Trent about the authority of the Vulgate. These writers insist that Fray Luis did not deviate from what were acceptable Catholic standards of exegesis and that in so questioning minor points of the Vulgate's accuracy, he was merely ahead of his time. Father Revilla points to the fact that there was nothing in his lectures on the Vulgate that was not in such accepted writers as Driedon and Sixtus of Sienna. This contention, according to them, adequately answers the charge that Fray Luis' exegesis is in any way rabbinical.

Another Augustinian author has noted that it was possible to accept both the norms of post-Tridentine Catholic exegesis and follow Jewish authorities with regard to the literal meaning of Scripture. Olegario García de la Fuente has observed that the exegetical principles of the *Bibliotheca Sancta* of Sixtus of Sienna, O.P., do admit the usefulness of rabbinical and cabalistical methods, a fact also noted by Secret. García, of course, rejects these as unacceptable and dangerous and denies there being any trace of them in Fray Luis.[8]

Fray Luis explicitly said he followed Sixtus of Sienna. A copy of the *Bibliotheca Sancta* was found in his library after his arrest and was sent to the Holy Office.[9] There is no question, then, that he was quite familiar with that work.

Following St. Augustine, Sixtus explains the division of Biblical exposition into the historical or literal sense and the mystical sense. The

[8] Olegario García de la Fuente, O.S.A., "Un tratado inédito y desconocido de Fr. Luis de León sobre los sentidos de la Sagrada Escritura," *La Ciudad de Dios*, CLXX (1957), p. 287. François Secret, "Les Dominicains et la Kabbale Chrétienne à la Renaissance," *Archivum Fratrum Praedicatorum*, XXVIII (1957), pp. 328 ff. *Doc. ined.*, XI, p. 81.

[9] *Doc. ined.*, X, p. 389. Sixtus of Sienna, O.P., *Bibliotheca Sancta*, (Venice, 1566), p. 142. Sixtus wrote: "Post illa quatuor potissima et apud omnes expositores resitatissima sacrarum expositionum genera, iam a nobis descripta, tres etiam reperiuntur particulares divinae scripturae explanationes, neminum Elementaris, Physica, Prophetica: quorum licet apud divinior interpretes rarus sit usus et sub jam praedictis communibus generibus quadammodo contineri videantur: tamen, ne quid a praesens institutum pertinens reliquamus intactum, eos; utpote scitur non indignos esplicabimus. . . ."

former is divided into proper and improper or metaphorical senses, and the latter is either allegorical, tropological (legal), or anagogical (mystical). Fray Luis seems to have used this traditional division as García has noted. But we also find that Sixtus has a section in which he discusses what he calls particular and useful examples of the above division, and here the cabalistical and rabbinical methods are explained.

These include the methods Sixtus seems to have derived from Pico and the other Christian cabalists. The "elementary" method depends on the significance of letters in Scriptural languages, Hebrew and Greek. The "physical" depends on the cabalistical belief that the description of the Tabernacle of Moses mystically contains the secrets of physical nature. The "prophetic" method depends on the idea that the literal words of Scripture contain prophecy of the future, not in the proper sense of literal, but by way of continued metaphors. This method, according to Sixtus, was used with great success by Joachim of Flore and Savanarola. It is also like the methods used in the midrashim and rabbinical commentators.[10]

Since there is no question that Fray Luis was familiar with Sixtus of Sienna's compendium of exegetical methods, it remains to be seen if he actually used the particular Hebraic ones suggested by him. I believe there is evidence that he did. One should remember that this would not have been an unusual practice in his time. Sixtus' book was widely known and he was merely laying down the principles followed already by many such as Pico, Galatino, Rici, and others, and many professional Catholic theologians as well.

Let us, as Father Gutiérrez did, turn to Fray Luis' treatment of the question of the purpose of the Incarnation and the creation of nature. Thus, we will be enabled to establish both the relation of the use of Jewish materials and his theory of society. Fray Luis treated this question three times. We find it in his academic treatise read during the year 1564-1565, *Commentarium in III Partem D. Thomae*. This lecture was not completed for he was transferred to the Durandus Chair where he again dealt with the same material in his *De Incarnatione* of 1566-1567.

---

[10] *Ibid.*, pp. 143-149. As stated previously, fourfold interpretations of Scripture were long in use by Jews and Christians. Pico was the first to identify them as a single set. However, the identity of the prophetic sense was already made by Lyra, if Reuchlin was right that he drew heavily upon Rashi, and therefore also by Pablo de Santa María who annotated Lyra. Hirsch, "Johann Reuchlin," p. 461. Sixtus, a converted Jew, was saved from the stake by the future Pope Pius V. He avoided the condemnation of cabala made by Trent by maintaining, like Pico, that there are two cabalas, a good and a bad. Secret, "Dominicains et la Kabbale," p. 329.

It is also treated in the *Nombre*: *"Pimpollo"* which was first published in 1583.[11]

The first indication that we have that Fray Luis was following the particular senses of Scriptures as suggested by Pico and Sixtus is the treatise of 1564-1565. He argues that God created all things in order to manifest His goodness and his Scriptural evidence is anagogical or elementary as we see.[12]

What is the purpose of nature? He says that it is that God may become man, and for this end mankind itself was created. The arguments he offers for this proposition are four. First, there is reason. If Christ is first, all else is secondary. Second, St. Paul says that Christ is the firstborn of all creatures and that God chose His elect before creation. The third argument is that in Scripture Christ is called "germen" (Zac. 6, Is. 4, Jer. 33, Ps. 67), and as the bud or fruit is the purpose of the plant, so Christ is that of nature. The fourth proof is from authority. The Council of Trent had stated (Ses. 7, cap. 7) that Christ is the final cause of grace.

These are traditional arguments. But, what is important is that the third explicitly refers to Galatino's Christian-Hebraic presentation as the authority on the meaning of these Scriptural texts. This must have been the feature resisted by the Dominicans.

In his second treatment of the Incarnation, we find the same arguments and again a reference to Galatino.[13] If we examine the *Nombre*: *"Pimpollo,"* we find the final cause of creation to be Christ. The Old Testament texts cited are the same as those of the lectures, plus others. All the

---

[11] Muñoz, *Fray Luis, teólogo,* p. 35-36. It should be noted that Fray Luis excludes the use of mystical or allegorical interpretation for proving propositions of faith except in those cases where it is based on the literal sense which explicitly states that it is being used. The classic example is St. Paul's use of Abraham's unions with Sara and Agar as a type of the two Testaments. In this matter Fray Luis opposes Cajetan's interpretation of St. Thomas. See: García, "Tratado inédito," pp. 283, 321-323. Another would be the use of the Greek letters "alpha" and "omega" in Apocalypse.

[12] Fray Luis de León, *Opera,* VII, pp. 257-258, 263-264. Istis rebus, ad hunc modum a Deo cognitis, scilicet, per simplicem intelligentiam, id quod Deus primo omnium voluit, atque decrevit, et ex quo volito reliqua omnia, quae voluit, volita fueruent, fuit suam bonitatem et perfectionem communicare, et manifestare gloriam suam. ... et Apocalipsis, capite ultimo: "ego sum Alpha et Omega, principium et finis," ratio est, quia Deus non potest habere pro ultimo fine rerum a se factarum aliquid aliud praeter se, ... Deus voluit ut essent homines, et universa alia, propterea ut esset Christus, qui finis fuit creationis: itaque, ordine et praesuppositione primo voluit esse Christum: secundo esse homines, et alias res, idque propter Christum. ... Hanc sententiam confirmant nobiles Haebraei, quos refert Galatinus, libro VII De arcanis catholicae fidei, capite II et III; qui Haebraei dicunt, quod Deus permotus amore Messiae, condidit universum, ... idque confirmant ex illis verbis Jeremiae, capite 33, "Nisi pactum meum esset, dies ac noctes, leges caelorum et terrae non possuissem," ex hoc testimonio ratione quodam cabalistica probant quod verbum pactum idem valet, quod Messias.

[13] *Ibid.,* IV, pp. 43, 47-49. See Appendix III.

texts with, perhaps one exception, are also cited in Galatino's *De Arcanis* where they are presented in connection with rabbinical expositions of the texts wherein the Jewish authorities are supposed to be defending the Christian doctrine of the Incarnation. The arguments of Fray Luis parallel those of Galatino almost exactly, if not quite literally.

In none of these places is the name of Scotus mentioned. It rather seems that the texts of Fray Luis indicate that his theory of the purpose of creation depends upon arguments drawn from Galatino's interpretation of Jewish books. That Fray Luis would use cabalistic arguments like Galatino's also is suggested when he argues the prediction of the Resurrection in the sephirothic name of God, *Ja,* in his *Expositio in Psalmos.*[14] There seems to be no other reason to believe Fray Luis' agreement with the Scotists is more than coincidental.

Galatino is not the only cabalistic authority cited by Fray Luis in the two treatises on the Incarnation. The *Apology for Thirteen Questions* is also referred to in the treatise of 1566-1567, in connection with the third of these questions about the veneration of images. Fray Luis states his agreement with Pico.[15] Regarding the fourth of these, about whether God could assume an irrational nature, Fray Luis disagrees with Pico.

In the same work, without explicit reference, Fray Luis adopts Pico's view that Jesus knew cabala. Fray Luis' first question on the matter is whether the soul of Christ was omnipotent. Christ had all the perfect knowledge which is possible to be had by the natural power of the agent intellect and he had it not, says Fray Luis, by infusion, as did Adam and Solomon. Rather he had it by virtue of his own human power, aided by his perfect knowledge of God.

The natures of things which Christ in his perfect science knew humanly were known by infusion to Adam and Solomon. The knowledge of Adam, who named all things in Hebrew according to their natures, and that of Solomon is presented with characteristic features of cabalism as found in Pico.[16] Science of nature is had by way of "numbers and figures"

---

[14] *Ibid.,* I, p. 222.
[15] *Ibid.,* IV, pp. 261, 264, 84, 297. Muñoz, *Fray Luis, teólogo,* p. 36, notes that not all this treatise is Fray Luis' since on January 7, 1567, Luis Sánchez substituted for him. Since the use of Pico's work is so diffuse one is lead to believe that such a continuity can only be that of Fray Luis himself.
[16] *Ibid.,* pp. 368-370, 379, 381, 385, 386, 389. "... illa propositio accipienda est in omni rigore: tum quia omnes Doctores concedunt, quod Adam habuit omnium istorum rerum perfectam scientiam, et etiam videtur de Solomone, ergo talis scientia non est neganda Christo, ... Christus habuit omnes species omnium numerorum et figurarum, quae erant in rerum natura, et quae ad cognitionem illarum scientiarum sunt necessaria ... Christus cognosceret mechanica non necesse habuit illa opera excercere, sed praestantia sui ingenii, visa quacumque re artificiali, potuit assequi, qua ratione illa conficienda esset. ... ingenium, quale erat Christo, non egebat nec

and to discover the secrets of nature one thus must ordinarily do experiments in mechanics. The book of Ecclesiates, attributed to the wise Solomon, indicates according to Fray Luis, that Scripture contains not only the doctrine of supernatural and moral science, but also the seeds of all natural philosophy and the rest of the arts and sciences as well.

There is good reason to suspect that Fray Luis was a cabalistic exegete. It seems his natural science of "numbers and figures" very much resembles the cabalistic modes of Pico and Sixtus.[17]

It is now time to see if Fray Luis' approach to Scripture seems to imply the interpretation of current historical events as his apparent use of Hebraic methods in other contexts seems to suggest. What is the nature of his prophetic interpretation? St. Augustine had, according to Sixtus, distinguished two allegorical senses of Scripture and Fray Luis follows him in this. The allegory of words is one where one thing is expressed in the literal meaning of the words, but another in allegorical meaning. Such allegories would be the use of metaphor or hyperbole, common to sacred and profane writings. This is the improper literal sense. The other allegory is that of deeds where things done in words signify other deeds. This is a mystical sense and is also called the typic sense.

The argument from the allegorical sense of the word *germen,* for example, is based on the meaning of the literal text by allegory of deeds. The nature of the future messiah and his relation to human history, is allegorically expressed in the operations of natural phenomena by the

multo tempore, nec otio ad alias omnes rationes et demonstrationes acquirendas, et comprehendendas. . . . Christi, anima concurrebat ad opera miraculosa, quae faciebat, non solum sicut causa, sine qua non; scilicet, orando et impetrando; sed, etiam ut causa effectiva instrumentalis, ipsa opera miraculosa attingens; et, item, non solum Deus faciebat miracula ad preces animae Christi; sed faciebat per ipsum animam Christi, et humanitatem."

For Fray Luis' notion of the significance of the figures of Hebrew letters, see his small preface to the *De los nombres de Cristo,* García, ed., *Obras completas,* I, p. 420. For another example see Egidio da Viterbo, *Scechina e Libellus de Litteris Hebraicis,* ed., by François Secret, (Rome: Centro Internazionale de Studi Umanistici, 1959), Two Vols., I, p. 28. For Fray Luis' remarks about Ecclesiates, see: Fray Luis, *Opera,* I, pp. 294-295. Scholem has observed that cabalistic physical science may be seen to rest on the double meaning of the Greek word "element," and "letter," whereby the letters of the Torah can be seen to parallel the elements of reality according to the Democratean theory of nature. Such a double use of this word occurs in Aristotle's critique of Democratus (*Gen. and Cor.,* 315b). Cabalists regard Greek philosophy as derived from Moses. Scholem, "Loi," pp. 101-102.

[17] If Fray Luis used this cabalistic "physical" interpretation of Scripture, as I think is most probable, we have an insight into his theory of physical science. Since it was cabalistic, i.e. "Jewish science," it may be connected to his theory of society and politics. Yet, in his case the physical sciences and their application in technology would be related for philosophical reasons, and religious ones, for he uses cabala as a Christian. One wonders if historically, Fray Luis' logic of science is based on religion, and on reason, as this seems to indicate. It may not, however, be based on Christian theology.

Hebrews whose allegories reveal the hidden sense of Scripture. For Fray Luis, this interpretation is certainly a matter of Catholic dogma and would be so because Scripture explicitly says that it is using this as an allegory. The other *Nombres* are also examples of this sense.[18] Fray Luis' concern with the "Hebraic truth" of Scripture led him to criticize the metaphors used in the Vulgate translation which did not always accord with those found in Hebrew versions and in cabalistical literature.[19]

In any case, prophecy of future events is also contained in Scripture in the improper literal sense and this is not a mode of determining matters of theological certainty. Examples are to be found in Fray Luis' exegesis on Deuteronomy 32, or Abdias, or some of the Psalms. In all these cases, the literal meaning is understood as predicting the history of the Jews by use of continued metaphor.

Complete treatments of Fray Luis' views on these matters are to be found in three of his commentaries. The *Tertia Explanatio Canticum Canticorum* was first published in 1589, as an addition to two previous editions of the *Explanatio Canticum Canticorum*.[20] The second lengthy treatment is found in his lecture *In Canticum Moysis*, an exposition of Deuteronomy 32, which was delivered from the Chair of Bible at Salamanca in May of 1582.[21] The third is the *In Abdiam Prophetam Explanatio* which he read in February of 1582. He published it with the 1589 edition of the work on Canticles.[22] Mention will also be made of the *Commentaria in Epistolam II B. Pauli Apostoli ad Thessalonicenses*, which lecture he gave in the academic year 1580-1581.[23]

[18] This method was apparently used by Ramón Martín, O.P. Scriptural and rabbinical texts are used by way of interpretation of this kind of allegory. See: Martinii, *Pugio Fidei*. Fray Luis held Scotus' view to be dogmatically certain. This was, it now appears, because he had introduced arguments from allegory like that of St. Paul's of Abraham's sons theretofore unrecognized in Salamanca but obviously used by Galatino and, perhaps Martín and others.

[19] Fray Luis discussed the value of using Hebrew texts in disputed translations of the Vulgate in his lecture *De Fide* of 1567-1568. His concern to recover the "Hebraic truth" is seen when he endeavors to determine the proper metaphors in Canticles. See: Fray Luis, *Opera*, V, pp. 306 ff. and Appendix II.

Millás has suggested that some metaphors found in the *Nombre*: *"Esposo"* derive from the *Midrash Sir ha Schirim Rabba*. An examination of the *Tertia Explanatio* of Canticles reveals that this *Nombre* is its condensation in Spanish. I believe that Fray Luis' interpretations of this midrash are primarily based upon those of the *Pugio Fidei*, though sometimes it seems that he follows midrashic imagery in cases where the text is not treated in the *Pugio Fidei*. If anyone were to suspect Fray Luis of deviating from Christian practice by drawing upon the midrash, he would be mistaken. See: Millás, "Probable influencia," p. 282, and Appendix I.

[20] Fray Luis, *Opera*, II.

[21] *Ibid., Opera*, I, pp. 3-104. See: Muñoz, *Fray Luis, teólogo*, pp. 72 and 74.

[22] *Ibid., Opera*, III, pp. 423-481.

[23] The 1891-1895, *Opera* was prepared under the direction of Father Marcelino Gutiérrez, O.S.A., and was financed by the Augustinian bishops of Spain. This set of

Fray Luis' commentary on Canticles is in three parts. The first treats the literal interpretation of the words of the Bible, the second is a treatment of the life of the love of God and the last is of the course of God's love for his Church from the beginning to the end of time. Solomon, he says, presents these latter by way of allegory in the image of the two lovers.[24]

History is the story of God's people and the significant events of the past are those which touch upon God's promise of rewards to man. Spiritual rewards were announced for the first time, not by Christ, but in the Old Testament period. However, the Old Law promised temporal rewards to the Jews. What is the outcome of these promises? And what place does the Christian Church have in this temporal history involved in the Jews' rewards?

Fray Luis says the history of the Church is divided in three parts just as Canticles can be divided into three. Here we have further indication of his view of natural law. It is somewhat like revealed law, and yet obtains without revelation. The Canticle recounts all history since Adam since it is nothing more than the story of the love of Christ and the Church.[25] The book tells us how man has striven to love God in all these periods and how God has aided His people.

The same theme is found in the work on Deuteronomy. God inspired

books is seven volumes; quite scarce, the one which I know is owned by Villanova University, Pennsylvania. It was made available to me through the kindness of its President, Father Robert J. Welsh, O.S.A. This edition was printed on paper of very poor quality and it is very important that a new edition of Fray Luis' latin works be forthcoming in the near future not only so that it might be studied, but that it might be used without physical damage to the texts. A new edition would also make available subsequent discoveries of works of Fray Luis made recently, for example, in Coimbra and Rome. I have learned from Dr. John Wang of the University of Montana that another set is owned by the Augustinian College, Washington, D.C.

[24] Fray Luis, *Opera*, II, p. 15. "Solomon . . . mutuum inter Deum et homines amorem exposuit, tum erga Ecclesiam totam, tum erga fideles singulos amorem." Neither of these readings is one arguing a matter of dogma. No point of faith is at issue here as is the case with the matter of the purpose of creation. Matters of dogma must be based on the literal sense of Scripture for Fray Luis. If explicitly so used the allegory of deeds may be used to establish dogmas. But, the prophetic allegory by continued metaphor and the mystical interpretation are not concerned with dogma because the texts in question make no explicit reference as to their interpretation. This can only be a matter of interpretation on the part of the exegete.

[25] *Ibid.*, pp. 116-118. . . . unum naturae, alterum legis, tertium Evangelii atque gratiae. Primum ab Adami pertinisse lapsu, usque ad lationem legis. Alterum a Mose usque ad Christum pervenisse. Tertium a Christo usque ad finem saeculi. . . . in quarum prima Ecclesiae in naturali lege constitutae ratio continetur, in secunda legitimus ejus status declaratur, tertia tota pertinet ad tempora gratiae. . . . Nam declaratur qualis, et quanta fuerit singulis aetatibus Ecclesiae et ejus in virtute praestantia, et Dei Erga ipsam beneficentia. Et quoniam omnis Ecclesiae praestantia, in colendo Deum consistit. Colitur autem Deus charitate, atque fide, id est, de ipso persuasione et amore: beneficentia autem Dei erga illam in hoc maxime extat atque eminent, quod eam tuetur in periculis, et consolatur in rebus adversis.

Moses to write, not to exhort the Jews to the observance of the Law, but following the interpretation of Pablo de Santa María, Fray Luis says that it was to tell them of the outcome of their pact with God before they entered Canaan. This book was written, then, specifically to Jews by their lawgiver to tell them that they were His special people, and that in return for their worship of Him, He was going to give them victory over their enemies.[26] In this the Promised Land is an image of the predestination of the saints.[27] Because of their goodness in worshipping God, and the evil of the Canaanites, the land was given to them. And he says that God lover those who love Him and He will take up His abode with those who love Him.

Nevertheless, Fray Luis says Deut., 32, 15, indicates the ingratitude of the Jews. The great benefits God gave them were deliverance from Egypt, the Promised Land and the messiahship of Jesus. They, however, were responsible for two great sins, that of idolatry and that of the rejection and killing of Christ. In retribution for these sins, the Jews received two punishments, first a light one, and then a heavy one. The light punishment, he says in commenting upon verse 20, was levied during the time of Judges and Kings when God "hid his face" from the Jews and allowed certain misfortunes to befall them. The heavy punishment corresponds to the greater sin of the rejection of the messiah and the punishment for this sin was that the Jews would be despoiled and conquered by the Romans and that the true religion and true love of God would be given to the gentiles. These punishments correspond to the two captivities, of Babylon and Rome, and the two destructions of the Temple. But, the first captivity is the prophetic figure of the second and just as the Jews were restored from the idolotrous city of Babylon, so at the end of time they will be restored to the Church and the possession of spiritual goods and the heavenly kingdom through faith in Jesus. In verse 24, Moses makes reference to the devouring beasts of Daniel and Zachariah in connection with messianic prophecies.[28]

The rejection of Jesus, according to Fray Luis, has resulted in the withholding of divine protection and its transfer to other peoples and the famine, plagues, wars, and envy of the gentiles endured by the Jews. Moses makes it clear that these disasters do not mean the gods of the gentiles are stronger than Him, but only that they are punishments and

[26] *Ibid.*, I, pp. 3-4, 22, 24.
[27] *Ibid.*, p. 21. . . . ut in illo beneficio praeparavit Deus Israelitis terram et regionem quam incolerent, sic in isto praeparavit sanctis regnum coeleste et terram viventium, quae vere promissionis terra est . . .
[28] *Ibid.*, p. 54, 57-60.

reminders. However, He will not continue His wrath lest the enemies of the Jews be satisfied or that they think they have overcome them by their own power or that the worship of the true God is without reward. "To me belongeth vengeance (Deut. 32: 35)." Punishment of the Jews belongs to God, not to their enemies. In fact, the fall of the Jews at the hands of Rome marked the beginning of the spread of the gospel and the beginning of the end of paganism. At the end of time, God will have mercy on the Jews and they will be converted to the faith of Jesus Christ and will be received into the Church and will again be His faithful people. This final conversion is not because of the Jews who deserve their extreme misery, but because of the pride of their enemies who detract from divine honor and power.[29]

God says in verse 39, that He is the master of life and in verse 40, He makes an oath to vindicate His honor and rescue the Jews. The arm of God which He will raise refers to the second coming of Christ who is the hand and sword of God. God calls His enemies those impious ones who are the enemies of the Jews, and therefore of God.[30]

These texts perhaps reveal to us the meaning of the *Nombre*: "*Brazo de Dios.*" It may be directed against those who hate Christian Jews. At the end of the world, Christ will vindicate the Jews as he vindicated them before the Babylonians, the Persians, the Macedonians and will, at length, vindicate them before the Romans who will have been inwardly defeated by the worship of the true God. At verse 43, God extends an invitation to the gentiles to join themselves to the Jews to remove from their own number those who will remain in impiety toward God. These final verses of the chapter, Fray Luis says, refer to the end of time when the Jews will be in the Church and the people of God of all times will be raised from the dead.

---

[29] *Ibid.*, pp. 60-61, 73, 77-79, 85-86.

[30] *Ibid.*, pp. 87, 91. "... et quemadmodum eos, quos diligo, quamvis primo castigatos et afflictos, tandem revoco ad bonam fortunam et felicitatem; sic, vos et idola vestra cum punire coepero, nemo erit qui possit vos eruere de manu mea, id est, afficiam vos sepiterno supplicio. ... Si acuero ut fulgur gladium meum, et arripuerit judicium manus mea: reddam ultionem ... idem Christus, qui in S. Scriptura appellatur brachium et manu Dei. ... qui unquam adversati sunt populo suo, populi, inquam, in ipsum credenti et religiosi ipsum colenti." See also: *Ibid.*, p. 95. The *Nombre*: "*Brazo*" says that the messiah promised to the Jews was not to be a military leader and it claims that it is obstinacy on the part of the Jews to believe this to have been the case. It proposes that Christ is a conqueror of idolatry by spiritual means and the spread of Christianity is evidence that this is the case. Yet, the enemies of Christ are pagans as well as Jews and since the *Arm* is the Jews' messiah, paganism is ultimately to be destroyed, not Jewish belief in its Christian form. See: García, ed., *Obras Completas*, I, p. 571. "Yo persuadido estoy para mi, y téngolo por cosa evidente, que sola esta conversíon del mundo, considerada como se debe, pone la verdad de nuestra religión fuera de toda duda y cuestión." Merino, ed., *Obras*, III, p. 271.

This prophecy was directed to the Jews especially, and it ends with their victory. Nevertheless, Abraham is the father of all men of faith whether by birth or by adoption. Before Christ, the Church was composed mostly of those who belong to Abraham by birth as well as faith, those who belonged by faith alone were few. Some of these were joined to him by faith and Mosaic observance and some by faith alone, i.e. gentiles not knowing Moses in the natural stage of history.[31]

On the other hand, after Christ, most of the people of God belong to Abraham by faith only, i.e. those converted from gentile peoples. Those belonging to Abraham by birth are now few and those by birth and faith, fewer still. As in the *Nombre*: *"Camino,"* Fray Luis observes that there are in the Church those who are just and those who are sinners, and among the sinners there are those who so far have kept the faith pure and those who have stained it by union with another religion. Those Christians who stain the faith by union with pagan gods seem to be those who hate the Jewish Christians. As the Ten Tribes of Israel mixed with the pagans, so after the time of Christ, the Church has parts. At the end of time the Jews will, as a whole, be joined to Christ. The Church will have many labors, but it will never be extinguished and it will always win over seemingly successful enemies.[32]

This doctrine also characterizes Abdias for Fray Luis. However, it will be fruitful first to touch upon his commentary on II Thessalonians. Here again, he says Christ is the author of peace. The Epistle was written because some "pseudoapostles" had taught them the world was about to end. Paul wrote, not to disuade them from desiring the coming of Christ, but to calm them for he knew that it would not occur in their time.[33]

The truth is, says Fray Luis, that the world will last 6000 years. This is proven by the interpretation of the prophecy of Eliah done by Pietro Galatino, Pico and Francesco Giorgio de Veneto, whose cabalism we have had ample occasion to discuss. Second, it is proven by the Sibyls and Hermes Trismegistus and by some of the Doctors of the Church, including among others he lists, Augustine, Irenaeus, and Jerome. It is further indicated, he says, by the account of creation wherein each day represents

[31] *Ibid.,* pp. 96-97, 98-101. . . . qui inter gentes colebant unum Deum et in Messiam futurum conferebant suam spem, vel implicite vel explicite.
[32] *Ibid.,* pp. 101-104. ". . . nam cui eam fidem penitus objiciunt, jam videntur plane in aliam familiam degenerare et in alium populum, contrarium populo Dei. . . . alii, enim, sunt justi; alii pecatores, integre tamen, retinentes professionem fidei, quales sunt omnes christiani; alii vero, qui unum Deum nobiscum colunt et spem suam collocant in Christo, sed tamen errant in eo, quod nondum venisse credunt, sed sperant venturum; quales sunt Judaei, qui ab Ecclesia hac de causa divisi sunt, ... unum cum reliquis fidelibus corpus efficiat."
[33] *Ibid.,* III, pp. 437, 468-470.

a millenium. But, it is especially indicated by the fact that the era of grace will be of same length as the time prior to the Flood, a view of Origen. This, says Fray Luis, puts the end of the world as occurring in the year 1656, A.D. Another argument is that when the gospel is preached to all the Jews and gentiles, Christ will come. The Bible says that no one knows the date certainly (Acts 1: 7), but Fray Luis says certain signs of it are expressed in the Bible and one cannot deny they are present.[34]

Fray Luis, like many others of his time, identified Islam as the antichrist.[35] His motives may well have been his conviction of the messianic destiny of the Jews and the unique place in history accorded Spain because of their conversion in that land. He seems to have connected this with the expulsion of the Moors from Spain which was also seen to have apocalyptic significance.

The vision of Abdias concerns Christ and the Church, says Fray Luis' commentary. The Edomites referred to in the prophecy have to do with the infidels and impious that Christ would one day subdue. Christ, who preached humility and poverty, broke their power, for as soon as he has ascended into heaven, the cult of idols began to abandoned. The power of Rome destroyed the Jews, and the gospel caused the Constantinian age and the fall of Roman gods. But, the antichrist, Fray Luis notes in a long digression, arose in a new form, Islam.

---

[34] *Ibid.*, p. 478.

[35] García, ed., *Obras Completas*, I, p. 603. For an outline of the various apocalyptic interpretations given Scripture at the time, see: Froom, *Prophetic Faith*, II, pp. 528-531. Melancthon also thought Islam was the antichrist. In a very persuasive article, the Jesuit scholar, Sandalio Diego, has noted that two years before Fray Luis published his work on Abdias, the famous Jesuit exegete, Francisco Ribera, published his first Biblical work, his lectures on the minor prophets. He has indicated that Fray Luis added material to his earlier lectures on Abdias and that these additions were directed against the Jesuit whom he attacked with extreme bitterness and abuse at the height of his own maturity and only two years before his death. Ribera is widely regarded as having been the initiator of Catholic Counter-Reformation exegesis. Specifically, he attacked the then current apocalyptic tendencies proposing the immancence of the end of the world to which many Protestant writers subscribed. According to Diego, the reason for Fray Luis' wrath was that Ribera was well known to have rejected the use of Hebrew sources, whether those of rabbis or Catholic Hebraists, in Biblical exegesis. Fray Luis accused Ribera of utter incompetence, saying that his Hebrew was worse than mediocre and that this was clear evidence against him having any professional ability in Scripture. See: Sandalio Diego, S.J., "Fray Luis de León y Francisco de Ribera en el Comentario de Abdias," *Estudios Eclesiasticos* (Madrid), VIII (1929), pp. 5-22. Ribera published his *In librum duodecim Prophetarum Commentarii* at Salamanca in 1587. Froom, *Prophetic Faith*, II, pp. 489-483. Ribera (1537-1591) thought that the apocalyptic events were not taking place. Perhaps, he was more against the use of Jewish sources than Protestants as Froom assumes. Froom, no doubt because of his own views on apocalyptic matters, wants to find a strict distinction between Catholic and Protestant exegesis of the book of Apocalypse that never existed. In the 16th Century, seemingly the difference concerned ,at most, the identification of the antichrist, i.e. whether Pope or Turk, not necessarily the use of prophetic interpretation as such.

On verse 17, Fray Luis draws upon the authority of such figures as Solomon, David, certain Hebrew commentators, as well as Lyra, Vatablus, and Montano, to say that Christ will save his people from their enemies according to Abdias.[36] The latter three commentators are Jewish Christians.[37] Not only will the just enjoy the heavenly rewards, but ". . . the House of Jacob will possess those who possessed them . . ." which, says Fray Luis, refers to the Apostles and those Jews who were converted to Jesus at the time of the early Church and who called the gentiles to their faith. These faithful Jews conquered the gentiles. The House of Jacob is the faithful Jews, and the House of Joseph mentioned are the gentiles who followed them, since Ephraim and Manasee were sons of Joseph by an Egyptian woman. But, the House of Esau is all the impious and idolatrous people. These are the straw and will be burned by the flame and fire of Jacob and Joseph. But, the faithful ones, he says, verse 19 indicates will fall heir to the whole world where ever they go as happened throughout the Roman world where the gospel was preached.[38]

Verse 20, merits an extraordinary commentary. Fray Luis clearly locates current events in prophecy. This verse prophesies the faithful Jews traveling to spread the gospel even to Sarepta, which, Fray Luis says, is all of Gaul.[39] These lines are like the parable where the steward was first sent to the invited guests, who refused to come to the feast, and then to those in the city and finally to those who lived in the country. Not only will the gentiles of the Roman world be called, but also those who live beyond it at the end of time. This Isaiah says. Fray Luis says here that Pablo de Santa María's gloss on Isaiah, 18, makes the prediction of the conversion of some unknown people to the faith of Christ whom Fray Luis seems to think are the native Americans.

The lot of fulfilling this prophecy has fallen to Spain. This is all the more clear because "Bosphoro" in the Hebrew texts is "Sepharad" which

---

[36] There is doubt whether Lyra was Jewish. But we are assured he was regarded as a virtual plagerizer of Rashi by Reuchlin. Hirsch, *Johann Reuchlin,* p. 461.

[37] *Opera,* III, p. 135.

[38] *Ibid.,* pp. 138-140, 147, 152. At the turn of the 17th Century there was much controversy about whether the New World's existence was indicated in the latin or the Hebrew version of the Bible. Ribera held that it is in the latin version. José Acosta, S.J. agreed that the prophecies concerning the spread of the faith could be applied to the Indies in a work given its ecclesiastical approval by Fray Luis himself. Abdias refers to the Church's role, not Spain's, says Acosta. Fray Luis using the Hebrew version says Spain is referred to, not the Church. Spain's claim would be based on the prerogative accorded to the Jews. It would suppose the preservation of Hebrew culture. See Grimston's English translation of Joseph Acosta, *The Naturall and Morall Historie of the East and West Indies,* (London: Blount and Asphy, 1604), pp. 50 ff.

[39] *Ibid.,* p. 154. ". . . certe . . . Massaliam in Narbonensi Gallia delati sunt." See also: pp. 153, 158.

is the rabbinical name for Spain. Sepharad was the place where Hadrian sent the captive Jews.[40] Once the gospel is preached everywhere, the end will come.

Fray Luis must have been interested in contemporary events and have considered them apocalyptic. His references to them include the identification of the Turks as the antichrist, the discovery and evangelization of the New World, and above all, the date of 1656. Furthermore, his view about the role of Spain in the apocalyptic process is that the final conversion of the Jews would occur there. All Jews in Spain were Christians – legally – after 1492. Also, it took no great perception to note the rapid propagation of the gospel then underway on a worldwide scale.

What is of special interest is the role of Jewish culture in the apocalyptic process. In each of the commentaries just examined, it is the history of the Jews that affords the key to understanding human history in general. This seems to be compatible with what was said earlier about his defense of the Incarnation as the purpose of creation, basing his claim on Jewish religious authorities. Lastly, just as the purpose of creation is the Incarnation, so also is the purpose of history the second coming of Jesus, the Jews' messiah.

This last point is of the greatest significance. The apocalypse is the last event of history for two reasons: First, because it is the purpose of Christian history and second, because the purpose of Christian history is that of all men as well. The first is true just as it is true that Jesus is the messiah. This is a point of Christian theology. The second is true just as the purpose of creation is the perfect man. This is also a point of Jewish belief. Fray Luis, however, may accept this last proposition as true, but not only for theological reasons, but also ones that concern his view of the relation of other religions and the Christian one.

Soto would say that the history of mankind and that of the Church are coincident. This is the view of Ribera as well, though he relegates the apocalypse to a distant few days' happenings. Soto's reasons would be that the only actual religious history is the Christian one, specifically the

---

[40] *Ibid.*, p. 172, 168-173. "Et certe non sine arcano Dei consilio in Hispaniam confluxit Judaeorum nobilitatis pars maxima, nam inquit: Transmigratio Hierusalem quae est in Bosphoro, id est, fideles, qui Hispanias incolunt, oriundi, tum a gentibus, tum praecipue ab iis Judaeis, qui Hierosolymis eversis in Hispaniam demigrarunt: Possidebunt civitates Austri, id est, novem orbem, qui Hispaniae Australis est, ... possidebunt. Possidebunt autem quia eum et Evangelii doctrina Idolorum everso cultu, fidei Christi subjicient, et armis suo adjicient imperio." The whole controversy over the relative merits of the Hebrew and Vulgate texts of Abdias in connection with the New World is discussed by Malvenda who sides with Ribera and Acosta. Tomás Malvenda (d. 1628), *De Antichristo libri undecim*, (Rome, 1604), pp. 151-154. This work is in the excellent collection of the Sutro Library, San Francisco, California.

Catholic one. Its end in history and that of the natural history of mankind cannot be other than coincidental if he is to remain faithful to Catholic belief. Fray Luis' view, on the other hand, also supposes philosophical reasons as well to support the second aspect of his opinion since in his view, it is this part that a Catholic can share with the Jews.

This seems to corroborate the claim made in the previous chapter about Fray Luis insisting upon the religious character of the Decalog. The moral law of Christians and Jews is identical as religious law just as certain aspects of their social theory are identical. All religious law does not have to be Christian law. However, one is inclined to add that for Fray Luis, the natural law is also a religious law and that men's societies and laws differ for him as their religious devotion to it. Here, perhaps, is the key to understanding what he means by saying that those Christians who deny Christian Jews their historical destiny are tainted with paganism. And, he insists, paganism will ultimately be destroyed.

One cannot help thinking that the *Nombres de Cristo* are, in part, veiled threats aimed at Ribera and his followers in apocalyptic exegesis as much as at Soto's followers in social theory.

Fray Luis' apocalyptic predictions can be considered failures in the eyes of secular historians. But, one should remember that for Fray Luis religious and secular history are not different in their apocalyptic termination. Neither are they for Soto and Ribera. Rather, as Fray Luis is careful to point out to his students, the date of 1656, is suggested as a possible term of a religious event which he sees as already in progress. This is the struggle of the messiah and the antichrist. It is also, for him, the last struggle of the God of Israel and the gods of Canaan, as well as that of Jesus and Satan. The date 1656, does not symbolize merely the term of the spiritual struggle between Christians and non-Christians, of the Church against the world, but also the end of the visible struggle of two social systems. One is identified with the religion he conceives of as common to just Jews, true Christians and good men in the natural state. The other he identifies with pagans and Christians whose obedience of natural law amounts to idolatry.

Those who question the propriety of his assigning such a date are not, insofar as they understand him, questioning either his orthodoxy or his historical judgment. What they question is the reality of the conflict of these social systems. Neither is theologically exclusive. On the one hand, there is the system common to certain gentiles and Jews, whether presently baptized or not. On the other, there is the system designated in general as being pagan. The first and ideal system can embrace Jew and gentile.

The second he condemns to destruction and is, like Islam, a false religion in guise of a true one.

Thus, Fray Luis' social theory has two aspects joined in one. First, there is that of traditional Christian thought in that it insists upon the final victory of the Christian Church in history. The second is a more philosophical one. This one he thinks of as common to faithful Judaism and reformed Catholicism. It asserts that the purpose of reality and human history transcends the cultures of Jew and gentile and is to be found in the universally expected just man, whoever he is.

Soto and Ribera would hold that history ends with Christ's coming, but for purely Christian theological motives. The Jews would agree that the messiah will come at the end of time for their own theological motives. What is new in Fray Luis' view is that the same religious element is essential to all just societies regardless of what theological of political differences there may be between them. This is his analysis of the problems of the 16th Century and the solution he gives in the *Nombres de Cristo* and elsewhere is to see that the ideal society, that of Christ, transcends men's differences, whether theological or political.

One can suggest now that his social thought includes the notion that some kind of ritual and public worship can be a feature of any just society. He himself holds an apparently orthodox view of the Christian sacraments which form an essential part of Catholic moral observance. Thus, Catholic moral practice after Trent can be seen as compatible with aspects of his social theory. On the other hand, the religious aspect is also compatible with the Jewish law which also commanded ritual worship of God. As a Christian, Fray Luis could accord this ritual no supernatural significance. Yet, such rituals might retain a moral status and as such no Catholic ought to object to them for theological reasons.[41]

Fray Luis' argument is that Christian morality and sacramental worship have fulfilled the purpose of the Jewish law in the impending defeat of paganism and that the Jews themselves are now blind to its religious significance.[42]

[41] Fray Luis thinks there is a natural worship of God besides that of the Jews and Christians. Cf. fn. 31. Vitoria and Cajetan had no objection to the custom of circumcision among certain Mexican Indians. Fray Luis seems to agree with them that certain practices of the Jews are legitimate if done in a spirit of Christian piety. Cf. Chap. III, fn. 9. Note the cabalistic flavor of his treatment of devotion to the Heart of Jesus. Cf. Appendix II. Perhaps the greatest observer of the Indians of the day, Acosta, himself draws a parallel between the rituals of the Mexicans and the Catholic sacraments.

[42] Cf. fn. 30, also Chap. V, fn. 41. García, ed., *Obras Completas*, p. 570. "Vengan ahora, pues, los que se ceban de solo aquello que el sentido aprehende, y los que, esclavos de la letra muerta, esperan batallas y triumfos y señorías de tierra, porque algunas palabras lo suenan así; y si no quieren creer la victoria secreta y espiritual,

All Catholics have a ritual law, just as each religious group has its own form of worship. But, by finding that ritual worship is one thing common to all social morality, an anthropological claim, he is able to identify those Christians whose social morality is akin to that of the Mosaic period, or even that of the Indians, and oppose these to those whose morality is not. Into the latter class would fall the moral philosophy of Aristotle.[43]

Both Catholic theology and the theory of society as a religious community seem to be part of Fray Luis' own social theory because he admits of only one possible moral law, that of Christ. And, to repeat, his reasons for this can be twofold. First, it may be a point of Catholic theology, and second, it is that religion is a basic mode of social organization, and ritual communion can characterize this kind of society no matter what the theology is of the religious society in question. With the prospect of an entirely new and universal moral order he seems to argue that membership in the Church could assure one of moral rectitude. It does not seem to follow from his principles, however, that only the Catholic Church would be morally correct. As far as his social philosophy is concerned it seems his view is that one needs a universal religious union to save society from disaster. The alternative to this kind of catholic social reform seems to be a kind of nationalism, whether pagan, Protestant, Catholic or Islamic, wherein the religious and rational aspects of social organization are confused.

---

y la redención de las animas que serían a la maldad y al demonio, que obró Christo en la cruz, porque no se ve con los ojos, y porque ni ellos para verlo tienen los ojos de fe que son menester, esto a lo menos que pasó y pasa publicamente, y que lo vió todo el mundo, la caída de los ídolos y la sujecíon de todas las gentes a Cristo . . ."

[43] One may recall Fray Luis' objection against Luther that purity of conscience does not free one from the obligation to obey canon law. Cf. Chapter III, fn. 19. His reasons for this are not to be found so much, I think, in Catholic theology as in his social theory generally. Goods works are necessary for salvation besides faith and the chief examples of these would be the sacramental worship of just men. Soto, as a Catholic, would perhaps insist upon the importance of sacramental worship, but he apparently would not regard this as a property following from the religious character of all just law, but of the supernatural law beginning with the death of Christ only. One notes, for example, his extreme opinion about the immorality of any circumcision. For him, the moral observances of the Jews and certain gentiles such as Hermes Trismegistus and Job did not differ, both being natural and of equal dignity. Pico regarded these as natural, but accorded a higher natural dignity to the observances of the Jews than to the gentiles' in line with his interest in natural magic, something Soto does not do. Fray Luis accomplishes this by observing that just moral law has a religious character as well as a rational one. Cf. Chapter III, fn. 8.

CHAPTER V

MORALITY AND NATIONAL DESTINY
IN FRAY LUIS

This examination and interpretation of themes in the works of Fray Luis de León relating to his moral theory opposes that of Menéndez y Pelayo and others that his moral thought is basically Hellenic in character, or that it is merely identical with Catholic moral theology. The position to be argued is, rather, that Fray Luis is not only to be considered a Christian cabalist, but that the Jewish cultural tradition may be considered an exclusive source of his own doctrine on mysticism. It is the universality of Jewish moral theory that is unique and special in his own moral thought. This characteristic will have relevance to this remarkable attitude toward Spain's national destiny.

The expositive part of this argument has several parts. First, salient themes from his major documents that refer to the spiritual life have to be presented. These can be compared to two possible sources, Pico and pseudo-Dionysius, in an effort to note parallelisms between Pico's ideas and those of Fray Luis. Second, it will be observed that Fray Luis' moral theory has elements showing the influence of the 16th Century ecclesiastical reform. Third, it will be shown that his moral doctrine manifests the influence of cabalism and that this is not to be seen as incompatible with his professed Thomism. Then, by comparison with authors whose ideas are similar, his own unique doctrine can be revealed. The last part will attempt to interpret these findings, especially as they seem to be related to Spanish national destiny in the New World.

It will be necessary to repeat only the barest essentials of Fray Luis' spiritual doctrine as already well presented by Father Welsh. Rather, the task at hand is to examine the crucial tests on the subject to establish philosophical sources.

The primary document for this is the *In Canticum Canticorum Expositio,* a three part work, the third of which we have already examined.[1]

---

[1] This work is in the *Opera,* II, pp. 9-462, which reproduces the 1589, *Triplex Explanatio* published by Fray Luis.

The first part of these treats the proper literal sense of the texts of Scripture. It roughly parallels the Spanish translation and commentary Fray Luis had done early in his career and which occasioned one of the complaints at his trail. Trent had forbidden the publication of vernacular translations of the Bible.[2] The second book is an allegorical exposition and is entitled *Altera Explanatio*. The allegory Fray Luis sees in this second reading is one of deeds, not that of words. He sees in the metaphors of the lovers the love of God and the soul expressed in the mystical sense of Scripture described previously.

The distinctive notion of Fray Luis' idea of unity in diversity is that Christ unifies the Church (and ultimately mankind) both because in him all find their common historic destiny, and also because each one is individually called by him to a life of divine love. Not only is the Church destined to an historic destiny of temporal rewards at the end of time, but presently it is characterized by union with Christ in the moral or spiritual life of its members. Inasmuch as the text of Canticles metaphorically expresses the life of the Church, it must also express, in the same manner, the degrees of the spiritual life of each of Christ's beloved. Just as there are three periods in the history of the Church, the natural, Mosaic and Christian, so there are three degrees of the moral life, that of beginners, the proficient, and the perfect. The metaphorical texts of each of the two sets of the stages correspond.[3]

Fray Luis says, further, that he is not entirely original in this. Older authors, he affirms, have interpreted parts of Canticles as referring to the Church and other parts as referring to individuals, but he states that his contribution is to treat the whole of Canticles as referring to each separately.[4] In this statement Fray Luis sets himself apart from St. Bernard, for example, whose *Sermones in Cantica* treat the beloved at times as

---

[2] See: Bell, *Fray Luis,* pp. 164-165, for details. Fray Luis had done this translation as a young man for a cousin who was a nun and who could not read latin. He claimed it was stolen from his rooms and circulated without his authorization. It was nonetheless enormously popular.

[3] Fray Luis, *Opera,* II, p. 40. Sed utrum hic singulorum tantum, an communiter omnium bonorum ratio explicetur, id est, utrum, in hoc carmine declaretur amor Dei erga singulos bonos, an potius erga ipsum coetum, et conventum bonorum, quae graeco vocabulo Ecclesia dicitur, in eo non omnes consentiut quamquam mea quidem sententia cur dissentiant causa nulla est: cum utrumque non solum verum sit, sed necesse sit esse. Nam et ratio totius semper ex partibus existit: et in natura ipsa qualis est descriptio universi, talis et ratio singulorum ejus partium, proportione tamen cujusque partis. Quare fateamur in his personis non Ecclesiae modo, sed cujuslibet etiam pii, ac fideles hominem imaginem inesse, et posse hoc divinium carmen apte referri ad utrumque genus.

[4] *Ibid.,* pp. 40-41.

the Church, as opposed to the Synagogue, and at times as the Christian soul, but certainly not both simultaneously.[5]

That Canticles is a guide for the moral life is a traditional Christian view. In the Hebraic tradition it is never interpreted as a dialogue between God and the soul until the 16th Century mystics of Safed did so in connection with its messianic significance. The mystical union is previously always pictured as one between father and daughter, not bride and bridegroom, Moses' case alone expected.[6]

The Hebraic nature of Fray Luis' themes in his treatment of the spiritual life are suggested when they are compared with those of Pico, especially his *Heptaplus,* or commentary on Genesis.

Pico held that Pythagoras, Plato, Aristotle, Jesus, St. Paul and Dionysius were all privy to a secret, unwritten doctrine of Moses by which the true meaning of the Law was to be understood, i.e. cabala.[7] The usage of numbers and whatever else he thought was great in Greek thought he conceived of as left over from this first source.[8] Pico expressed the view that the Jews found justification because they did not worship the stars, but God, and their Law is distinguished as the "supercelestial waters" or "fire" are from "celestial waters" or "fires" which the gentiles made their gods. Because they observed the Law, spiritually, the Jews were able to conquer the Promised Land, but when the did not obey God, the gentiles were as "incursions of water and the sea." [9]

Fray Luis compared the "waters" to the enemies of the Church and the fire of love of the perfect is said to be unable to be quenched by adversity.[10] In the Christian Scriptures, Pico said, water also refers to the gentiles, but now as if they were the supercelestial waters of Christ. Because the Jews were found wanting, it was the gentiles who received their

---

[5] J.-P. Migne, ed. *Patrologiae Latinae* Tomus 183, (Turnhalt, Belgium: Brepols, undated), cols. 785-1198.

[6] M. Simon, trans., *Midrash Rabba, Song of Songs,* (London: Soncino Press, 1951), p. 93, etc. Scholem, *Major Trends,* pp. 226-227.

[7] Fray Luis, *Opera,* III, p. 475. It is likely that St. Paul was regarded by Fray Luis to have been a cabalist for he knew the time of the end of the world, a point Fray Luis drew from Pico.

[8] Pico, *Opera,* unpaginated incunabulum. *Oratio.*

[9] Giovanni Pico della Mirandola, *Heptaplus,* (Florence: Vallechi, 1942), pp. 343-348.

[10] Fray Luis, *Opera,* II, p. 432. Ignem infusa aqua extingui: illorum vero amore, atque ira aestuantem et ardentem animum ne ipsis fluminibus infusis posse mitigari: quae duo maxime saeva maximeque inexorabilia esse viduntur, mortem, et infernum, pene exorari facilius illis posse. . . . Nam quibus multa dedit Deus, ab iis plurima exigit: . . . Nam in hoc genus hominum proprie . . . Paulus invehitur, cum ad Haebraeos . . . scribit: . . . See also: pp. 448-449. . . . aquarum enim nomen in his litteris ad maximas calamitates transfertur; . . . aquae multae, id est, res adversae, . . . non potuerunt tuam erga me aut charitatem extinguere, aut obruere pietatem.

inheritance. The time of plenitude, said Pico, was the fourth of the six thousand year periods, then the messiah was born. Fray Luis said that the return of the Jews to the spiritual observance that once characterized them and that now belonged to the Christians would be difficult, for God expected much of them. Fray Luis used Pico's imagery of the elements in the same way.

Pico's explanation of the six days of creation and the one of rest was based on the theory of a secret doctrine of Moses. The morality prescribed for the Jews was a universal morality, first revealed only to them because of their election, but later, through Christ, promulgated to the whole world. This morality the Jews abandoned and do not now recognize as the same as that of the Christians. This proved for Pico, from the testimony of the Jews, that by the work of the fourth day the coming of Christ was indicated. The sin of the Jews was a sin against their own law and one of perfidy because they did not accept the Christian law which was actually their own as understood by a cabalistic interpretation of their own books. Pico's cosmology is that there are three worlds, the sublunar or world of fire and water which burns and dampens. The higher world is that of the heavens where the sun is a lifegiving fire and the rains vivifying waters. This is the world known by pagan philosophy. The highest world is the supercelestial one where the fire and water are the angelic minds. The science of this world is cabala or Jewish philosophy. This highest world is that of God, the first and immovable unity. The middle world, like God's is unchanging, but only with respect to the earthly world of flux. So, Aristotle's first mover is associated with the stars. These three worlds are depicted in the construction of the Tabernacle of Moses. Jewish philosophy embraces pagan wisdom, yet goes beyond it.[11]

A fourth world exists wherein everything is found that is in the three others, and this is man himself. Man's form is the form of a microcosm in which are mixed aspects of plant, animal, angel and likeness to God. Each world is contained in the other in man so that the image of man is the image of the world and there is no multitude which is not this one in

---

[11] Pico, *Heptaplus,* pp. 186-190, 192-194. According to Walker, *Spiritual Magic,* pp. 55, 90 ff., Pico and Agrippa were able, by this threefold division, to explain the significance of sin and redemption with regard to the course of history. They were able to show that the stars were not the only or ultimate influence on earthly events as was the case in Aristotelianism. Nauert notes that Pico's cosmology is not cabalistic though it is based on Hebraic sources. Agrippa follows Pico whereas Galatino apparently has a more authentically cabalistic view. Charles G. Nauert, Jr. *Agrippa and the Crisis of Renaissance Thought,* (Urbana: University of Illinois Press, 1965), p. 266.

some way, and no discordance not tied to man's basic harmony, nor is there any unconnected multiformity. The first day of creation is that of the creation of the physical world, the second of the celestial world, the invisible angelic world is third, and the fourth is that of the creation of man. Since the number four is man's, this is the millenium of the Incarnation in whom all are redeemed as in Adam all sinned. The exposition of the fifth and sixth days has to do with the division of each of the worlds in order, and the knowledge of the relations of all things among themselves. The seventh day is presented as one of rest and deals with eternal life.

The angels of the supercelestial realms are the heavenly waters over whom the Spirit of Love brooded. These angels have an earthly service to man, who, because of Christ, is the final cause of the whole created order.[12] The orders of angels correspond to the three degrees of the mystical life and order cosmological tasks.

It is true that the doctrine of the three stages of the spiritual life and the roles of the three orders of angels correspond. It is found in Dionysius but nowhere does he compare them with the "waters" of the three levels of the universe.[13] Nor do we find the messianic interpretation of the texts of Genesis nor the significance of the human form in him either. Pico draws upon themes traditional in Christian literature and carefully weaves them into a cabalistic fabric in an attempt to argue the common source of Platonic philosophy and the cabala in the revelation to Moses.

Fray Luis says that beginners on the road to perfection enter the "galleries of the King" (Cant. 1: 3) which is the heavenly temple, the house of God. In the innermost parts of this temple one would encounter, not images of God, but God Himself.[14] In the present life no one sees God, so He calls the beginner into the three galleries where they know Him

---

[12] Pico, *Heptaplus*, pp. 232, 262, 266.

[13] See: Dionysius the Areopagite, *The Mystical Theology and the Celestial Hierarchies*, (N. Godalming: Shrine of Wisdom, 1949).

[14] Fray Luis, *Opera*, II, pp. 56-57. "Sed quaenam sunt ista cellaria quaerat aliquis, ad quae pias mentes Dominus introducit? ... ut praeteream coeleste templum, quod est Dei proprium domicilium, id enim est maxime interius penetrale, in quo, qui introducuntur non imaginem aliquam Dei, sed ipsum qualis est, Deum aspiciunt, sed ut hoc praeteream, quoniam ad id nemini patet aditus in hac vita, tria reliqua cellaria sunt, triaque penetralia, in quae dum hic vivitur, introduci a Deo incipientes solent, ad gaudia ex ipso capienda. Incipientes inquam, nam qui robustiores jam ac perfectiores sunt, interdum corporis omni sensu deposito, mente obeunt, altiora quaedam et coelestic, ac intelligibilis lucis magis plena loca. Igitur minores verari solent interius, et jucunde cum Deo ab ipso intromissi: primum ad rerum naturae inspectionem deinde ad cognitionem sui ipsorum: postremo ad earum rerum contemplationem, quas Christiana dispiclina, ac litterae continent." See Welsh, *Introduction*, pp. 72 ff. where the role of the senses and the relation of the physical and spiritual life is discussed.

through sensible knowledge. Fray Luis indicates the temple has three other inner rooms or *"penetralia"* wherein advance the more perfect who know God without recourse to feeling and sense.

Here we find an image like Pico's where we see God in the lowest of the three worlds, that of the senses, precisely because of His presence in man who sums up in himself all three worlds. The novelty of this view is suggested by comparing it with the traditional view of pseudo-Dionysius. He does not have the idea of the temple with galleries or the idea that man unifies the three worlds. However, according to Pico and Fray Luis, the Tabernacle of Moses represents the heavenly temple.[15] Dionysius speaks of the Incarnation of God as a condescension and the angels of God ministering to Jesus, not as summing up in his humanity all creation, but because of his obedience as man to the Father.

For both Pico and Fray Luis, the object of devotion is the humanity of Christ which blossoms forth from nature as its supreme goal. As Christ is the purpose of nature, his grace flows to men who desire to be like him because of their humanity. For this reason Christ calls all men to perfection. For Dionysius, advancement in the spiritual life is reserved for the few, whereas Fray Luis advocates it for both layman and monk.[16]

It is interesting to note that Fray Luis describes the Church as a palace adorned by the virtues of its members, where God's glory dwells.[17]

---

[15] Fray Luis, *Opera,* II, p. 71. Hic si ex tabernaculorum natura rem interpretamur, necesse est intellegamus significari quaedam naturae partes, sensu et ratione carentes; quarum tamen ex inspectione et contemplatione inducitur homo ad cognoscendum, et amandum Deum: quale coelum est, et astrorum ignes, et mundi totius species, amatus et descriptio.

[16] See: Dionysius, *Mystical Theology,* pp. 36, 42. Welsh *Introduction,* pp. 37, 51, 53.

[17] Fray Luis, *Opera,* II, p. 173. "Nam sicut qui domum aliquam suo sumpto magnifice aedificavit, et aedificatam ornavit rebus omnibus, libenter in ea moratur, sic Deus in iis, quos ipse aedificat, atque ornat, libentissime habitat, itaque id Ecclesia cum sciret, omnia quae ab eo accepit eidam ornamenta explicat, sub aspectumque ponit lectuli flores, domus magnificentiam suam, ipsius pulchritudinem, ea ut ratione, magis se illius in amorem insinuet . . ."

The image of a castle is found in the *Nombre:* *"Pimpollo"* in connection with the Incarnation. All the magnificence of the appointments of the castle is but a reflection of that one for whom it is built. Insofar as the Jews in the Old Testament were the Church, he says the following about the "litter" of Solomon in Cant. 3: 7 in *Opera,* II, 223. "Propitiatorium . . . lectulum Salomonis figurate et apte nominavit . . . Salomonis nomen atque persona in his litteris ad Christum significandum transfertur . . . Id autem propitiatorium erat intra velum, quae interior pars tabernaculi erat: tabernaculum porro ipsum in medio castrorum locatum a fronte et a tergo, et ab utroque latere cingebant Israelitarum tentoria, id est, cingebant Hebraeorum familiae duodecim fixis tentoris, ita ut ternae familia singulas ejus partes, quae ad mundi relatae plagas erant quatuor, obsiderent." Here the arrangement of the Israelites indicates their spiritual relation to Christ by their positions with respect to the tabernable. The love of God has also a geographical dimension as well as a spiritual one, it will be noted. This theme is developed also in the *Nombre:* *"Esposo"* as it is in Alonso de Orozco's *Nueve nombre:* *"Esposo."*

However, in another place in the commentary, he says it is of the essence of their office that the leaders of the Church be spiritual guides and so bishops ought to be learned in Scripture and theology. Here we see in Fray Luis what Bataillon so correctly regards as the spirit of the Counter-Reformation.[18]

In the previous chapter it was suggested that Fray Luis' social theory has reference to Jewish and Christian ritual or ceremonial observances. A further indication that this is so is found here where virtue is referred to as contributing to the splendor of the Church. God's glory dwells primarily in the Church as a whole, and secondarily in the virtue of the perfect.

The Church is supposed to lead men to virtue. Fray Luis' attitude toward the hierarchy is not incidental to his spiritual doctrine. Just as the early Christians were persecuted by the chiefs of the Jews in the *Tertia Explanatio,* so also the spiritual Christians are persecuted by the evil watchmen of Canticles 5: 4, who now are identified as the bishops of his day.[19] Rejected by the leaders of the Church, the perfect turn away from them and seek aid from the humble and simple.

Their apostolate to the downtrodden is an essential part of the moral life of the perfect.[20]

For Fray Luis, a good bishop must be a good man. Moral righteousness depends upon the care of the meanest person, not on the episcopal office. His new morality is clearly related to the reform of the Church in that the oppressed perfect are victims of the Church itself. Also, the

---

[18] Cf. Chap. I, fn. 4. Fray Luis, *Opera,* II, pp. 206-209. Nam hoc fortitudinis genere praelatos Ecclesiae praestare debere, Israelis facta commemoratio significat. . . . Quo certe gladio, id est, rerum atque legum divinarum cognitione, atque scientia, Ecclesiae ministri armabuntur; si modo id futuri sunt, quod se esse volunt, atque cupiunt, populi Christiani rectores, doctores veri, magistri vitae, lumina Ecclesiae.

[19] *Ibid.,* p. 302. An est credibile, qui fidelium conventibus praesunt, quique praesident Ecclesiis Dei, nam iis urbis Ecclesiae, atque murorum custodia concreditur, eos non modo praesidium nullum afferre, sed detrimentum etiam et calamitatem bonis, et Dei amatoribus viris saepe importare?

[20] *Ibid.,* pp. 304-305. In Ecclesia porro sua futuros servos praedicit, qui quod viderent ipsum moram facere, et ab eam causam sibi persuaderent, eum non esse venturum, ipsius servos et ancillas percussari essent, id est, futuros religionis suae atque doctrinae dispensatores, atque ministros infideles et pravos, qui communis domini servos, hoc est, mystici corporis maxime Deo chara, et praestantissima membra vexarent, calumnis opprimerent, ferro atque flammis persequerentur. . . . Itaqui illos relinquunt crudeles hostes, fautores qui esse debebant, seque ad privatos convertunt, eisque dicunt: "Adjuro vos filiae Hierusalem." Semper enim nescio quomodo simplex et humile vulgus, quippe quod amitione et avaritio vacuum animum habeat, aequum se atque audiens sanctis hominibus exhibet, semperque lumen illud verae pietatis, in quocumque elucere incipiat, statim perstringit oculos privatorum et humilium hominum. . . . "Qualis est dilectus tuus." . . . Haec pii atque simplices homines adurati respondent, quia etsi se juvare minus possint, studio tamen juvandi arere solent.

care of the humble, is a duty that the perfect who are despised by the bishops freely undertake.

The point that seems to be implied in these passages is not only that the bishops ought to be virtuous, or that it would be helpful if they could be spiritual guides, but that without them the perfection of the spiritual life is impossible. It is the Church that is virtuous, as a whole, not merely individuals, bishops or not. As the bishops are the sign of the Church's unity, so they are indispensable to the moral observances of the perfect. Once again, then, one has the sense that Fray Luis regards ritual social communion as a condition of moral living. The perfect recognize this in the bishops, even if they persecute them.[21]

Without discussing this point further now, let us go on to suggest that cabalism forms the basis of Fray Luis' spiritual doctrine and that this phenomenon is related to current theory for Church reform. In his gloss on Canticles 5: 10-16, in the *Tertia Explanatio,* Fray Luis says that the mystical description of Jesus, the Sponse, to whom the chief priest and the Romans were blinded, was evidence of advancement in the knowledge of divine things on the part of the early Christians. The gloss on the same text in the *Altera Explanatio* says the mystical description is the doctrine sought by the humble and taught by the perfect.[22]

Fray Luis glossed the same texts in the *Nombre: "Faces de Dios"* where the description of the beloved is proposed as the object of mystical contemplation in accord with his idea that Christ in his human nature ought to be the object of devotion. Fray Luis' glosses on this and similar

---

[21] The Council of Trent (Ses. VII, 1547, and Ses. XXIII, 1563) and Pius IV (*"In suprema,"* 1564) taught that bishops are obliged to reside in their dioceses to personally fulfill the obligations for which they are supported by benefice. This obligation was insisted upon as early as 1517, by Cajetan and reform elements in the Church, including the Augustinian Prior General, Seripando. These regarded this obligation as one of divine positive law, not admitting of any dispensation, even by the Pope, except for extreme causes. In Jedin's opinion, this forms the pivotal ecclesiastical reform of the Council. The point of this reform is that Catholics have an obligation to assist at the ritual worship of God which can, in the ordinary course of things, be performed only through the bishop's functioning among them. This obligation the Council saw as a divine law and so the Pope cannot give dispensations for prelates to be absent from their jurisdictions. This abuse was common in the preceding period, as was the holding of several benefices at once.

Fray Luis seems to see the Counter-Reformation as much as a program of general and universal social reform as an ecclesiastical reform as such.

On the Council of Trent see: Hubert Jedin, *A History of the Council of Trent,* (St. Louis: Herder, 1961), Two Vols., II, pp. 321, 326.

[22] *Ibid.,* p. 305. Sed quid perfecti de Christo sentiant, qualisque illis esse videatur, audimus: "Dilectus meus candidus et rubicundus." Prisci scriptores haec de Christo, qua homo est interpretantur; quorum ego sententiam maxime probo; quanquam scio nonnullos esse, qui de ipsa natura Dei ista intelligi debere contendant; sed sequamur antiquos, quorum fere semper est praeferenda sententia. Igitur haec in Christum ita quadrant, ut quacumque ipsum spectes, ei apte conveniant. *Ibid.,* pp. 334, 337.

texts clearly indicate their cabalistic nature when compared to actual texts of the *Zohar* or the *Portae Lucis* or other cabalistic books available in his time.[23]

One does not find this emphasis on Church reform in Pico. His interest in cabalism seems to have been centered primarily in a method of converting the Jews, not of ecclesiastical reform as such. One must look in other authors for the development of this aspect of Fray Luis' thought. The conversion of the Jews is a matter connected with the apocalyptic age and it is related to the moral reform which was believed to have to accompany it. Aspects of cabalism, apocalyptic messianism, and moral reform are all found connected in Renaissance Christian cabalism. Examples of this are the identification by such as Pico and Rici of the traditional moral doctrines of the Jews and Christians. This identity of Greek and Jewish moral doctrine is characteristic of Renaissance Jewish authors.

One must look to Christians of the first half of the 16th Century to find cabala being used as the basis of the much needed moral reform of Christian society. The greatest of these was, no doubt, the general of the Augustinian Order, Cardinal Egidio da Viterbo. His work, *Scechina,* of 1530, is considered the finest example of an attempt to adapt Christianity and the world of cabalism.[24]

---

[23] See Appendix II for evidence of Fray Luis' dependence upon the section of the *Zohar* known as *"Idra Rabba"* in his spiritual interpretation of Cant. 5: 10-16. The source of Fray Luis' knowledge of the *"Idra Rabba"* is as yet unknown to me. However, the liklihood that he knew it in translation and in Christian cabalistical literature is such that an authority on Spanish Hebraic literature has kindly informed me that it would be beside the point to mention that the *Zohar* was published in Aramaic in Mantua many years before this time. Letter of Yosef H. Yerushalmi to Karl Kottman, Haifa, Israel, June 15, 1969. I was made aware of Mr. Yerushalmi's work by Professor Raimundo Lida of Harvard University.

[24] Egidio da Viterbo, *Scechina.* Secret speculates that this work is connected with the incredible Reubini-Molcho affair. According to Silver, David Reubini (c. 1490-after 1535) capitalized on the messianic fervor after Abravanel. He appeared in Rome in 1524, and obtained from Clement VII an introduction in the interest of his supposed embassy to the Christian powers. These he wished to rally to the side of his brother, allegedly king of part of the lost Ten Tribes, in the final defeat of Islam. The Marranos of Iberia were much excited at this and one Diego Pires sought out Reubini who spurned him. Pires went to several Jewish mystic centers in the Near East after he had circumcised himself and taken the name Solomon Molcho (1500-1532). He became inflamed with the ascetic-messianist practices of Safed whence word went to Rome in 1521 that the messiah was approaching. Molcho, in a book written in 1529, said the messiah would appear in 1540. The same year, 1529, he visited Rome and joined Reubini. He prognosticated the great Tiber flood of October 8, 1530, and his fame became widespread. He was received by the Pope and he and Reubini set out to see Charles V at Ratisbon. This was in 1532, the year the dead of Palestine were to arise according to the *Zohar.* Both were seized at Mantua and Molcho was burned at the stake as an apostate Christian. According to Molcho's calculations, Elijah was to appear in Rome before 1540. For complete details of this incident and the many

Cardinal Egidio's *Scechina* is rich in Jewish lore, and references to Canticles are but a part of its complex composition though the very title indicates that he identifies the midrashic term for the presence of God among His people with the female aspect of the cabalistic divinity. It very clearly reflects the identification of Dionysius' mysticism and cabala that was worked out by Rici. What is altogether remarkable is that the theosophy of the cabala is linked with the messianic themes of rabbinical literature in such a way that Christian history is seen to follow the pattern of the divine life with which the mystics are intimately related. What Egidio proposed was that the approach of the second coming would be first heralded by evidence of the divine presence in men. Therefore moral reform was a part of the apocalyptic drama. The mystic was a sign of the last days, as it was believed by both Christian Joachimites and the Jewish cabalists.

In accord with this belief he addressed this work to Pope Clement VII who took him quite seriously if we are to judge from the Reubini incident, and to the Emperor, Charles V, whom he regarded as the new Cyrus. The Emperor and the Pope were to be the ministers of the messiah to lead the Church to triumph over the Turks and to introduce the coming age of peace.

The impact of Egidio's *Scechina* upon Fray Luis' work seems evident in that Fray Luis' commentary on Canticles, like that of the *Scechina,* weds the historical and mystical interpretations of Canticles based on the imagery of the midrashic and cabalistical literature. Like Egidio, Fray Luis tries to show that Canticles can be interpreted both as a prophetic account of the history of the Church as well as an account of the individual mystical life of its members. Fray Luis also believes these are not unrelated. He remarks in the *Altera Explanatio* that the discription of Christ in Canticles 5: 10-16, can be taken both as an object of mystical contemplation and as a description of Church history.

Fray Luis says the form of Christ in Canticles is like the statue seen by the king of Babylon and interpreted by Daniel. The gold of the head is the age of the early Church when there were many Jews in it. Its virtues under duress until the age of Constantine were outstanding. The second age, that of ivory, is the time to Pope Gregory, an age of greatness, but of lesser virtue then before. After him is the age of marble, one wherein the Church lost most of its early moral spendor. The fourth age of the Church is seen by Fray Luis to be dawning, a time when the practice of virtue is

other cabalistic calculators and false messiahs of the 16th Century see: Secret, *Kabbalistes Chrétiens*, p. 117. Silver, *Messianic Speculation*, pp. 110-192.

being revived, when the enemies of the Church are being driven away, when contemporary events leave no doubt about the truth of the prophecies concerning the end of time. This last age will be marked by the final calling of the Jews to Christ, their final liberation from servitude, and the universal preaching of the gospel. God, in this last age, will return the Church to its pristine glory and then there will be peace.[25]

This very account of history, based on colors, is found in the *Scechina*.[26] For the Augustinian cardinal, this is partially a history of the Roman Empire, and the age of reform is that of Charles V. In Fray Luis, the distinction between the Roman Empire and the Roman Church is quite clearly made whereas it was not only fifty years beforehand.

A second person, I think of more direct influence upon Fray Luis, is Girolamo Seripando who was a longtime secretary and associate of Egidio da Viterbo. This Neopolitan cleric was elected general of the Augustinians in 1539, at the insistence of Pope Paul III, for the precise purpose of effecting a general reform of the Order that Egidio had begun while he was general. As general, Seripando participated at the first session of the Council of Trent and was responsible for the production of the first draft of its decree on grace and justification. Later in life he was made cardinal by Pius IV, and was papal legate at the same Council. Recently this famous theologian's adoption of cabala, no doubt under Egidio's influence, has been brought to light by Secret. By 1540, he was surely holding the doctrine of the Sephiroth, only a short time before he drew up the draft on justification at Trent.

However, it is his visit to Spain in 1541, that interests us most for Fray Luis joined the convent at Salamanca probably in 1543, and could not have escaped the influence of the changes instituted by Seripando.[27]

The general outline of Seripando's theory of reform seems clear enough. Like Egidio's, it was centered around an apocalyptic view of contemporary events. He quotes such figures as Reuchlin and Galatino with ap-

---

[25] *Opera,* II, pp. 314-324, 357.

[26] Egidio da Viterbo, *Scechina,* II, pp. 174 ff., fols. 291v-292.

[27] For an outline of the history of the Spanish Augustinians of this period see: David Gutiérrez, O.S.A., "Del origen y carácter de la escuela teológica hispano-agustiniano de los siglos XVI y XVII," *La Ciudad de Dios,* 153, 1941, pp. 227-255. During the late Middle Ages Augustinian observance of the monastic rules of the Order had become lax. During the 15th Century a reform had been initiated so that by 1505, most of the houses of Spain were restored to the old discipline. These, however, considered themselves independent of the unreformed houses and the unity of the Order was threatened. Seripando came, armed with full papal authority, to unite these houses under himself, an effort which, in Spain, caused much resentment among the observing monks.

proval and his conviction of the impending coming of Christ is indicated even while he was at Trent.[28]

There is no clear evidence on the degree to which Seripando influenced the revival of Biblical studies that occurred immediately after his visit. He was a longtime friend and correspondent of the Coimbra Augustinian theologian Francisco de Cristo (d. 1587).[29] There is no indication of such direct contact with Fray Luis, but there is reason to believe Seripando influenced him. He was the Order's head and was then legate at Trent during the period of Fray Luis' education (1544-1560). Seripando's example would normally have been important to him, since during this period he was the major spiritual force behind the reform and unification of the Order. Fray Luis' wholehearted support of this reform is indicated by his speech at the Chapter of Dueñas (1557).[30] Surely his own support of such Church reform must have been inspired in some degree by its great exponent at Trent and later model archbishop of Salerno, Seripando.

Another possible indication of Seripando's influence is the fact that one of the Definitors of the Castilian Augustinians named at the Chapter of Dueñas of 1541, at which the general presided, was Alonso de Orozco (1500-1591).[31] This man's *De nueve nombres de Cristo,* written perhaps around 1560, is the model of Fray Luis' *De los nombres de Cristo.* Among the things for which Orozco is famous is his insistence upon the use of Spanish in theological writing. Another notable thing is that his *Nueve nombre: "Esposo"* adopts the three stage theory of history one finds in Fray Luis. It also refers to the midrashic designation of the breasts of the

[28] This aspect of his thought is only suggested by Jedin, *Papal Legate,* pp. 42, 57, 284, 513, 582. He says that he accepted prediction of future events by prophets as a proof of Christian religion, that he used Hebrew texts to correct the Vulgate, that he had a religious devotion to the concept of the Empire and that he preached the impending apocalypse in the 1530's. In the light of Egidio's better known position and of the texts published by Secret, we have a much stronger suggestion of his relation to Christian cabalism. François Secret, "Girolamo Seripando et la Kabbale," *Rinascimento,* XIV (1963), pp. 251-268. It may be significant that Seripando continued Egidio's *Historia XX Saeculorum.*

[29] This is Jedin's view. He remarks that "intimate relationships, such as he had with Francisco de Christo ... were quite rare" for Seripando. Jedin, *Papal Legate,* p. 212.

[30] See the texts and commentary of A. Coster, ed. "Discours Prononcé par Luis de León au Chapitre de Dueñas (15 mai 1557)," *Revue Hispanique,* 50, 1920, pp. 1-60. The authenticity of the speech has been seriously questioned, but Coster's remarks made the present point nonetheless.

[31] D. Gutiérrez, "Del origen y carácter," p. 233. E. J. Schuster, "Alonso de Orozco and Fray Luis de León: *De los nombres de Cristo,*" *Hispanic Review* 24, 1956, pp. 261-270. See also *Enciclopedia Universal Ilustrada* (Madrid: Espasa-Calpe), Vol. 40, p. 663. The *"Nueve nombres de Cristo"* are published in García, ed., *Obras completas,* I, pp. 831 ff.

bride as Moses and Aaron. This could be a point taken from the *Pugio Fidei* or some work based on it. He seems to draw from the work of Christian Hebraists like Martín. The brief *"Esposo"* and *"Jesus"* manifest the double interpretation of Canticles one finds in Egidio's work. Seemingly Orozco, like Seripando, draws moral lessons from Christianized Hebraic themes.

I suggest that Hebraic methods of exegesis of Canticles, and their being a possible basis for Christian morality, were present among at least some Castilian Augustinians at the time of Fray Luis' education. If cabalism was not present before (as suggested by Ciruelo's attack on it in the 1530's) it must have been introduced by the example of Seripando. The cases of Orozco and Fray Luis seem to indicate that the seeds of Seripando's reform fell on fertile ground.

One might ask how Fray Luis can be seen as a cabalist since he usually seen as a Thomist of some kind. This question is further complicated by the fact that it was Giles of Rome who was the official doctor of the Augustinians according to the Order's statutes going back to 1287. Seripando himself renewed these statutes.[32] The word "Thomist" is most ambiguous when one examines the writings of Renaissance figures who claim this name. Father David Gutiérrez helps little when he calls such men as Fray Luis and Orozco "independent Thomists." He gives a hint as to what route one must follow to explain in what sense one can call Fray Luis a Thomist and a cabalist. He notes that Seripando called himself a Thomist and was, in fact, one of the promoters of placing the *Summa Theologiae* on the altar at Trent next to the Bible and the Code of Canon Law. The name of Aquinas was the name of reform, and surely the differences between Aquinas and Giles always were not thought as great as they are now. Men like Fray Luis' student, Alfonso de Mendoza, thought they both were teaching the same or, at least, basically the same doctrine. The case of Thomas Sutton and others shows their differences on the nature of the distinction of essence and existence in finite being was a matter of small concern to many in the 13th Century as well.[33]

There is a history of Spanish Augustinians following Giles of Rome. One of the earliest was Bernardo Oliver (d. 1348)who was bishop of Tortosa. This theologian was probably a nephew of Arnold of Villanova,

---

[32] D. Gutiérrez, "Del origen y carácter," p. 239. Jedin, *Papal Legate*, p. 214. Jedin treats Seripando as a Thomist and a follower of Giles of Rome on many questions.

[33] E. Gilson, *History of Christian Philosophy in the Middle Ages*. (New York: Random House, 1955), pp. 423-424, 742. Grabmann, *Historia de la teología*, pp. 131-132. D. Gutiérrez, "Del origen y carácter," p. 247.

the Christian apologist in whom we see elements of cabalism, apocalyptic vision, and moral reform joined for the first time. Oliver himself was a polemicist against the Jews and a preacher of the impending apocalypse. Another follower of Giles was the Paris theologian who became bishop of Toledo, Alfonso Vargas (d. 1366).

However, it is generally known that there was a severe intellectual decline among the Spanish Augustinians of the late medieval period and this raises the question of the nature of the reappearance of the study of Giles during the 16th Century. Father David Gutiérrez' opinion is that the emphasis on the Order's official doctor was lessened in this period and that the medieval tradition was reestablished only in the late 17th and early 18th Centuries by such theologians as Noris and Berti.

It is true that some Augustinians such as Fray Luis never mention the name of Giles of Rome. However, there is abundant evidence that some of his Augustinian students and others of his Order who published during his lifetime claimed to be followers of Giles. The influence of Giles on Seripando is also manifest. Scholars of other orders of those years were reading him, and it was Soto who objected that Giles was not a true Thomist on the grounds that the nature of his distinction of essence and existence was radically different than that of St. Thomas. Quintana reports that he finds that Fray Luis held a position similar to Giles' in that he held that there is an existential difference between the essence of Christ as man, and his divine subsistence.[34] Essence and existence in St. Thomas differ only as principles of being, not as beings in themselves as in the case of Giles. In view of Giles' influence on other contemporary Augustinians it is difficult to believe that Fray Luis did not follow him on this point. Perhaps he did not quote him in order to emphasize his belief that on important issues he was substantially in agreement with Aquinas and so sought to declare the universal application he believed his own teaching to have.

In any case, to settle the relation of Thomism and Hebraism in Fray Luis, one must settle it in such figures as Ramón Martín and, more especially, in Seripando and Orozco. The fact that all Catholic theologians accepted Aquinas as a universal doctor is evidence that the issues that divided them on the interpretation of his doctrine were other than those clearly arising from his own writings themselves. It seems, according to Father Gutiérrez' account, that Mendoza's defense of Giles of Rome as an authentic interpreter of Aquinas indicates that this question

[34] Quintana, "Las bases filosóficas," p. 746.

was a matter of difference among Thomists. But at least nominal attachment to him was nearly universal.

The choice at the time was not between slavish fidelity to one scholastic doctor or another. Fray Luis followed Scotus' opinion on the matter of the purpose of the Incarnation. Francisco de Cristo followed St. Thomas. Yet, both are called Thomists for their positions on other matters. Surely, Fray Luis thought himself an authentic interpreter of Aquinas when he lectured on law. Francisco de Cristo followed Giles on some matters.[35] The general confusion on this indicates there is no necessary conflict in calling Fray Luis both a Thomist and a cabalist, at least in the sense in which those terms applied in Renaissance and Counter-Reformation theology.

There was solid and immediate precedent for Fray Luis to have given his moral doctrine a Hebraic character. We have already mentioned Egidio da Viterbo, Seripando and Orozco. Egidio and Seripando argued that the apocalypse was near. In the expected moral reform that was to accompany it, they saw the Emperor Charles as the agent of its political dimension.

Both hoped that the Emperor would take up arms against the Turks and lead Christendom to its final victory in the last struggle with the antichrist. Seripando was disgusted by the involvement of the Pope and Emperor in wars with the French whose military policy in that period is clear evidence of rising Gallican nationalism. By the late 1540's it was clear from events that Hapsburg imperial fortunes were in decline and in the early 1550's Charles V began to liquidate his universal empire.[36] Never again could any Christian emperor hope to get the universal support of Europe for a crusade against Islam.

Another precedent is found in the work of Guillaume Postel (1518-1581). In 1548, at Venice, he published his *Candelabri Typici in Mosis Tabernaculo*. This work also involves a double interpretation of Canticles along cabalistical lines. Canticles is seen as a prophecy of history and a model of Christian spirituality. However, the central political role is assigned to the French king, not the emperor. The *fleur-de-lis* is taken as the mystical rose of Sharon. According to Postel, signs of the antici-

---

[35] U. Domínguez, O.S.A., "La predestinación y reprobación en Francisco de Cristo y Alfonso de Mendoza," *La Ciudad de Dios,* CLIV (1942), pp. 300, 306. This author notes a similar though not identical doctrine on predestination in Francisco de Cristo and Fray Luis who had treated these questions at Salamanca already. Often the difference is that Fray Luis says is certain what Fray Francisco takes as probable. Perhaps this is a mark of caution inspired by Fray Luis' trial for heresy and also a mark of discipleship.

[36] Jedin, *Papal Legate,* pp. 503 ff., pp. 442 ff.

pated moral reform could be seen in contemporary mystics, the founding of the Jesuits in France, his remarkable Virgin of Venice, and the reputed moral superiority of the French people. What is significant here is that the Hebraic methods are used both as the basis of anticipating Christian moral reform and of establishing the temporal claims of the French king apart from a universal Christian sovereignty.[37]

There is no mention of Egidio or Postel in the writings of Fray Luis. It is supposed that Postel may have known Egidio's work through their common friend Witmanstetter.[38] But, a cabalistic interpretation of Canticles is present in all three. All use Canticles to refer to the history of the Church and to Christian spirituality. The combination of these elements in such as these men who looked for the reign of Christ in the near future, assures us that moral reform, as they conceived it, was connected with what they took to be apocalyptic happenings in the current events of the day.

In Fray Luis' case the perfect of the spiritual life are clearly persons of his own time. He mentions the resistance of the bishops to their good works. He says that they are able to accomplish good which many had wished to do, but were unable to carry out themselves. One gathers that his praise and efforts on behalf of the Teresian reform of the Carmelites may be taken in this vein.[39] He mentions the concern of the perfect for the poor and humble and how they are actually admired by all because of the excellence of their qualities of soul.

In all this Fray Luis may not differ much from Egidio and Postel. However, one must account for the historical dimension characteristic of the Hebrew interpretation of Canticles.

---

[37] Guillaume Postel, *Candelabri Typici in Mosis Tabernaculo,* François Secret, ed., (Nieuwkoop: De Graaf, 1966), pp. 137-139. Bouwsma, *Concordia Mundi,* has a full presentation of details mentioned here.

[38] Johann Albrecht Witmanstetter was a common friend of Postel, Egidio and Seripando. Seripando was his patron who introduced him to Egidio in Rome in 1530. This Bavarian thought that Seripando was Egidio's chief disciple in the field of oriental studies. He and Seripando were in correspondence during the 1540's. Jedin, *Papal Legate,* pp. 19, 57, 185. Secret, *Kabbalistes Chrétiens,* pp. 115, 121. It is possible that Orozco knew of Egidio's work through Seripando. Orozco himself published his *Commentaria Quaedam in Cantica Canticorum* in 1581, at Burgos. I have been unable to consult this work.

[39] Fray Luis interceded with Philip II so that he would publish the Brief of Sixtus V concerning Carmelite reform without delay. P. B. Ibeas, "El carácter de Fr. Luis de León," *Religión y Cultura,* II (1928), pp. 363-364. Fray Luis was also an author of the first constitutions for the Discalced Augustinians, outlining the character of their spirituality and the rigorous nature of their life. There are indications that, had he lived, he would have taken part in the actual founding of this reformed group of monks. Pedro M. Bordoy Torrents, "Momentos históricos de la gloria de Fr. Luis de León," *La Ciudad de Dios,* CLIV (1942), pp. 461-462. In the original text of her *Interior Castle* Sta. Teresa explicitly praised the Jesuits. In both places in the first

In the cases of Egidio and Postel the emperor or king is presented as the political agent of moral reform. This is not so for Fray Luis. Even more than Postel, Fray Luis must have realized that the universal sovereignty of the Christian empire was no longer more than nominal. The king of Spain was then Europe's most powerful monarch. Fray Luis could have made a reply to Postel by saying that some passage of Canticles referred to Philip II or the Hapsburgs. As we have seen, he did interpret Abdias as a prophecy of Spanish greatness and its position in America. But, such a historical prophecy affords no claim to universal moral preeminence. It is here that Postel's extravagant Gallican views break down as, perhaps, St. Ignatius saw.

It may be useful to add other details regarding his moral theory. This general exposition of Fray Luis' thought is a starting point and it is now possible to offer some interpretations.

Fray Luis denies that prophetic interpretation of Scripture could form a basis for the moral and political character of Postel's Gallicanism. Historical interpretations are not dogmatic in nature. Mystical interpretation has to do with spiritual morality for the individual, not historical events. Fray Luis' attitude that the perfect should attend to the humble indicates that he was aware that temporal power in itself is not a licence of moral right. He observes there are limitations on the king's right to rule. Political power belongs to the people first.

A second point is that Fray Luis seems to find an acceptable moral life in both Judaism and Christianity. We are not considering his theological opinion here, only his philosophical one. What is to be emphasized is that elements essential to Christian morality are also found in Judaism under the Old Law.

The Jews in pre-Christian times were in possession of the true morality and Fray Luis cites Galatino to show that the Fathers of the Old Law were believers in the promise of the spiritual rewards of eternal life as well as the temporal.[40] Jesus extended this morality and the promises of rewards to all men and the Church in the beginning practiced this

---

edition of this work produced by Fray Luis, these remarks are missing. This would be consistent with the editor's differences with Postel's French version of apocalyptic events. St. Ignatius himself expelled Postel from the Society for his Gallican bias in 1545. Vallejo, *Fray Luis,* pp. 245 ff. Bouwsma, *Concordia Mundi,* pp. 13, 235.

[40] Fray Luis, *De Legibus,* Real Academia de la Historia, Madrid, MSS, 9/2081, fol. 182. "... patres veteris testimenti et sancti qui in illa lege vixerunt habuerunt notitiam atque fidem premiorum eternorum alterique vitae ... videte Galatinum, lib. 12, c. 6." This statement is marked out for special attention by an official of the Inquisition which confiscated this copy, Fray Luis' own, at the time of his arrest on charges of heresy.

morality. According to Fray Luis' account the early Church, with its many Jews, preached it to the gentiles who were thus enabled to receive eventual temporal rewards with the Jews.

It seems reasonable, therefore, that Fray Luis should have looked as he did to the spread of Christendom as an evidence of divine favor upon spiritual morality. He seems to refute the claim of Abravanel, made eighty years before, that a lack of universality counted against the election of Christians and God's favor with the Jews.[41]

Fray Luis says in the *Nombre*: *"Brazo,"* as elsewhere, that the special merit of Christianity is its proper worship of God and its success over idolatry. He denounces legalism and materialism, but not religious morality as such. Christ, for Fray Luis, vindicates the religious as opposed to the rational part of Mosaic morality by destroying idolatry by spiritual means. This means is emphasized when Fray Luis treats the special characteristics of the perfect of the Christian life. Here its fulfillment is among Jewish Christians. Indeed, the Christian moral life, for Fray Luis, seems to coincide with the godly object of the Mosaic Law, the moral perfection of man. Here the perfect are praised precisely because of their religious morality which is distinct from both the law of reason and Christian theology.

Indeed, one finds that the perfect of whom he speaks in the *Altera Explanatio* are such Christians. He continually compares their virtues to those of the early Christians who he regards as having been mostly Jews. He explicitly calls them blood brothers of Christ, indicating that they are special children of God by a physical as well as a spiritual right. He

---

[41] García, ed., *Obras completas*, I, pp. 571-572. In the *Nombre: "Brazo de Dios,"* he says that the conversion of the world is to be in spiritual terms, not by means of a military conquest as he claims the Jews hold. He says: "Yo persuadido estoy, para mi, y téngolo por cosa evidente, que sola esta conversión del mundo, considerada come se debe, pone la verdad de nuestra religión fuera de toda duda y cuestión y hace argumento por ella tan necessario que no deja repuesta a ninguna infidelidad, por aguda y maliciosa que sea; sino que, por más que ... se esfuerce, la doma y ata y la convence; y es argumento breve y clarísimo, y que se compone todo él de lo que toca el sentido. ... Evidente cosa esto, sin duda; porque aquellas obras maravillosas que las historias de los mismos infieles publican, la conversión de toda la gentilidad que es notoria a todos ellos y fue las más maravillas y milagros tan grandes, necessaria cosa es decir que fueron o falsos o verdaderos milagros; y si falsos, que los hizo el demonio y si verdaderos, que los obró Dios. Pues siendo esto así como es, si fuere evidente que no los hizo el poder del demonio, quederá convencido que Dios los obró. Y es evidente que no hizo el demonio, porque todas las gentes lo vieron, como todas las gentes lo vieron, fue destruido el demonio, y su poder y el señorio que tenía en el mundo, derrocándole los hombres sus templos, y negándole el culto y servicio que le daban antes y blasfemando de él. Y lo que pasó entonces en toda la redondez del orbe romano, pasó en la edad de nuestros padres, y pasa abora en la nuestra, y por vista de ojos lo vemos en el mundo nuevamente hallado; en el cual, desplegando por él su victoriosa bandera la palabra del Evangelio, destierro por dondequiera que pasa la adoración de los idolos."

implies that they were previously in ill favor with their countrymen, but have become esteemed because of their virtues which others seek to follow.[42]

The crucial question is, of course, what type of morality the ancient Jews and, especially, these contemporary ones practice. What are the elements and foundations of Fray Luis' moral theory? Are they to be found in Greek thought? It seems not, for the Jews were never required to practice a merely rational or pagan morality. The spiritual interpretation of the Law was known to some of the Jews long before Plato and Aristotle. Fray Luis shares Pico's view that Moses was the source of all spiritual morality. He differs with Pico, however, about whether spirituality was central in Jewish moral observance. Morality in both Laws seems to require observance of the Decalog according to Fray Luis. This is a specifically religious law that is not recognized in Greek moral thought.[43]

Domingo Soto also says Christian morality requires an obedience to the Decalog. Both he and Fray Luis grant this. However, Fray Luis seems to follow Ramón Martín and others in saying that it obliges as well as divine positive law and not merely as deduced from reason. If the Decalog is a divine law for Jews and Christians, are ceremonial practices to be excluded from being legitimate moral expressions? The natural law of the Decalog obviously entails divine worship, but Soto is most anxious to insist this is not ceremonial and ritualistic.[44] On the other hand, part of the Jewish moral observance is ritualistic. This aspect can be preserved in Christianity. This need not be a matter of faith. Catholic theology like Jewish law enjoins ceremonial worship on its subjects, not all men as such. The problem is whether Fray Luis considers ritual worship as commonly expressive of the religious character of the moral law. Certainly his interpretation of the Decalog does not preclude this, and, indeed, it rather suggests it.[45]

---

[42] Fray Luis, *Opera,* II, p. 420. He writes: "Itaque quod hic figurate describitur, quoad rerum natura patitur, ipsi faciunt atque imitantur: cum Christo, tamquam cum fratre germano in oculis omnium dulcissime et conjunctissime vivunt, neque quid de se alii judicent, curant: imo constantia, et libertate in amando, ipsaque tandem veritate assequuntur, ut qui illorum amoribus antea obtrectabant, jam ipsi sibi displiceant, illasque admirentur: oraque sua impia a detrahendo et ab loquendo ad laudandum et celebrandum convertant, dicantque, et praedicent illos esse Deo similes, in quo minime certe falluntur. ... Sic enim censendum est, que ad hanc magnitudinem pervenerunt amoris, quique id jam assequuti sunt, ut spiritu et veritate Deum colentes, nulla aut rerum humanarum, aut hominum judiciorum ratione habita, et privatim, et publice in Dei amore occupentur, eos fratres Christi germanos esse; ac proinde Dei filios praedicari et haberi, ut diserte Paulus testatur de hoc genere ad Romanos scribens: 'Qui spiritu Dei aguntur, hi filii Dei sunt.' "

[43] Cf. Chap. III, fn. 19.

[44] Cf. Chap. III, fn. 9.

[45] Fray Luis states that it is probable that in every nation and in the natural state

Our first interest in this chapter is what specifies mystical and spiritual practices for Fray Luis. On this point Soto may seem to agree with St. Thomas and, perhaps, Martín and older Thomists that it may be natural reason and Hellenic philosophy. Fray Luis' position cannot merely coincide with Catholic moral theology. The Jews of old and men in the natural state practiced a worthy morality and some Jews even had a spiritual one. The Greek or solely rational source has already been excluded.

I suggest that in view of the impossibility of the alternatives considered and the circumstances surrounding its formulation, that the basis of Fray Luis' theory of spiritual morality is Hebraic and cabalistic, based on the mystical interpretation of Scripture used by the Jews and adapted to Christian belief during the Renaissance. This theory would meet the qualification of being suitable to Judaism and Christianity.

Would it, however, be a rational morality? According to Fray Luis, cabala was known to Adam. He apparently lost his understanding of it when he sinned.[46] Adam's loss did not involve a loss of reason. Cabala was infused knowledge in the Mosaic period. Those who had it by tradition had it from those to whom God revealed it. Fray Luis says that only in Jesus do we find it to have been completely natural. In him the whole purpose of the race's existence, even Adam's, is supposed to have been accomplished.[47]

Before Jesus cabala was not a rational mode of moral practice. It was not rational for those who had it by infusion, nor for those who learned of it by tradition. It was not even a natural revelation of a spiritual morality as Pico suggests. Fray Luis insists that the moral observances of the Jews were supernatural by way of expectation of the messiah.[48]

As a matter of fact, the supernatural observances imposed upon the Jews were of a legal sort and did not require spirituality. Only in the New

there are men free from the vices of the rest through whom God reveals Himself. Fray Luis, *Opera*, III, p. 163. This freedom is not a spiritual one, but only a sense of an expectation of a deliverer from the effects of sin. In general, it seems, Fray Luis thought the American Indians to be quite immoral. Pereña, "Descubrimiento de America," pp. 590-593. He was not opposed to Indian religions as such, but only insofar as they were perverted. Acosta reported Indian rituals were Satanic parodies of the sacraments and had to be destroyed. I do not think Fray Luis would accept this extreme measure. He seems to call for the purification of their culture, not its destruction.

[46] García, ed., *Obras Completas*, I, p. 417. It is interesting to note that as late as 1651, one finds Hobbes rejecting a theory of language like Fray Luis' which depends on Adam's knowing ". . . names of figures, numbers, measures, colours, sounds, fancies, relations . . ." Sir William Molesworth, ed., *The English Works of Thomas Hobbes*, (Scientia Aalen), *Leviathan*, p. 19.

[47] Cf. Chap. IV, fn. 12.

[48] Cf. St. Thomas' view in *S.T.*, I-II, 98, 5.

Law are spiritual observances required. Fray Luis says that the New Law consists in precepts, e,g, the Decalog, and the infusion of grace interiorly and in a spiritual manner. It is made up of each of these aspects. Only Jesus knew cabala naturally and only after him is spiritual morality natural to man.

Fray Luis does not seem to regard rational modes of spirituality as natural unless they are associated with cabalistical ones. Historically speaking, he indicates that the Platonic mysticism stems from the Mosaic. Earlier Christian cabalists did not insist that cabalism and Greek philosophy present incompatible moral systems. Pico seems to imply that Christian mysticism from Greek sources is not different from that of cabala in kind, only inferior in quality. Rici notes the moral excellence of cabala but quotes Aquinas to the effect that it is perfect accord with natural reason.[49] Egidio da Viterbo wrote a treatise on Platonic mysticism with no explicit reference to cabala, though it does identify Mosaic mysticism and that of Plato.[50]

Fray Luis seems to follow them in this and the point for all of them appears to have been that cabala is the highest form of a spiritual morality, though not necessarily the exclusive one. He follows Edidio da Viterbo in noting that the virtues of the early Church, with its many Jews, exceeded those of the post-Constantinian period. The gentiles of the latter epoch were not cabalists, yet were advanced spiritually. The example of Jesus' own human perfection argues best for the superiority of cabala as a mystical doctrine.[51]

In what sense is cabalistic spirituality rational? It involves a certain agreement with reason in the sense that Christian morality is natural. Jesus' moral qualities are those that are natural for all men after him. Those who lived before him were able to benefit naturally from it though they knew of it by divine inspiration. If the Incarnation is the purpose of creation, then even Adam's moral perfection before his fall is not to be considered as having been that fully proper to him as man. Only Jesus is the perfect man, and he would be accepted as such by all and allowed to rule as king without laws.[52]

---

[49] Cf. Chap. IV, fn. 12.

[50] The Vatican Library MSS, Vat. Lat., 6325, is entitled "Agid. Vit. S.R.E. Card. P. Sent. ad Mentem Platonis."

[51] Cf. Chap. IV, fn. 16.

[52] Cf. Chapter III, fn. 16. Fray Luis argues in the *Nombres* that Christ, not Adam, is man's spiritual father. Besides his obligation to obey the natural law, Adam was bound by a divine positive law regarding the tree: "homo in omni statu indiget lege supernali ut ad foelicitatem coelestem perveniat." *Expositio in Genesim*, Ms., Bib. Cat. Pamp., #83, fol. 46v.

Cabala, after Jesus, seems to meet the requirement of being a natural form of spiritual morality. This does not indicate that a rational, even a spiritual, morality is a complete natural morality. What is to be considered natural seems to fulfill some kind of religious expectation beyond what one may hope for by reason alone. It seems to involve an element of historical expectation not available to rational expectation. For Fray Luis this expectation is not capricious for Christ too is our natural father.

Our interpretation suggests that cabalism is the basis of Fray Luis' theory of spiritual morality. However, he says that both the Old and New Laws are also characterized by the imposition of religious precepts, both enjoin a cult of God. Other precepts were given by Jesus that were common to the Old Law such as obedience to rulers, care of the poor, and so forth. These preceptive elements are noted by Fray Luis to have been part of natural morality as well.[53] Thus, it seems to be Fray Luis' view that no spiritual morality, as such, is a natural morality unless it entails an observance of the natural law of the Decalog. This is something cabalistic mysticism would do. Yet, no morality based on reason alone would seem to qualify on this count. Fray Luis insists upon the religious character as well as the rational one of the Decalog.

Perhaps one can suggest that Fray Luis sees ritual social organization as a significant aspect of man's moral life. Such practices are not asserted in the Decalog and they do not, in themselves, justify. Yet, this would explain, at least in part, Fray Luis' rejection of mere reason as an adequate basis for human morality. The natural, Mosaic and Christian periods are each distinguished by a characteristic cult.[54] Also, this interpretation would be consistent with a basic feature of Counter-Reformation theology about the need of a material worship of God. Also, it would help us understand him as both a creator and devotee of Baroque art.

A third feature of Fray Luis' thought is that cabalistic moral observance characterizes persons of his own day. He seems to think that the most perfect examples of spiritual living since primitive Christianity are his contemporaries. This point brings us to the relevance of cabalism to his theory of Spanish national destiny.

---

[53] Cf. Chapter III, fn. 20.

[54] There was no spiritual worship in the natural stage and in the other two God imposed the manner of worship in some detail. There are many examples of natural material worship in the Bible. Cf. Chap. IV, fn. 25. It may be observed that Fray Luis was no partisan of sentimentalism in religion. His *La perfecta casada* is an attack on excesses in piety. If we are to judge by his *"Oda a Salinas"* Fray Luis was very conscious of movements in Baroque music. Baruzi notes he was student of Cipriano de la Huerga on the subject of ancient Hebrew music. Jean Baruzi, *Luis de León: Interprète du Livre de Job,* (Paris: Presses Universitaires de France, 1966), p. 12.

Fray Luis is not the first to relate cabalistic spiritual morality and political affairs. The moral law is associated with positive law in the temporal state. Egidio da Viterbo and perhaps Seripando also identify cabalistic mysticism and the law of the Christian Empire. This is clear from the former's appeal to Charles V in 1530. He also indicates that the Pope's role is to be co-leader in the final defeat of Islam, so he seems to be sensitive to the fact that spiritual morality or political authority are not the only components of the ideal society. The priest is also a minister of God's law. The king's victory must also be a religious one.

After the 1550's the Holy Roman Empire was breaking up and hopes for a universal state by political means were at an end. Fray Luis takes from Egidio his general plan of history, but he does not join the Empire and religion in a single cause. Perhaps the success of the Reformation plays a part in this. Germany no longer observed the ritual aspect of its moral union with the rest of Christendom.

Postel is an early proponent of French nationalism on a religious basis. It is clear to see how Fray Luis would find his moral claims unsatisfactory. His exegetical methods are suspect.[55] His claim is in the interest of the French king, not the French people.[56] Postel seems to regard the French as a morally superior people. His argument is nationalistic because it proposes the universal sovereignty of the Bourbons on a Biblical basis. The emperor stood above all nations by their consent, not divine right. Furthermore, to Fray Luis' eyes, the French can be morally superior only by being cabalists.

Here is where Fray Luis seems to be able to argue the moral superiority of his own countrymen. Many Christianized Jews of Spain were familiar with cabalism. One may see traces of it, perhaps, in the writings of Sta. Teresa, Fray Luis, and Fray Juan de los Angeles to mention but three fundamental authors of Spanish spiritual books.[57] Fray Luis' moral and political theory was apparently developed and taught at least by his

---

[55] Cf. Chap. IV, fn. 24.

[56] Fray Luis, following Aquinas, says that the primary recipient of political power is the people, especially because of their religious characteristics. Cf. Chap. III, fn. 15.

[57] Cf. Chap. II, fn. 21. Fray Juan de los Ángeles (1536-1609) was preacher at the court of the Empress María. His *Consideraciones* show the influence of his teacher, Fray Luis. His *Diálogos* make use of the image of the Mosaic temple with four doors leading into the spiritual realm of God where the soul ought to live. He also makes the point that human rationality is an inadequate moral guide and that human nature has to be divinized before it can converse with God. Does this mean cabala is proposed as the mode of spirituality? Fr. Jaime Sala, ed., *Obras Místicas del M. R. P. Fr. Juan de los Ángeles,* (Madrid: Bailly-Bailliere, 1917), Vol. 24 of the *Nueva Biblioteca de Autores Españoles,* pp. 13 ff. Fray Juan de los Ángeles, *Diálogos de la Conquista del Reino de Dios,* (Madrid: Aguirre, 1946), pp. 71-72, 116-117.

Augustinian students.[58] The extent of his influence on Suárez has yet to be determined. Perhaps a whole field of research stands open to show that cabalistic spirituality was very common in that day.

If this were to be the case, it could be argued that, like Fray Luis, many others saw Spain's destiny in the light of the old beliefs about the significance of the presence of the chief families of Israel in Spain, and then of the Jews' conversion to Christianity. Their vision of Spain's role in history perhaps can best be understood in the light of the common messianic beliefs of Judaism and Christianity as they merged after the time of Vicente Ferrer.

Just as in the early medieval period, the Jews hoped that their religion would be vindicated before the Christians and Moslems, so also their baptized descendents in the late 16th Century were apparently still awaiting the fulfillment of their fathers' dreams, though now as Christians. It must be kept in mind, however, that Fray Luis' argument was that the messiah was to convert the world by spiritual means, not political ones. Nevertheless, this conversion seemingly was, for him, a uniquely Spanish task because of the universal moral significance of Jewish culture especially that of Iberia. It was not so because of papal grants or political imperialism. For the same reasons, he held, the Christian Church spread before the time of Constantine.[59]

---

[58] In this regard there are two very interesting articles to be noted: Bonifacio Difernan, O.S.A., "Miguel Bartolomé Salón, fundador del Derecho Internacional," *Revista Española de Derecho Internacional*, I (1953), pp. 83-126, and "Estudio especifico de Derecho natural y Derecho positivo según los clásicos agustinos españoles del siglo XVI," *La Ciudad de Dios*, CLXIX (1956), pp. 253-285. Father Difernan thinks that the honor of developing a natural right theory of law to oppose Soto belongs to Salón. His *Commentarium in disputatione de Justitia quam habet D. Thoma* appeared in Valencia in 1591. He thinks Pedro de Aragón, O.S.A. (d. 1592) shares the honor. His *De Justitia et Jure* appeared in Salamanca in 1590. Another article of theological interest in this connection is the development of the theology of Christ the King. See Eusebio Cuevas' article on Alfonso de Mendoza in *La Ciudad de Dios*, 1942, cited earlier. For a bibliography of Augustinian authors of this period see: E. Domínguez Carretero, O.S.A., "La escuela theológica Agustiana de Salamanca," *La Ciudad de Dios*, CLXIX (1956), pp. 638 ff.

[59] See the works of Professor Lewis Hanke on the Spanish struggle for justice in the New World. There is a suggestion that Fray Luis' moral views may have been influenced by contemporary missionary work in: Ernest J. Burrus, S.J., "Alonso de la Vera Cruz's Defense of the American Indians," *The Heythrop Journal*, IV (1963), pp. 225-253. Fray Alonso de la Vera Cruz, O.S.A., returned to Spain after his theological lecturers, the first ever given in the New World and which dealt with justice to the Indians. Maybe he was in contact with Fray Luis before the latter's lectures on law. Their views seem similar. Cf. Ernest J. Burrus, S.J., ed. *The Writings of Alonso de la Vera Cruz, O.S.A.*, (Rome: Jesuit Historical Institute, 1968). Three volumes, two more forthcoming. I find Father Burrus' work both enlightening and complementary with regard to my own. We have wondered if Fray Luis' moral view may not have been anticipated in the writings of Vera Cruz and thereby have a Mexican source, perhaps?

On the basis of this study, I think some new conclusions must be drawn about the moral thought of Fray Luis de León. First is that the philosophical basis of his moral doctrine is not to be identified as Hellenic. In this one opposes Bell's Aristotelian theory, as well as Father Marcelino Gutiérrez, O.S.A., in his Stoic characterization. One must reject the notion that Platonism or neo-Pythagoreanism is, as such, an adequate explanation. This was espoused by such eminent critics as Marcelino Menéndez y Pelayo and Dámaso Alonso. The libertarian character ascribed to Fray Luis' thought by Américo Castro is confirmed and further defined, against Claudio Sánchez-Albornoz, to have a clear Christian-Hebraic character.

Perhaps a more general result of this investigation is what I think is a new hypothesis about Fray Luis' thought which has not yet been suggested by recent students of Christian Hebraicism and Renaissance occultism. Unlike many earlier Christian students of cabalism, such as Pico and Agrippa, Fray Luis did not regard Jewish traditions as merely one antique heritage among many. He insisted that Hebraic traditions were not only different in degree from Platonism, Hermeticism, etc., but were specifically different as well. Names in Hebrew, for him, stand for things in a way differently than in any other language. To be noted is the Hebraic character of his social theory as well and his cabalistic moral doctrine. Also, he was clearly anti-Aristotelian, and anti-nominalist and non-Thomistic in these respects.

This feature should be of interest to the legal philosopher and social theorist. Society, according to him is not constituted on a merely rational model, nor is it merely an association in obedience to divine positive command. Both explanations exclude the religious significance of social organization. His differences with Soto on this point were not theological, but more anthropological. Perhaps he was anticipated in this by the Augustinian priors general and orientalists, Egidio da Viterbo and Girolamo Seripando. The cabalism of these latter is better understood within the Joachimite tradition. Fray Luis, I believe broke from it and his views are more richly Hebraic.

It is not uncommon today to read that a theory of morality should involve a religious element. Perhaps this interest in diverse aspects of moral theory is common in many Renaissance thinkers as well. For Fray Luis, however, the Hebraic tradition in Christianity affords something more than a moral norm of a higher degree. His view is not that religion is simply more profound, or more appealing than some other moral system, but that there is something about it without which the others are of no significance at all. He does not necessarily propose an Hebraic morality as the only one. But, it does conform with the natural conditions for the possibility of correct moral action.

Is moral freedom for Fray Luis merely indeterminacy of choice, or does it also suppose adherence to an objective, perhaps natural, standard of some kind? He seems to think that men's implicit or explicit faith in God and the material and spiritual change He is to cause in human life is something common to all times and places. This faith, for him, is a condition of moral righteousness in natural, Mosaic and Christian history. There is some objective standard of moral action. Also, his view seems to have been that ritual elements of divine cult along with apocalyptic expectation (not a theology of Jesus) are indeed elements of the study of morals and legal philosophy. Faith in God perfected Abraham, the Jews, and gentiles such as Job, not ritual as such. Yet he thought that public manifestation of this belief is useful to man. Thus, while there is a standard of morality that is objective, it is apparently not something limited to rational intelligibility in an *a posteriori* manner, nor is it coincidental with theological dogma. In what sense is it objective?

According to Fray Luis an objective moral standard is found in law. However, law is not merely a matter of reason as though moral disorder affected only man's mind. Rather moral disorder has its consequences in his body, its affections and in society and its institutions. It infects his very culture. Though presently disordered, Fray Luis seems to believe human nature can bring itself, in thought and action, to an intended wholeness. What is significant in his theory is that Adam, our material father, and source of our disordered life, was never our moral and spiritual father. Isaiah, says Fray Luis, calls Christ the "Father of the Age to Come." The wholeness of human nature, on this apocalyptic view, must still transcend the disorder of history and can be found in a spiritual quality possessed by men, i.e. Jesus, the early Christians, and almost certainly, the Carmelite mystics.

For this reason, Fray Luis writes in his *Nombre*: *"Padre del Siglo Futuro,"* that man must be reborn in Christ. Such a rebirth is both spiritual and moral. But it is, nonetheless, a principle of the restoration of nature in its material dimension as well. Material disorder, that is the disorder of human affections and society, is but a condition of sin, not a defect in nature itself. This moral rebirth, then, can transcend cultural limitations imposed by the effects of sin.

A moral standard can be objective in nature insofar as a new material and spiritual world order is a possibility. But this possibility is not in itself a moral standard. Lacking this new order are our moral obligations undefined? Even if it is present among saints and mystics, is their example adequate guidance for the management of society and the justice of citizens?

Human law can afford us moral norms insofar as it does by way of representation what nature accomplishes in actuality. Human law is based on the natural law, but not only by way of deduction from rational principles. Natural law is perfected by religious law. Political law can impose a certain form of moral unity upon men in a divided society, according to Fray Luis. Very little should be left to the discretion of the ruler. Also, ritual can accomplish in representation the restoration that nature accomplishes. In neither case is absolute justice achieved in the sense that men's moral and physical disorders are relieved by mere observance of the law. On the other hand, these laws can afford a conditional justice. The order of human law is not an end in itself, but must look beyond itself to a new order latent in nature and that it is incapable of creating of itself.

Thus, objective moral standards are of two kinds, the natural and the artificial. Both are available to us and the second follows the first much as spiritual regeneration is the beginning of social reform. For this reason Fray Luis insisted that governors and prelates be good men. The office does not make its occupant just any more than the institutions of society are good in themselves. There is a moral standard in nature which even the powerful must obey. At the same time this supposes material recognition of the equal rights of citizens.

Moral freedom, for Fray Luis, involves adherence to the natural order. At the same time the moral aspect of this natural order is not apparent except in the perfect of the spiritual life. Human law, whether civil or ecclesiastical, can never be identified with natural law. Furthermore, natural law is something other than divine positive command. And, unlike Aristotelianism, Fray Luis de León's theory maintains that the naturally just moral order is now found in religious, not secular society as it is presently constituted. Rather, social justice supposes the natural possibility of a radical change of an apocalyptic kind.

As I mentioned in the beginning, consciousness of this possibility is not new. It is found in Joachimism in the Christian tradition and in cabalism in Judaism. What is new in Fray Luis is the point that the mysticism of the apocalyptic era, not only in early Christianity, but also in his own time, is noted for its unique observance of natural law. He sees the radical change expected by others to have already occurred in Jesus' time and the apostolic age and to have been recovered in his his own.

One can imagine Fray Luis' thought, therefore, as standing at the head of a phase of human consciousness where the development of man's natural capabilities is to be emphasized, not his religious hopes. Joachimism and cabalism thrived into the 17th Century, but they were eventually debilitated by what are usually considered rationalistic forces developing along side them. Perhaps one may say they were translated in the Enlightenment into the elements of romanticism.

These two trends, reason and prophecy, are not opposed in the thought of Fray Luis, but joined together. So, I think, his esteem of the Hebraic tradition goes far beyond an inclination to compare it favorably with Joachimism, Platonism, Hermeticism or Pythagoreanism. Hebraic apocalyptic consciousness and its attendant manifestations has shown itself to be expressive of nature's own law for him. This cannot be said of the others.

This book must close before the study of Fray Luis' moral thought can be called complete. Fray Luis claimed that the basis of moral life is natural. This means it is objective and available for scientific consideration.

The sum of moral truth is Scripture, he often said. His office as moralist is to interpret Scripture, not as theologian, but as a "connoisseur of painting." [61] Fray Luis was moralist as exegete, not theologian. One must seek the key to moral judgment among his tools of exegesis, especially in his theory of the natural character of names in Hebrew which is explained and developed in the *De los nombres de Cristo*. This naming quality of Hebrew, in its meanings, its sounds, and its letters and figures is surely connected with his view that the Mosaic moral law is both divine and natural law.[62] Fray Luis' view about names deserves to be explored in its own right. However antique his exegesis is in other respects, he is contemporary in his search for an ethical language.

This book is historiography. Much more could be added to support my assertions. In the interest of brevity I favored key illustrations. Its right to be a philosophical interpretation rests upon the substance of my claim that Fray Luis was an innovator in the history of philosophy. My view is an awkward one because Fray Luis would have rejected this himself. He saw himself as a discoverer of the truth of history, not an originator of history himself. The truth was that Christian history is the same as universal natural history and being religious, these cannot be conceived of exclusively in terms of time and space. These are usually thought to be the limits of the historians' work.[63]

---

[61] Alice P. Hubbard, trans., *The Perfect Wife, Translated from the Spanish of Friar Luis de León, 1583,* (Denton, Texas: The College Press, 1943), p. 5.

[62] This is what Ribera, Acosta and Hobbes deny and what probably was the basis of the charge of heresy against him in 1572.

[63] In this connection there is the famous thesis of Edmundo O'Gorman that America

When one says that historiography is not limited to the interpretation of beings in space and time, two questions are involved. One is logical. Can history be conceived of as being represented in the Bible as interpreted by cabalistic exegesis? Is it logically possible that history is written in the figures of the Hebrew alphabet? That is not the same question as whether a history concealed in sacred figures, sounds and meanings is true. This is a problem of value and is more metaphysical, not to say religious.

In his religious thought, Fray Luis has been seen as standing within a number of traditions, from cabalist to Stoic. Certainly his values are religious as I show. I do not think anyone can say, once and for all, how Fray Luis saw himself as religious. Nor does one have to in establishing the substance of his thought. I know his writings show cabala is fundamental in his thought and there is good reason be believe he met the canonical standards of the Church, but who can know his private beliefs?

His adoption of cabalistic moral and historical interpretation of the Bible was perhaps a discovery of divine truth and not mere invention. It depends upon the ontological status of his values. On this score, I find it difficult to answer whether Fray Luis was Christian or Jewish in other than a descriptive sense. One reads that the Vatican Council allows that the religious or metaphysical issue among the Christian Church and Judaism and paganism is open, though the theological one is not. Orthodoxy aside, it may be there is no difference between theology and religion as the Council implies there is. Or it may be that all religions are equally true.

Apart from the value question, I do think Fray Luis would have accepted my claim that he was inventive in a philosophical sense. He insisted upon the importance of a distinction between questions of logic and those of value. He conceived of a language which would embrace and properly name each thing, moral and physical. This is the language of Christ. The rules of Hebrew and all the intricacies of cabala served him as the names and grammar of this language. Whether or not this language qualifies as true is the value question. But, whether or not it is true,

---

(and American history) is an idea invented by Europeans and one that Americans have come to believe themselves. John Leddy Phelan has exemplified this with the case of Gerónimo de Mendieta, O.F.M. (1525-1604). A more fundamental problem, which Phelan does not account for in terms of his analysis of 16th Century prophetic interpretation, is whether American history and Christian or any religious history are analogous ideas in writers like Fray Luis and Alonso de la Vera Cruz as they are in Mendieta. John Leddy Phelan, *The Millennial Kingdom of the Franciscans in the New World,* 2nd Edition, Revised, (Berkeley and Los Angeles: University of California Press, 1970), pp. 5-16, 76.

it remains a logical possibility and its may have a truth distinct from a value attached to it by man.

Luis de León's genius was to raise a new moral question. He proposed that since man can, for example by using cabalistic exegetical principles, conceive of himself as capable of being other than he is now, he must be able to choose between this possibility and its opposite. Every man can choose the remarkable qualities attributed to Christ, or reject them in favor of those of a more ordinary kind. His error about the length of history does not negate the thesis about the apocalyptic element in human law. Man's freedom is to decide his own history with respect to whether its logic is divine or not.

Can anyone say, without fear of contradiction, whether man's history is his discovery of a divine plan or only his mental invention? Fray Luis, no doubt, hoped his readers and students would take him as expressing the truths of prophecy, and not merely his poetic genius. The interesting thing about him is he would insist the choice is entirely our own. No scholar should presume to make it for others, and I will not.

APPENDIX I

Correspondence of Commentaries on the Texts of Canticles as Found in the *Tertia Explanatio* and the *Pugio Fidei*.

Key: TE: *Tertia Explanatio,* Fray Luis, *Opera,* II.

PF : *Pugio Fidei.*

Cant. 1: 1-3.

TE, 118. Quare Solomon, eam ut adumbret, puellam hic inducit, pro aetatis simplicitate et candore [Ecclesia in naturae lege] sui sponsi osculta aperte petentem.

PF, III, 3, 20, 8. Ecclesia desiderat lege Messiae: . . . Porro Sponsa, i.e. Ecclesia hae legitur, ac postulasse, ubi in Canti. Cant. Glossa ejus sic dicit cap. 1, v. 1. . . . "infusa est doctrina legis in cor illorum, et fuerunt dicentes, et non obliviscentes. Venerunt itaque a Moysen, et dixerunt ei, Moseh magister noster esti tu sequester, et legatus inter nos . . ."

Cant. 1: 4.

TE, 124-125. At o vitae commutationem miseram, ut brevi id amisi bonum. Verum ut amiserim, tamen iterum recuperata sum: Nam "Exultabimus et laetabimus in te," id est, futurum est, ut meae pristinae foelicitati restituar . . ."

PF, II, 5, 2. In Midrasch schir haschirim . . . R. Abbin dixit, non erant scientes in quo esset gaudendum, utrum in die, sive in Deo, donec dixit Salomo, et exposuit: "Exultabimus, et laetabimur in te." In te, id est, in Deo sancto benedicto; in te, id est [in Jesu vel in salutari tuo].

Cant. 2: 13-14.

TE, 181. Surge, inquit, quia dura servitute oppressa jacebat. Nam qui in moerore sunt constituti, et rebus angustis urgentur; jacere, in sacris dicuntur litteria . . . Servitutem quam in Aegypto serviebat figurate hyemem nominat, . . . Et quoniam ejus libertatis tempus instabat, hyeme, id est, servitute finita, ideo flores germinare, et apparere incipere dicit, hoc est, libertatis advenare ver, quod describit elegantissimis a conjunctis, et consequentibus, uti supra docuimus, ut intelligamus eam libertatem, ad quam hic Ecclesia vocatur, fuisse perfectam ex omni parte.

PF, III, 3, 11, 14. . . . in Midrasch Schir haschirim . . . super illud: . . . hyems est regnum nequam, quod concitavit totum mundum, et errare fecit illum in mendaciis idolatriae suae, . . . Hic est servitus; . . . "Flores visi sunt in terra" . . . id est, triumphatores visi sunt in terra . . .

Cant. 3: 9.
TE, 223-224. Et lectulum Solomonis sexaginta fortes ambiunt ex fortissimis Israel; intuemini illum, qui versatur mecum, quem habeo intra ambitum castrorum meorum, id est, arcam Dei et propitiatorium auream, Cherubinis item aurei innixum, in quo quiescit apud me et commoratur Deus: nam is mihi omnes istas felicitates profundit. . . . lectulum Solomonis figurate et apte nominat: lectulum, quod in eo quiesceret: Solomonis, quod Solomonis nomen atque persona in his litteris a Christum significandum transfertur. . . . Fericulum fecit sibi Rex Solomon . . . Quod autem in hujus fericuli descriptione dicitur; . . . tabernaculi parte inerat arca, et propitiatorium, in quo residebat Deus, quem ardebant filii Israel, et qui amoris erga ipsos igne flagrabat.
PF, III, 1, 11, 13 and 14. Quod autem in Deo sit aliqua proprietas, quae vocatur dilectio seu charitas, ex eo innuitur, quod in Midrasch Schir haschirim . . . Hic est thronus, *vel sedes gloriae* divinae. "Fecit sibi Rex Salomoh." Rex cujus est Pax. . . . Medium ejus stratum, vel accensum dilectionem, sive Charitate. R. Asarias dixit: Hanc dilectionem esse ipsam Divinitatem, vel gloriam Dei. . . . Nota quod nullus melius hoc in loco per Solomonem quam Christus videtur intelligendus . . .
Cant. 2: 1.
TE, 173. . . . et hebraice . . . est Habozeleth, quamvis de eo utrum lilium an rosa sit Hebraeorum doctores dissentiant; tamen quin colore negro flos sit, de eo dubitat nemo. Quod et vocabulum ipsum quod a nigore et umbre ducitus, praesefert.
[Fray Luis seems to continue the imagery of the Midrash with regard to the flower (Israel) among thorns (gentiles). There are no texts of these parts of this Midrash quoted by Ramón Martín in the *Pugio Fidei*. For purposes of translation of this section of the Midrash on Canticles from Hebrew: M. Simon, trans., *Midrash Rabba, Song of Songs*, (London: Soncino Press, 1951), p. 93.]
And why is it called habiozeleth? Because it is hidden in its own shadow (habayah bezillah) . . . Not to the lily of the mountains; which soon withers, but to the lily of the valleys, which goes on blooming.
Cant. 4: 1-5.
TE, 263-267. Expositis superiori capite, ex persona Ecclesiae, iis, quae Deus denique, et amanter cum illa fecit in Aegypto, et in mari: . . . in hoc capite, quo intelligatur, quam ea Ecclesia Deo grata esset, quamquam ejus reipublicae ratio atque forma ipsi esset ex omni parte probata, ejus Ecclesiae membra singula laudans, personae sub qua loquitur decoro servato. . . . Quas omnes similitudines atque res, non necesse est cum totidem aliis Ecclesiae conferre rebus, aut minutatim manus (ut ita dicam) aptare manibus, atque oculos oculis. . . . Ergo, animo quasi oculis sponsus hauriens, spectaculum, et quam sibi ejus Ecclesiae partes omnes gratae essent, oculis igneam significat nubem, qua praemonstrante viam, illi carpebant iter, quaeque ideo illis erat porro oculis. Judae tribus, et duarum tribuum, quae in eadem regione, qua illa, castrametabantur cohortes, siquis spanis nubem sequentes, capillis assimilat; . . . Ad extremumque Mosen et Aaron eximie laudat, duo illi populo data quasi ubera eos esse dicens . . .

[Fray Luis connects a part of the body with each of the groups of the tribes arranged in the desert. He does the same in the *Nombre de Cristo*: *"Esposo,"* (García, ed. *Obras completas,* I, p. 676). Alonso de Orozco has a similar though briefer treatment of the same matters, including Solomon's litter as the ark, the eyes of the dove as a cloud and the breasts as Moses and Aaron. See the *Nueve nombre*: *"Esposo," Ibid.,* p. 854.]

PF, III, 3, 12, 20. Prolatio labiorum tuorum dilecta est mihi sicut filium spledoris. R. Abhu dixit ... "Quid reddemus pro vitulis et hirco emissario, qui scilicet emittebatur in desertum? Confessiones, et laudes labiorum nostrorum." ... Ex praedicta igitur satis patet, qualia sacrificia velit Deus; ...

PF, III, 3, 3, 2. Messias Redemptor generis humani: In Midrasch quoque Schir haschirim super ... "Glypeus suspensis mille super eum" ... Omnia illa millia et decem millia eorum qui steterunt super mare, et protexi eos; ... Omnia illa millia, et decem millia eorum qui steterunt coram me in monte Sinai, et protexi eos, non protexi eos nisi propter meritum illius venturi mille generationibus.

PF, III, 3, 16, 21. Nota quod "iste clypeus suspensis in turri David" ... non potest esse nisi Messias.

PF, III, 3, 21, 18. Duo enim ubera Synagogae, de quibus his locutus est Salomo ...; hi sunt Moyses et Aaron. Non igitur duo Messiae, ... post istos vero duo ubera Synagogae fuerunt Prophetae et Sapientes.

Cant. 4: 6.

TE, 267-268. "Ad montem myrrhae, et a collem thuris." ... figurate Palaestinam nominat montem et collem ... certe quod iis in montibus primo tabernaculum Dei figendum erat, deinde templum magnificentissimo opere construendum, et in his thymiorum Deo singulis diebus odolendum ...

PF, III, 3, 16, 26. In hora, qua circumcidit Abraham seipsum, et filios suos, fecit de praeputiis eorum collem: illuxitque sol eis et vermificata sunt. Ascendit autem inde coram Deo ... sicut odor fumi aromatum ... istud quod scribitur ...

Cant. 5: 9-10.

TE, 336-338. Inducuntur enim Hierosolymitanae quaedam foeminae de dilecto ipsium rogantes ipsam, quarum in persona illi significantur Judaei atque Gentiles, quicumque Christi praeconium commoti vocibus eis adhaeserunt, et se ab eis disciplinam Christianam exacte doceri vehementer optarunt, in quorum scilicet cordibus ingressa fides alte radice egit ... Deinde rogant eos [doctores evangelii] ut se doceant, qualis sit dilectus iste, id est, volunt ut exactius ipsis exponant totam rationem et doctrinam Christi, ... ejus sub imagine Christi vitae, atque omnium actionem ejus praestatium et excellentiam ante oculos ponit ... In quo adverti primo debet quantum in cognitione rerum divinarum jam haec Evangelica Ecclesia profecerit, quantumque ipsa se in hac re superarit, aliarum ejus, quae praecesserunt aetatum ratione habita.

PF, III, 1, 4, 4. Item in Midrasch Schir hasirim (sic) ... "Qualis est dilectus tuus de dilecto?" qualis est Deus de diis? qualis patronus ipse de patronis? Israel vero furunt iis dicentes: "Dilectus meus candidus, et rebeus electus ex millibus." ... dilectus ... sit Messias.

PF, III, 3, 6, 9. . . . legitur in libro Mechilta . . . "Ecce enim gentes saeculi erunt interrogantes Israelem dicendo . . . 'Qualis est [etc.]' "

PF, III, 3, 16, 32. . . . unum de nominibus Messiae esse . . . Candidus, vel perforatus; . . . rubincundus, et perforatus clavis ferreis . . .

Cant. 7: 1.

TE, 399. . . . illos primo laudant, laudant autem quando gressus Ecclesiae ac pedes commendant, nam iis vocabulis celeritatis in annunciando Evangelio, et ex eo Evangelii praecones ipsi figurate significari solent, ut videre licet in Esaia (52:7) . . .

PF, III, 3, 20, 4. Fideles novus foedus suscipient: . . . quod in Midrasch Cant. Cant. dicitur super illud Cap. 2, 12, . . . Quae est ista? ista est vox regis Messiae, qui annunciat et dicit Esias 52, 7: "Quam pulcri sunt pedes evangelisantis, . . ."

Cant. 7: 3.

TE, 401. Quae nominentur in Ecclesia ubera, . . . sunt duos Apostolorum principes Petrum et Paulum praecipuos Ecclesiae altiores et institutores . . .

PF, III, 3, 21, 18. Non igitur duo Messiae, ut Judaei impudentissima fatuitate delirant: post istos vero duo ubera Synagoge fuerunt Prophete, et Sapientes . . . Hoc tunc fuit impletum, quando Dominus abstulit spiritum prophetiae; ac Sapientes ipsorum permisit a diabolo infaturari, et spiritualiter excoecari.

Cant. 8: 7.

TE, 448-449. . . . aquarum enim nomen in his litteris ad maximas calamitates significandas transfertur . . . aquae multae, id est, res adversae, pertulisti, non potuerunt tuam erga me aut charitatem extinguere, aut abruere pietatem. . . . Itaque haec oratio et manifestam admonitionem continet, et tacitam praedictionem, et totum illud Ecclesiae tempus complectitur, quod a Constantino Imperatore ad haec usque tempore effluxit.

PF, III, 3, 13, 14. Notandum autem, quod Gentes vocantur Aqua in Midrasch Tillim: " 'Aquae multae non sufficient ad extinguendum amorem.' Hae sunt gentes saeculi, . . ." Romani itaque, ac gentes aliae sunt spiritualiter aquae, super quarum aliquos invisibiliter volitavit Spiritus Dei, i.e. Messiae, ab meritum poenitentiae . . .

[Fray Luis may well be using the double application of "water" suggested by Pico's *Heptaplus* where it at once stands for the "waters" of the celestial realms or the skys worshipped by the pagans, and those of the supercelestial realm or the Holy Spirit or baptism. Fray Luis, unlike Martín, seems to be accusing the post-Constantinian Church of lapsing back into paganism, but reminding it that God loves it nonetheless.]

Cant. 8: 8.

TE, 450. Nam sub persona hujus sororis natu minoris, et parum forma praestantis . . . multi significantur populi atque gentes longe a nostro orbe remotae, ad Christum adducendae nova quodam Evangelii tradendi ratione: hoc est, significatur Hispanorum navigationibus reperti orbis, ejusque incolarum ad Christi fidem nuper facta conversio. Id enim certe his significari figuris Hebraei quidam Doctores viderunt, quodammodo ac tradiderunt . . . "Ubera non habet" id est, doctrina caret . . .

PF, II, 3, 29. Et in Midrasch Schir haschirim . . . dicitur: "Soror nobis," illi sunt ascendentes de captivitate: "parva" quia fuerunt pauperes, vel inops in (exercitibus), et "ubera non ei," hae sunt quinque res, in quibus domus ultima extitit diminuto.

[The *Pugio Fidei* applies this text to the return of the Jews from Babylon under Cyrus. Fray Luis, three hundred years later, says it refers to the evangelization of the Indians. This would be more consistent with his view that Canticles can be read as a three part history of the Church in its natural, Mosaic and Christian stages. Martín, of course, does not use this method.]

APPENDIX II

Translations of Brief Sections of Fray Luis' Commentary on Canticles 5: 10-15, 7:5, 6:7, 4: 1-5, and Its Dependence Upon the Section of the Zohar Known as *Idra Rabba* or "Greater Holy Assembly."

KEY

IR : Runes, Dagobert, foreward author, *The Wisdom of the Kabbalah,* (New York: Citadel Press, 1967).*

F : *Nombre de Cristo, "Faces de Dios,"* García, ed., *Obras completas,* I, pp. 448-450.

PE : *Prima Explanatio,* Fray Luis, *Opera,* II.

AE : *Altera Explanatio, Ibid.*

TE : *Tertia Explanatio, Ibid.*

CC : Cantar de los Cantares, García, ed., *Obras completas,* I, pp. 70-210.

DF : *Tractatus De Fide,* Fray Luis, *Opera,* V.

AB : Archangelus de Burgonovo's explanation of Pico's *Cabalistic Conclusions* as found in Pistorius, *Artis Cabalisticae.*

Cant. 5: 10. My beloved is white and ruddy, the chiefest among ten thousand. IR, 512. " 'Like as the appearance of a man'; because that (form) includeth all forms. Like as the appearance of a man; 'because He includeth all names.' Like as the appearance of a man." Because he includeth all secret things which have been said or propounded before the world was created, even although they have not been substituted herein."

IR, 547. And that dew hath in itself two colours. From the White Head there is a whiteness in it, which entirely comprehendeth all whiteness.

IR, 548. But whensoever it remaineth in that head of Microprosopus, there appeareth in it a redness, like as in crystal, which is white, and there appeareth a red colour in the white colour.

IR, 794. "And come, behold! There is an Arcanum hidden in this thing; and wheresoever in this passage mention is made of the word ADM, *Adam,*

---

* This book contains the *Idra Rabba.* The body of the *Zohar* text was taken from the English translation by S. L. MacGregor Mathers. His English version, *The Kabbalah Unveiled,* is now out of print, but is based on the Latin edition of Knorr von Rosenroth, and collated with the original text. The Sperling-Simon edition of the *Zohar* in English is abridged and omits the *Idra Rabba.*

thereunto the Holy Name is joined; and truly for a reason, seeing that man subsisteth through that which is analogous unto himself.

F. . . . the color in the body, which results from the mixture of the qualities and humors which are in him . . . correspond to the mixture and texture which the perfections of God make among themselves. Then as it is said of that color which is colored red and white so all this secret mixture is colored simply and lovingly.

AE, 306. Here the color mixed from red and white signifies the union and the mixture of the divine and human nature in the one person of Christ. For in white is to be understood the nature of the word of God . . . red however is the proper note of human nature from which the first parent of the human race is Hebrew is call Adam, because . . . it signifies reddening or ruddy.

TE, 338. . . . thus it signifies that in it; translated to the notion of Christ because from the mixture of two natures, by which he is tempered, results certainly that concentration of human and divine.

AB, 823. Salomon sings of the bridgegroom in Canticles. . . . It results from these colors of his beauty which is called beautiful before the sons of men. . . . In the right is the white . . . of grace and mercy; but in the left red in respect to . . . justice and punishment. This Spouse is *Tipheret* (according to the cabalists) who hears the Bride *malchut* . . . pausing in the gateway.

Cant. 5: 11. His head is the most fine gold, his locks are bushy and black as a raven.

IR, 536. This is the tradition. When the White Head propounded unto Himself to superadd ornament unto His own adornment, He constituted, prepared, and produced one single spark from His intense splendour of light. He fanned it and condensed it (or conformed it).

IR, 837. "And because those locks are black and obscure, it is written, Job xii, 22: 'He discovereth deep things out of darkness, and bringeth out to light the shadow of death.' "

IR, 834. "This is that same which is written, Cant. v. 11: 'His locks are busy. THLTHLIM, *Teltelim,*' as if it were THLI THLIM, curls heaped upon curls.

F. And he says that the head on the body is the same as that which in God is the height of his knowledge. That, then, is of the gold of Tibar, and it is the treasures of wisdom. The hairs which come out of the head, are said to be bushy and black; the thoughts and counsels which come from that knowledge are great and mysterious.

PE, 283. THALAL, to the Hebrews signifies to stand out: from which THAL is said to be mounded, as you say erect, and THALTHALIM, since it is transferred to hairs it signifies they are curly.

AE, 307. The secret meaning of gold is varied in Scripture. Sometimes the divine nature is signified by gold. All aproved writers acknowledge that Tabernacle constructed by the command and description of God by Moses the lawgiver was made to the likeness of the universe. And in that holy ark, surrounded with Cherubim, and remaining in its interior part, it contained an image of the divine nature, which likewise in the region of the highest heaven is surrounded by the choirs of angels . . . If we are willing that in gold the virtue of charity is to be understood, doubtlessly the charity of Christ is the head of the rest of his virtues.

TE, 339. ... they are black as a raven, because things done in the light of history are hidden in darkness.

Cant. 5: 12. His eyes are as the eyes of doves by the rivers of waters, washed with milk, and fitly set.

IR, 612. And (the eyes of Microprosopus) behold the open eye (of Macroprosopus shining down upon them), and they are rendered brilliant with a certain brilliant whiteness of the good eye (i.e., that of Macroprosopus, because in Him "all is right" – i.e., good – and there is no left).

IR, 613. Like as it is written, Cant. v. 12: "Washed with milk." What is "with milk?" With this excellent primal whiteness.

IR, 614. And in that time is there found with Him (i.e., Microprosopus) an intuition of mercy, and therefore the prayer of the Israelites ascendeth, because His eyes are opened (i.e., those of Microprosopus), and are whitened with that whiteness (of the eye of Macroprosopus).

IR, 642. Nevertheless, the sense is that this whiteness of them is as that whiteness of the eyes (of Microprosopus) when they are made brilliant by the white brilliance of the supernal eye (of Macroprosopus).

IR, 643. And the just are about to understand and behold that thing in the Spirit of Wisdom.

F. The eyes of the providence of God and the eyes of this body are the same; these latter, as doves bathed in milk, look at the water; those former attend and foresee the universality of things with delicacy and great sweetness, giving to each one his sustenance, as we say, his milk. [N.B. the simile of two faces in one.]

PE, 285. This beauty ... and the lightening of the eyes shines and appears more, they bathe themselves in the river. ... The Bride says ... that the eyes of the Bridegroom are like the eyes of doves ...

AE, 310. In a dove is declared that meekness and gentleness which Christ himself said of himself ... I wish that when I say "of waters" that the Holy Spirit be understood ... Who believes in the Son, from his heart flow rivers of living waters.

TE, 339. ... certainly because in that part of the life of Christ which contains in itself the gifts of the Holy Spirit, of which the dove and water are symbols, it brings out these things into the open and into the light.

Can. 5: 13. His cheeks are as a bed of spices, as sweet as flowers ...

IR, 585. Like as it is written, Ps. xxv. 6: "All the paths of Tetragrammaton are mercy and truth unto such as keep His covenant and His testimony."

IR, 658. And the mercy of Microprosopus, which is called mercies plain and unqualified, seeing that in Him there are right and left, (symbolizing the balance of) Justice and Mercy. And therefore is it said: "And in great mercies will I gather thee"; those, namely, of the Ancient of Days.

IR, 761. What are the places of fragrance? Like as it is said, Cant. v. 13: "like a bed (singular) of spices," and not "beds" (plural).

IR, 768. The fourth conformation. The hair goeth forth and is disposed in order, and ascendeth, and is spread over His cheeks, which are the place of fragrance of the Ancient One.

IR, 769. The fifth conformation. The hair is wanting, and there are seen two apples on this side and on that, red as a red rose, and they radiate into two hundred and seventy worlds, which are enkindled thereby.

IR, 891. "The fifth conformation. The hair is wanting, and there appear two apples, on this side and on that, red as roses, and they radiate into two hundred and seventy worlds.

IR, 892. "As to those two apples, when they shine on either side, from the light of the two supernal apples (*the cheeks of Macroprosopus*), redness is removed therefrom, and a white brilliance cometh upon them.

F. What will I say of the cheeks which here are olorous as plants, and in God are his justice and mercy ... and in the one and in the other side of the countenance, and which spreads its odor throughout all things? Which, as it is written (Ps. 24, 10) "all the ways of the Lord are mercy and truth." [N.B. *Idra Rabba* quotes the same Psalm in the same context.]

PE 285. She commends the cheeks from their color, purple and white mixed, as are seen ... where flowers are varied, some purple, others white.

AE, 310. ... therefore in the cheeks we rightly understand modesty, gentleness, probity of soul, ingenuity and other virtues to be meant, by which the face of Christ is outlined and colored ... Which such a concourse of Christ and so many virtues, rightly is said to be like spices made of pigments, because where many flowers of various colors conspire into one form of beauty, so here that multitude and diversity of various virtues conspires into a certain wonderful concentration and wonderfully do they match one another, as out of all these one dignity makes a most beautiful form.

Cant. 5:13. ... his lips like lilies dropping sweet smelling myrrh.

IR, 877. "Secondly, because the passing over of that path descendeth even unto the commencement of the mouth.

IR, 878. "But concerning this it is written, Cant. v. 13: 'His lips like roses (that is red as roses), dropping sweet-smelling myrrh while passing over'; which denoteth notable redness.

IR, 879. "And this path of that place is a duplex form, and is not mitigated, whence he who wisheth to threaten toucheth that path twice with his hand."

IR, 904. "And by that mouth, when that path is opened, are clothed many true prophets; and they are all called the mouth of Tetragrammaton.

IR, 904. "And in that place where the Spirit goeth forth no other thing is mingled therewith; for all things wait upon that mouth, that they may be clothed with the Spirit going forth therefrom.

F. And the mouth and the lips, which are in God the advice which he gives us and the Holy Scriptures where he speaks to us, so as in this body they are violets and myrrh, so in God they have much burning and bitterness, with which they burn for virtue and embitter and kill vice.

AE, 311. Grace is diffused in your lips because God blessed you in eternity.

TE, 340. ... the certain purple kind of lilies means that each word of Christ was filled with the most fervent love.

Cant. 5:14. His hands are as gold rings, set with beryl:

IR, 1059. Rabbi Schimeon spake, and said: Let us behold. The superiors are below, and the inferiors are above. (Note: Which is equivalent to the great magical precept of Hermes Trismegistus in the second clause of the Smaragdine Tablet: "That which is below is like that which is above, and that which is above is like that which is below, for the performance of the miracles of the one substance.")

IR, 1060. The superiors are below. That is the form of Man which is the Universal Superior Conformation.

IR, 1063. We have learned in the "Book of Concealed Mystery" that in man were comprehended the Superior Crowns in general and in special; and that in man are comprehended the Inferior Crowns in special and in general.

IR, 1065. (*The Superior Crowns*) in special (*are comprehended*) in the fingers of the hands, which are CHMSMKNGD CHMSH, *Chamesh Ke-Neged Chamesh*, Five over against (or opposed to, of chief above) Five.

F. ... that which in God are the hands, which are his power for working and the works done by Him, are like those of this body ... they are perfect and beautiful and all very good as the Scripture says (Gen. 1: 31). [N.B. from this and the following texts, it is clear that cabala is the key to understanding Fray Luis' theory of natural science.]

PE, 286. My spouse, she says, has gold hands and fingers, ... most beautiful ...

AE, 311. The hands of Christ, that is all his works are very perfect.

TE, 341. To be admired above all is the way by which are signified what works Christ did by which the laws of nature were superceded. But nothing was more admirable, nothing more fertile in secret testimony than was his death and burial, which of all things Christ did seemed to be most degrading as the belly is seen to be the most contemptible part of the human body.

CC, 158. The stone *tarsis* which is named as the province where it is found, is a little between red and white, according to the description of an ancient Hebrew called Ibn Ezra. And according to this the Bride gives to understand the fingernails ... which are a little red and shining as the precious stone of *tarsis* ... of that color [of the hands] it has already been said they are white, when I spoke above "my Spouse is white and red."

Cant. 5: 14. His belly is as bright as ivory overlaid with saphires.

IR, 955. This Tiphereth, Beauty, hath been extended from the heart, and penetrateth it, and passeth through unto the other side, and instituteth the formations from the Countenance of the Woman even unto Her heart; so that from the parts about the heart it taketh its rise on this side, and in the parts about the heart it terminateth on that side.

IR, 956. Moreover, this Tiphereth is extended, and it formeth the internal parts of a Man.

IR, 957. And in entereth into and disposeth therein all mercies and aspects of mercies.

IR, 1128. Adam, truly, is the interior conformation, wherein consisteth the RVCH, *Ruach*, Spirit; like as it is said, I Sam. xvi. 6: "Because Adam seeth according to the eyes, but Tetragrammaton seeth according to the heart," which is within the interior parts.

IR, 1129. And in that formation appeareth the true perfection of all things, which existeth above the Throne. Like as it is written: "And the appearance as the likeness of Adam upon it from above" (Ezek. i. 26).

F. Then for the bowels of God and for the fertility of his virtue, which is as the belly, where all things are engendered, what image will be better than that white belly as if made of marble and adorned with saphires.

PE, 287. With the word of "belly," the breast and the remaining parts of the body are comprehended and it is called ivory from its whiteness and shininess.

AE, 311. *Meghaim* not only pertains to the belly but to the heart and all the parts of the body extending from the neck to the genetals and also to the Hebrews it signifies the internal viscera as well; however in a figurative and secret word they are transferred to mean the heart . . . insofar as it is understood to be the seat and principle of animal sense and the recepticle of the desire for all things. . . . His belly is white as ivory . . . not only is white meant but also thought and that agitation of mind in which light illumines something of truth. . . . What is the heart of Christ? White as ivory, she says, that is, knowing, decorated with saphires, that is not only alien to all evil, and turbulent movement, not so much subjecting itself and its desires to reason, but also doing everything from the prescription of reason as unless it goes first, it is able neither to desire anything nor to grieve. [Fray Luis' devotion to the Sacred Heart of Jesus is here clearly a Christianized form of Jewish mysticism.]

TE, 341. His belly, thus are named his cross and his burial either because lowly as a belly as we said, or certainly because in the belly nearly all the vital organs are contained, as in it are digested every manner of food, so in the sepulchre and cross of Christ we all are enclosed and were as digested.

Cant. 5: 15. His legs are as pillars of marble, set upon sockets of fine gold:

IR, 1061. We have learned this which is written, "And the just man is the foundation YSVD, *Yesod,* of the world, "Prov. x. 25, because He comprehendeth the Hexad in one enumeration.

IR, 1062. And this is that which is written, Cant. v. 15: "His legs are as columns, SHSH, *Shesh,* of the Number Six." (Note: the ordinary translation of this passage is: "His legs are as pillars of marble." SHSH may be translated either "marble" or "the Number Six," according to the pointing.) [Yesod, like Tiphereth, is one of the ten Divine eminations in cabala.]

F. And the legs of the same one, which are beautiful and strong, as marble on golden foundations, are clear pictures of the divine firmness, unmovable, . . .

AE, 312. The strength of Christ is declared in these words. Strength, I say, not only that which is in his deeds, and by which he broke the powers of the devil, but those things, however, which he makes in us, who by faith and charity are joined with him.

TE, 341. For in the legs there is the type and symbol of the Resurrection of Christ . . .

CC, 159. In which is shown the firmness and noble posture and their proportion . . . signifying his beauty by his parts from the head to the feet . . .

Cant. 5: 15. His countenance is as Lebanon, excellent as the cedars.

IR, 916. "Concerning this it is written, Prov. 29: 'The beauty of a young man is his strength.'"

IR, 917. "And He appeareth upon the (*Red*) Sea, like a beautiful youth, which is written in Cant. v. 16: 'Excellent (or young) as the cedars.'"

IR, 918. "Like a hero hath He exhibited His valour, and this is that THPARTH, CHILA, VGBVRTHA, VRCHMI, *Tiphereth, Chila, Ve-Geburatha, Ve Rechemi,* Beauty, Strength, and Valour, and Mercy."

F. It is also his features as those of a cedar, which is as the height of his divine nature, full of majesty and beauty.

AE, 313. By which we are taught that . . . there is nothing higher neither on earth nor in heaven . . . that mountain . . . and the tree which it produces are able to be transferred to Christ . . . because he abounds in all that material which was necessary for the building of the temple at Jerusalem constructed by Salomon. For there was in that temple the image of the heavenly and spiritual temple because Christ, from whom first all men first come to be, began to build, and always establishes . . . what is the one and true temple pleasing to God.

Cant. 7: 5. Thine head upon thee is like Carmel, and the hair of thine head like purple; the king is held in the galleries.

IR, 952. And all hairs red gold are produced in Her head; yet so that other colours are intermixed therewith.

IR, 953. This is that which is written, Cant. viii. 5: "The hair of Thy head like ARGMN, *Argaman,* purple."

IR, 954. What is Argaman? Colours intermixed with other colours.

IR, 955 and 956, see above.

PE, 387. . . . that is watery and captivated by the love of those hairs which in translation are called galleries (channels), from the similarity of water which since it rushes through channels is said to by many: just as the long hairs of women are curled flowing over their shoulders, and they are said to pour on the shoulders, the word taken from waters [pouring].

DF, 308-309. [The following is part of Fray Luis' support for his proposition in his lecture *De Fide* that the translations of certain passages of the Vulgate are only one of two possible renderings, and that the Hebrew version is sometimes better translated differently for the sake of more certainty of meaning. This proposition is one of the main complaints of those who charged him with heresy in 1572. As we see the argument was over whether cabalistic exegesis was permissible.]

Also in Chapter 7 of Canticles, the Vulgate has: "The hairs of thy head as the purple on the king bound in the channels." There is however a sense of the Hebrew words, as not only able to be translated in that way, as the Vulgate, but also in that way in which more recent ones translated it, namely: "The hairs of thine head like purple, the king is held in the galleries," which version makes the sense more elegant and easier; . . . in that however, namely "the king is held in the galleries," there is a poetic figure in love songs; vehemently he exaggerates the beauty of the hairs; they are beautiful so that the king or bridegroom is held and bound in his love for them; he calls the hairs channels, by likeness to water, which, as it flows from channels is wavy, as are long and copious locks, flowing and spread out on the shoulders. And these things according to the literal sense. For according to the mystic one, the hairs of the head are thoughts . . . therefore the thoughts of the bride are as purple, which burn with charity, and also the king is bound by these thoughts, or vehemently rejoices in them . . .

Cant. 6: 7. As a piece of a pomegranate are thy temples within thy locks.

IR, 548. See above.

AE, 360. Which virtues are here praised in these words, by which they were praised above, nevertheless in proportion to his charity, from which all take their origin and start, here, that is, in the perfect man, whose much the most perfect charity teaches that these [of the bride] are greater and more perfect.

TE, 372. That he may teach that both the old and the new Church had almost the same gifts, the same faith, the same grace, promises, doctrine, so here he attributes to both the same members [Cant. 4: 1-5, and 6: 4-7, are descriptions of the Bride, first as the Synagogue, then as the Church] and praises the attributes in almost the same way to declare these very ornaments of soul and heavenly gifts common to both Churches to be greater in the Church of the Gospel and more distinguished, so he joins it with the old Synagogue and puts it before the Synagogue.

DF, 315. [This part of *De Fide* has the same end as the above.] Also the Vulgate has in Chapter 6 of Canticles, "Thy cheeks are as the bark of a pomegranate," for the Hebrew word . . . *felaj* does not mean "bark"; and in the same book, Chapter 4, the Vulgate turns the same word as "piece" and the notion of likeness, which is there used by the Holy Spirit, demands that we read it as "piece"; for he compares the cheeks of the bride as somewhat and fittingly as red, and mixed with red and white; he compares them with a piece of pomegranate whose grains grow together from red and white, thus redden slightly and fittingly.

Cant. 4: 1-5. Thy hair is as a flock of goats, that appear from Mount Gilead.

IR, 575. The curling locks are parted on this side and on that above the head.

IR, 576. Also we have learned that they remain in curls because they proceed from many fountains of the three canals of the brain.

IR, 577. For from the fountain of one cavity of the skull proceedeth the hair, and it becomes curls upon curls (*formed*), from the fountains proceeding from that cavity.

IR, 578. From the second cavity there go forth fifty fountains, and from those fountains the hair issueth, and it becometh curls upon curls, and they are mingled with the other locks.

IR, 579. From the third cavity there go forth a thousand times a thousand conclaves and assemblies, and from them all the hair issueth; and it becometh curls upon curls, and they are mingled with the other locks.

IR, 580. And therefore are those locks so curling, and all the progeny of them is produced from the three cavities of the brain of the skull.

IR, 581. And all those curls hang down and are spread over the sides of the ears.

IR, 582. And therefore it is written, Dan. ix. 18: "Incline thine ear, O my God, and hear."

IR, 583. And in those curls there are found alike right and left, light and dark, mercy and judgment, and everything (*that hath in itself and the qualities of*) right and left dependeth thence (*from Microprosopus*), and not from the Ancient One.

IR, 584. In the parting of the hair appeareth a certain slender path, which hath a certain connection with that path of the Ancient of Days, and from that path are divided six hundred and thirteen paths, (Note: The precepts of the Law are said to be 613 in number, which is also expressed by Gematria in the words "Moses our Rabbi"; MSHH RBINV, *Mosheh Rabbino,* $40 + 300 + 5 + 200 + 2 + 10 + 50 + 6 = 613$.) which are distributed among the path of the precepts of the law.

IR, 585. Like as it is written, Ps. xxv. 6: "All the paths of Tetragrammaton are mercy and truth unto such as keep His covenant and His testimony."

IR, 586. We have learned that in the single locks a thousand times a thousand uterances of the speech of Tetragrammaton are found, which depend from the single locks.

IR, 587. Among them some are hard (*rigorous*) and some soft (*merciful*), as (*belonging unto*) the Lord of the equilibrium (or, the Lord of mercy, who is an equilibrium between these); and therefore is He (*Microprosopus*) said to include right and left.

AE, 243, 244, 247. I see that it is generally accepted that in these secret things of sacred letters the thoughts of the soul and the mind are to be signified by reason of speaking with the name of hairs, and fittingly. For as the hairs arise from the head, so from the mind do thoughts proceed which are to the soul as the head, in great number and nobility they seem like hairs as well. . . . Therefore these pertain to this order [that of the proficient of the spiritual life]; the splendor or thoughts consists in this, or they are taken as splendid things themselves are, that is as concerning brilliant and sparkling things, that is as the heavens, or as pertaining to the celestial life.

APPENDIX III

Relation of Texts from the *Nombre de Cristo*: *"Pimpollo"*
and Texts of *De Arcanis Catholicae Veritatis*

KEY:

P : García, ed., *Obras completas* I.

G : Galatino, *De Arcanis*.

P, 426. Introduction: El primer nombre puesto en castellano se dirá bien Pimpollo, fue en la lengua original es *cemah*, y el texto latino de la Sagrada Escritura unas veces lo traslada diciendo *germen*, y otras diciendo *oriens*. Asi le Llamó el Espiritu Santo en el capitulo 4 del profeta Isaias: En aquel dia el Pimpollo del Señor será en grande alteza, y el frute de la tierra muy ensalzado. Y por Jeremias en el capitulo 33; Y haré que nazca a David Pimpollo de justicia y haré justicia y razón sobre la tierra Y por Zacarias en el capitulo 3, consolando al pueblo judaico, recién salido del cautiverio de Babilonia: Yo haré, dice, venir a mi siervo el Pimpollo, Y en el capitulo 6: Veis un varón cuyo nombre es Pimpollo.

1.

P, 426. Pues viniendo al primero, cosa clara es que habla de Cristo, asi porque el texto caldaico, que es de grandisima autoridad y antigüedad, en aquel mismo lugar adonde nosotros leemos: En aquel dia será el Pimpollo del Señor, dice él: En aquel dia será el Mesias del Señor, como también porque no se puede entender aquel lugar de otra alguna manera.

G, III, 16. Quod quidem in una Messiae persona complendum fuisse, Esaias et Jeremias, secundum Targum, hoc est, secundum Chaldaicam translationem evidentissime insinuant. Nam Esias quidem quarto capite sic ait ... Jeremias (ch. 33) autem sic inquit ... sicut dictum est Zachariae sexto capite, Ecce vir ... *tsemah*, id est, Germen nomen ejus.

2.

P, 428. Porque en la destructión que hicieron de Jerusalén los caldeos, si alguno por caso quisiere dicir que habla aqui de ella el profeta, no se puede decir con verdad que creció el fruto del Señor, ni que fructificó gloriosamente la tierra al mismo tiempo que la ciudad se perdió. Pues es notorio que en aquella calamidad no hubo alguna parte o alguna mezcla de felicidad señalada, ni en los que fueron cautivos a Babilonia, ni en los que el vencedor caldeo dejó en Judea y en Jerusalén para que labrasen la tierra, porque los unos fueron a servidumbre miserable, y los otros quedaron en miedo y desamparo, como en el libro de Jeremias se lee.

G, IX, 8. ... propterea dixit Dominus (ut scribitur Jer. 39) Eruens eruam te ... Fuit insuper tunc Jeremias, ac alii permulti viri justi, ac sancti, qui en Babylonem transmigrarunt.

3.

P, 428-429. Porque decirle a David y prometerle que le naceria o fruto o Pimpollo de justicia, era propia señal de que el fruto habia de ser Jesucristo, mavormente añadiendo lo que luego se sigue, y es que este fruto haria justicia y razón sobre la tierra, que es la obra propia suya de Cristo, y uno de los principales fines para que se ordenó su venida, y obra que El solo y ninguno otro enteramente la hizo. Por donde las más veses que se hace memoria de El en las Escrituras divinas, luego en los mismos lugares se le atribuye esta obra, como obra sola de El y como su propio blasón. Asi se ve en el salmo 71, que dice: "Señor, da tu vara al Rey y el ejercicio de justicia al Hijo del Rey.... Dará su derecho a los pobres del pueblo, y será amparo de los pobrecitos, y hundirá al violento opresor."

G, VI, 4. Primum contra eos [Judeos] illud affero quod Psal. 72, qui a vetustis Hebraeorum totus de Messia exponitur, hoc modo legitur, ... Parce Pauperi [etc.]

4.

P, 429. Pues en el tercero lugar de Zacarias, los mismos hebroeos lo confiesan; y el texto caldeo, que he dicho, abiertamente le entiende y le declara de Cristo.

G., III, 21. Hic est, Messias filius David. Sicut dictus est Psal. 118. Lapidem reprobaverunt aedificantes, etc. De hoc etiam lapide apud Zachar. 3. capit., its legitur ... Ecce ego adduco servum meum Germen. Quia ecce lapis quem dedi coram Jehosua.

5.

P, 429. Y asimismo entendemos el cuarto testimonio, que es del mismo profeta. Y no nos impide lo que algunos tienen por inconveniente, y por donde se mueven a declararle en diferente manera, por lo que dice luego que este Pimpollo fructificará después o debajo de si, y que edificará el templo de Dios; pareciéndoles que esto señala abiertamente a Zorobabel, que edificó el templo y fructificó después de si por muchos siglos a Cristo, verdaderisimo fruto. Asi que esto no impide, antes favorece y esfuerza más nuestro intento.

G, III, 16. Inter caetera Messiae nomina Germen eum saepissime vocatum invenio, et praesertim apud Zachariam, cum sexto capite ait ... In hoc enim palam ostenditur, divinam incarnationem, ac naturae humanae assumptionem ... See also VIII, 2.

6.

P, 430. ... si Esaias en el capitulo 11 le llama unas veces rama, y otra flor, y en el capitulo 53 tallo y raiz, todo es decirnos lo que el nombre de Pimpollo o de Fruto nos dice. Lo cual sera bien que declaremos ya, ques lo primero, que pertenece a que Cristo se llama asi, está suficientemente probado, si no se os ofrece otra cosa.

G, II, 6. Hunc insuper Spiritum Sanctum super Messiam fruisse venturum, quietemque perfectam habiturum, Esias optime ostendit ... Egreditur virgula de stirpe Iissai et virgultum de radicibus eius fructificabit ...

G, VIII, 1. Et de Juda natus est Messias, juxta illud Isaiae, 11, cap. dictum, Et egredietur ...

G, X, 4. Hic est Rex Messias, de quo dictum est Isa. scil. 11 ca. Egredietur ...

7.

P, 436, 437, 439, 440. Por manera que Cristo es llamado fruto porque es el fruto del mundo, esto es, porque es el fruto para cuya producción se ordenó y fabricó todo el mundo. Y asi Isaias, deseando su nacimiento, y sabiendo que los cielos y la naturaleza toda vivia y tenia ser principalmente para este parto, a toda ella se le pide diciendo: Derramad rocio, cielos, desde vuestras alturas; y vosotras, nubes, lloviendo, enviadnos al Justo: y la tierra se abra y produzca y brote al Salvador. ... Pero entre otros, pare este propósito, hay un lugar singular en el salmo 109, aunque algo obscuro según la letra latina; mas, según la original, manifiesto y muy claro, en tanto grado que los doctores antiguos, que florecieron antes de la venida de Jesucristo, conocieron de alli, y asi lo escribieron, que la Madre del Mesias habia de concebir virgen, por virtud de Dios y sin obra de varón. Porque vuelto el lugar que digo a la letra, dice de esta manera: En resplandores de santidad del vientre y de la aurora, contingo el rocio de tu nacimiento. ... Y demás de esto, lo que luego se sigue de aurora y de rocio, por galana manera declara lo mismo; porque es una comparación encubierta, que si la descubrimos, sonará asi: En el vientre, conviene a saber, de tu madre, serás engendrado como en la aurora; esto es, como lo que en aquella sazón de tiempo se engendra en el campo con sólo el rocio, que entonces desciende del cielo; no con riego ni con sudor humano.

G, III, 17. Sicut etiam ros per herbarum superficiem se suaviter diffundens, herbis, et plantis virorem vigoremque tribuit, et quod aestu diurno desiccatum et consumtum declinaverat, ros nocturnus humectat, favit et erigit: sic verus noster Messias in se credentibus, ac in bono perseverantibus, virorum atque vigorem tribuit, eosque regit, atque ad vitam aeternam erigit ... Quas ob res Messias non inepte a patribus antiquis Ros vocatus est: ut ex hoc, occulta et incomprehensibilis Filii Dei incarnatio atque nativitas designaretur. Quocirca non abs re Esa. 45 cap. dicitur ... Rorate vel stillate coeli desuper. ... De eodem quoque rore David Psalmo secundum Hebraeos 110 sic ait, ..., De matrice aurorae vel ex aurora tibi ros nativitatis tuae. Quod aurora hic pro matre Messiae aptissime accipiatur, ... De eo quoque sit David Ps. 110. De matrice aurorae tibi, ros nativitatis tuae. Messias igitur non incongrue Ros appellatur. Primum quidem propter descensiones similitudinem. Ros enim de alto descendit, eiusque descensus nostris aspectibus est occultus.

8.

P, 440, Y a la verdad, asi es llamada en las divinas Letras en otros muchos, lugares, esta virtud vivifica y generativa con que engendró Dios al principio el cuerpo de Cristo, y con que, después de muerto, le reengendró y resucitó, y con que en la común resurrectión tornará a la vida nuestros cuerpos deshechos, como en el capitulo 26 de Isaias se ve.

G, VI, 11. Quod igitur mundus iste universus qui propter Adae peccatum corruptus quodammodo fuerat, per Messiam reparandus esset (et mors ipsa destruenda [esset]) ... Illud quod scriptum est Isa. 26. ... Id est, Quia cum *joth he,* formavit Deus secula: cum his enim duabus literis creavit secula Deus sanctus et benedictus. Haec traditio [cabala].

9.

P, 441. Muchas otras cosas pudiera alegar a propósito de aquesta verdad; mas porque no falte tiempo para lo demás que nos resta, baste por todas, y con ésta concluyo, la que en el capitulo 53 dice de Cristo Isaias: Subirá creciendo como Pimpollo delante de Dios, y como raiz y arbolico nacido en tierra seca. Porque si va a decir la verdad, para decirlo como suele hacer el profeta, con palabras figuradas y obscuras, no pudo decirlo con palabras que fuesen más claras que éstas. Llama a Cristo arbolico; y porque le llama asi, siguiendo el mismo hilo y figura, a su santisima Madre llámala tierra conforme a razón; y habiéndola llamado asi, para decir que concibió sin varón, no habia una palabra que mejor ni con más significación lo dijese, que era decir que fue tierra seca. Pero, si os parace, Juliano, prosiga ya Sabino adelante.

G, VIII, 2. Redemptor quoque, quem constituam, vel suscitabo ex vobis, absque patre erit. Sicut dictum est Zachar. 6. cap. Ecce vir, Germen nomen ejus, et de subter te gernimavit. Et sic etiam ipse ait Isaiae 53 cap. Et ascendit sicut virgultum coram eo, et sicut radix ex terra sicca. De ipso quoque David inquit Psalm. 110. De matrice aurorae tibi ros nativitatis tuae.

BIBLIOGRAPHY

PUBLISHED WORKS OF LUIS DE LEÓN LISTED IN AVAILABLE EDITIONS:

Opera. Salamanca (Episcopali Calatravae Colegio), 1891-1895. Seven Volumes. Contains:

In Canticum Moysis. Opera, I, pp. 1-104.

In Psalmos. Ps. XXVI, *ibid.,* pp. 111-168. Also published at Salamanca, 1580, 1582, 1584; Venice, 1604; Paris, 1608, 1649.
    Ps. XXVIII, pp. 169-191.
    Ps. LVII, pp. 192-203.
    Ps. LXVII, pp. 204-270.

In Ecclesiastem. ibid., pp. 271-508.

In Psalmos (fragments). Ps. XV, *ibid.,* pp. 512-519.
    Ps. XVI, pp. 519-527.
    Ps. XVIII, pp. 528-530.
    Ps. CXLV (?), p. 530.

In Canticum Canticorum Triplex Explanatio. Opera, II, pp. 1-472. First and second explanations published at Salamanca, 1580, 1582. All three at Salamanca, 1589; Venice, 1604; Paris, 1608, 1649. Second explanation in Italian at Naples, 1796.

In Abdiam Prophetam Explanatio. Opera, III, pp. 5-174. Published at Salamanca, 1589.

In Epistolam Pauli ad Galatas. ibid., pp. 175-418. Published at Salamanca, 1589.

Commentaria Epistolam II ad Thessalonicenses. ibid., pp. 419-481.

De Incarnatione Tractatus. Opera, IV.

Tractatus de Fidei. Opera, V, pp. 9-447. Includes "De Ecclesia," "De Conciliis," "De Summo Pontifice," "De Infidelitate," "De Haeresibus," "De Apostasia," and a lecture on the Vulgate.

Tractatus de Spe. ibid., pp. 449-618. (Doubtful)*

Tractatus de Caritate. Opera, VI. (Doubtful)*

Quaestiones XXIII Sancti Thomae De Praedestinatione Elucidata. Opera, VII, pp. 2-133.

De Creatione Rerum. ibid., pp. 135-182.

Commentaria in III Partem Divi Thomae. ibid., pp. 183-338.

De Utriusque Agni, Typici atque Veri, Immolationis Legitimo Tempore.

ibid., pp. 339-359. Published at Salamanca, 1590, 1592, 1611; Madrid, 1604; in French translation by Gab. Daniel, S.J., Paris, 1695.

Panegiricus Divo Augustino Dictus. ibid., pp. 365-384.

Oratio Funebris Habita in Exequiis Mag. Dominici Soti, Segoviensis. ibid., pp. 385-405.

In Psalmum XXXVI. ibid., pp. 405-455.

Obras completas castellanas. Felix García, O.S.A., ed. Madrid (Biblioteca de Autores Cristianos), 1957. Fourth Edition. Two Volumes. Contains:

De los nombres de Cristo. Obras completas, I, pp. 397-825. Two books published at Salamanca, 1583, 1586; Barcelona, 1583. Three books published at Salamanca, 1587, 1595, 1603 (with "Cordero"); Barcelona, 1587, 1846, 1848, 1885; Valencia, 1770 (twice); Madrid, 1805, 1885, 1872, 1907, 1910, 1914-17, 1917, 1925, 1934, 1944 (twice), 1947, 1951 ...; Paris-Lyons (French by Postel), 1856, 1862; London (Abridged English by a Benedictine of Stanbrook), 1926; St. Louis (Abridged English by Edward Schuster), 1955.

La perfecta casada. ibid., pp. 243-360. Published at Salamanca, 1583, 1586, 1587, 1595, 1603; Zaragosa, 1584; Venice (Italian), 1595; Naples (Italian), 1598; Madrid, 1632, 1776, 1786, 1799, 1805, 1819, 1865, 1868, 1872, 1873, 1877 (twice), 1878, 1882, 1884, 1885 (twice), 1886, 1887, 1897, 1899 (twice), 1900, 1903, 1906, 1910, 1914 (twice), 1917, 1918, 1928, 1929, 1930, 1933, 1935 (four times), 1939, 1941, 1943, 1944, 1946, 1950, 1951, ... ; Florence (Italian), 1712; Valencia, 1765, 1773, 1875, 1876; Paris (French by Guignard), 1845, (Spanish) 1847, (French by Postel), 1857; Barcelona, 1846, 1848, 1884, 1885, 1889, 1898, 1899, 1904, 1905, 1912, 1913, 1930, 1931 (twice), 1935, 1942, 1950, 1951; Vienna (German), 1847, (Spanish) 1847; Seville, 1878; Chicago (Spanish), 1903; Pontendra, 1906; Paris (French by Dieulafoy), 1906; Valencia (?) (Esperanto by Jiménez Loira), 1909, 1913 (?); Amsterdam (Dutch by Wierdels), 1925; Denton, Texas (English by Hubbard), 1943; Vetusta, 1931; Mexico, 1899; Buenos Aires, 1938, 1940, 1942, 1943, 1944, 1946; Brescia, 1608.

Expositión del libro Job. ibid., II, pp. 27-696. Published at Madrid, 1779, 1804, 1853, 1855, 1872, 1885, 1899, 1910, 1951 ....

Traducción literal y declaración del libro de los Cantares. ibid., I, pp. 70-222. Published at Salamanca, 1798; Madrid, 1806, 1847, 1872, 1885, 1899, 1910, 1940, 1946, ... ; Barcelona, 1884, 1905; Mexico, 1944; Bardón, 1950; Naples (Italian), 1796.

Traducción y expositión del salmo 41. ibid., I, pp. 891-899. Published at Madrid, 1806, 1885; Barcelona, 1905.

"Carta-Prologo a 'Los libros de la Madre Teresa de Jesús' a los M.-M. Priora Ana de Jesús y Religiosas Carmelitas Descalzas del Monasterio de Madrid." *ibid.,* I, pp. 904-914. Published at Salamanca, 1589, 1806; Burgos, 1915; Madrid (BAE, LIII, p. 18).

"Apologia de los libros de la Madre Teresa de Jesús y de su impresión en lengua vulgar." *ibid.,* I, pp. 915-920. Published at Rome, 1610; Valencia, 1623; Madrid, 1885.

"De la vida, muerte, virtudes, y milagros de la Sta. Madre Teresa de Jesús." *ibid.*, I, pp. 921-941. (Found in *Revista Agustiniana,* V, pp. 61-66, 95-102, 195-203.)

Explanación del salmo 26 por Mto. Fr. Luis de León. ibid., I, pp. 900-903.

Twenty-nine letters. *ibid.,* I, pp. 942-1009.

Poems and poetic translations (Spanish and latin). *ibid.,* II, pp. 742-1040. Published in numerous other editions.

Obras del M. Fr. Luis de León, de la Orden de San Agustin. Antolín Merino, O.S.A., ed. Madrid (Ibarra), 1804-1816. Six Volumes. Contains (in addition to works in the García edition):

"Repuesta que desde su prisión da á sus émulos R. P. M. Fr. Luis de León en el año de 1573." *Obras,* V, pp. 281-292. Published at Salamanca, 1798; Madrid, 1872, 1885, 1899, 1910; Barcelona, 1884, 1905.

Sermon *"Vos estis sal terrae." ibid.,* pp. 369-399.

Fragment of sermon *De Kalenda. ibid.,* pp. 400-404.

De Legibus o tratado de las leyes (I, 1-VIII, 20). Luciano Pereña, ed. Madrid (CSIC), 1963.

In Psalmum "Quemadmodum Desiderat Cervus." Salamanca, 1583 (?).

Biblioteca de Autores Españoles. Madrid, 1907.

Contains (in addition to works in other editions):

"Censura de 'Los libros de la Madre Teresa de Jesús.'" BAE, LIII, p. xl. Published at Salamanca, 1589.

"Advertencia puesta al principio del libro de Las Moradas, acerca de las correcciones y enmiendas hechas en él." BAE, LIII, p. 133.

"Extracto del processo que la Inquisición hizo al Mto. León." BAE, XXXVII, pp. 102-108.

Archivo Agustiniano contains:

Various autographs. Miguel de la Pinta Llorente, O.S.A., ed. XLIV (1950), pp. 293-325. (Various letters of Fray Luis identified by several scholars are collected here.)

Archivo Historico Hispano-Agustiniano contains:

"Processo de la Cathedra de Biblia que vacó por muerte del Rmo. M. D. Gregorio Gallo, Obispo de Segovia." Gregorio de Santiago Vela, O.S.A., ed., VI (1916), pp. 192-209, 255-268, 325-337. (Contains statements of Fray Luis.)

"Memorial contra algunas determinaciones del capitulo provincial de 1586." Gregorio de Santiago Vela, ed., XVI (1921), pp. 15-33; XXII (1924), pp. 302-312; XXIII, pp. 37-51. (Known only in Italian copy, MS, Archives of the Spanish Embassy to the Holy See, I, Index of XVI Cent. Doc., p. 97, leg. 35. Doubtful.)*

"Alegato en favor de las Monjas Carmelitas." Gregorio de Santiago Vela, O.S.A., ed. XVIII, pp. 274-281. (See XIX, p. 55, for evaluation of authenticity.)

"Discurso sobre la differencia que hay entre Frailes y Monjas Carmelitas Descalzas acerca del gobierno." Gregorio de Santiago Vela, O.S.A., ed. XIX, pp. 39-52.

Augustinianum contains:

In Epistolam ad Romanos (portions). David Gutiérrez, O.S.A., ed. I (1961), pp. 299-309.

La Ciudad de Dios contains:
"Carta sobre la enmendación de la Biblia, y Advertemiento acerca de la corrección de las obras de los S.S. Padres." XXXVI, pp. 97-102. (*Religion y Cultura*, II, pp. 528-530.)
"Parecer acerca de la clausura y votos del Monasterio de Sancti Spiritus de Salamanca." CLXIII (1951), pp. 323-328 .
"Quaestio Quodlibetica (XIII) cum Argumentis: Utrum Christus Omnis Gratiae Causa ex Nunc Sit et in Omni Rerum Statu Futurus Fuerit." Angel Custodio Vega, O.S.A., ed. CLXVI (1954), pp. 140-157.
"*De Sensibus Sacrae Scripturae.*" O. García de la Fuente, O.S.A., ed. CLXX (1957), pp. 328 ff.

Religión y Cultura contains:
"Processo de la Cathedra de propriedad de Philosophía moral que vaca por muerte de el Rmo. Sr. M. Don Francisco Sancho, Obispo de Segovia." Gregorio de Santiago Vela, O.S.A. and Pedro Abella, eds. III, pp. 145-152, 309-313; IV, pp. 151-159.

Revue Hispanique contains:
"Discours prononcé par Luis de León au chapitre de Duenas (15 mai, 1557)." Ad. Coster, ed. L (1920), pp. 1-60. (Doubtful)*
Colección de documentos inéditos para la historia de Hispana. M. Salvá and P. Sainz de Baranda, eds. Madrid, 1847. Contains:
Ninety documents by Fray Luis de León. Volumes X and XI to p. 358. (The titles of these are listed in ZC, see below.)

Felipe Picatoste Rodriguez. *Apuntes para una biblioteca cientifica del siglo XVI.* Madrid, 1891. Contains:
"Parecer y dictamen dado juntamente con el maestro Fray Luis de León a la Universidad de Salamanca por encargo de la misma sobre la reducción del calendario, despues del Santo Concilio general de Trento." (See: Marcelino Gutiérrez, O.S.A., *La Ciudad de Dios*, XXII, pp. 333-336.)

Gregorio de Santiago Vela, O.S.A. *Ensayo de una biblioteca Ibero-Americana de la Orden de San Agustín.* El Escorial (Monasterio), 1931. Eight Volumes. Contains:
"Carta de 7 de Dic., 1561 (portion)." (This letter concerns the treatise *De Decimis* of Fray Alonso de la Vera Cruz, O.S.A., delivered in the University of Mexico, 1555. Both are found in the Real Biblioteca de El Escorial, MS iii-K-6, xiii, 354 fols. Fray Luis' letter is dated at Salamanca.) VIII, p. 170. *Revista Agustiniana*, II, p. 158.

Ecclesiastical approbations and censures given by Fray Luis include the following:
"Aprobación." Fr. Tomás de Mercado, O.P. *Tratos y contratos de mercadores y tratantes discididos y determinados.* Salamanca (Mathias Gast), 1569. (Approbation is also given by Alonso de la Vera Cruz.)

"Aprobación dada en San Felipe de Madrid, 4 de mayo de 1589." P. José de Acosta, S.J. *Historia natural y moral de las Indias.* Sevilla, 1590.

"Aprobación, Madrid, 10 de junio de 1589." Pedro Simón. *Apuntamientos de como se deben reformar las doctrinas.* Madrid, 1589.

"Censura, 10 de dic. de 1587." Pedro López de Montoya. *Libro de la buena educación y enseñanza de los nobles.* Madrid, 1595.

"Aprobación y licencia dada por Luis de León en Madrid, 15 de julio de 1587." Fr. Marcos de la Camara, O.F.M. *Quaestionarium conciliationis simul et expositionis locorum difficilium Sacrae Scripturae.* Alcalá, 1587.

WORKS DRAWING ON THOSE OF FRAY LUIS DE LEÓN:

Fr. Hieronymo Almoncario, O.P. *Commentaria in Canticum Canticorum Salomonis.* Alcalá, 1588.

Fr. Alfonso de Herrera Salcedo, O.F.M. *Espejo de la perfecta casada.* Lima, 1627; Granada, 1638.

WORKS ATTRIBUTED TO FRAY LUIS DE LEÓN:

"El perfecto predicator, exposición del Ecclesiastés." *Revista Agustiniana,* XI, pp. 340-348, 432-442, 527-537; XII, 15-23, 104-111, 211-218, 322, 330, 420-427, 504-512; XIII, 32-38, 106-114, 213-222, 302-312; XIV, 9-17, 154-160, 305-315, 449-459, 581-591, 729-743.

"Forma de vivir de los Frailes Agustinos descalzos, ordenado por el Provincial y Difinidores de la Provincia de Castilla." Fr. Andrés de San Nicolas, agustino descalzo. *Historia general de los Padres Agustinos.* Madrid, 1664. Tome I, pp. 138-148. (Probably co-authored with Fray Luis.)*

A comedy by Fray Luis de León has been mentioned. See Astrana Marín, "Sobre el Renacimiento español," *Archivo Historico Hispano-Agustino,* XXVII, p. 237.

A translation of the first six books of the *Aeneid* attributed to Fray Luis in 1777 and 1795 is the work of Fr. Antonio de Maya, O.S.A.

TRANSLATIONS OF FRAY LUIS' POEMS:

In German (Schlueter, Starck): *Obras poeticas proprias de Fray Luis de León.* Muenster, 1853.

In French (Rousselot): *Les Mystiques Espanols.* Paris, 1867, 1869.

— (Coster): *Frère Luis de León, Poésies Originales classées pour la première fois dans l'ordre chronologique.* Chartres, 1923.

In English (Phillips): *Poems from the Spanish of Fra Luis Ponce de León.* Philadelphia, 1883.

— (Beall): "The Quiet Life," *Hispania-California,* VII (1924), pp. 266-268.

— (Bell): *Lyrics of Luis de León.* London, 1928.

— (Morgan, Tobin, Sackett) *An Anthology of Spanish Poetry.* A. Flores, ed. New York (Doubleday Anchor), 1961. Pp. 45-58.

In latin (Viñas): *Versiones latinas de Poesías Hispanas.* Barcelona, 1927.

UNPUBLISHED MANUSCRIPTS OF WORKS OF LUIS DE LEÓN:

De Incarnatione. (In III, 20-27, 1568) MS, Library of the Seminary of Valladolid, no number, fols. 88-103.

De Eucharistia. (1569, substitution for Mancio de Corpus Christi, O.P.) MS, Provincial Library of Evora, Portugal, 123-2-27; Library of the Seminary of Valladolid, no number, 230x173 mm., 607 fols, XVI Cent.

De Trinitate. (1569-1570) MS, Library of the University of Coimbra, Portugal, 1834, fols. 1-114. (1843?)

De Angelis. (1570-1571) MS, Library of the University of Coimbra, 1834 (1843?), fols., 22v-53.

De Legibus. (1571-1572) MS, Library of the University of Coimbra, 1843, fols. 113-223. MS, Library of the Royal Academy of History, Madrid, 9/2081, fols. 176-187v. The latter is a fragment dealing with the promises of the Old Law a photocopy of which is held by Library of Iowa State University, Ames, Iowa. (The MS attributed to Fray Luis by Pereña appears partly illegible. Vatican Library, Ottob. Lat. 1004.)

De Libero Arbitrio. (1571-1572) MS, Library of the University of Coimbra, 1984.

De Gratia et Justificatione. (1571-1572) MS, Library of the University of Coimbra, 1843, fols. 69-111.

De Simonia. (1576-1577) MS, Municipal Library of Oporto, Portugal, 1202, fol. 146.

—. (1577) MS, Library of the Cathedral of Pamplona, cat. 111, no number fols. 323r-359v. Photocopy held by Library of Iowa State University, Ames, Iowa.

De Trinitate. (1577) MS, Provincial Library of Palencia, fol. 200-200v.

Expositio in Genesim (cap. I, II, III, 3). (1589-1590) MS, Library of the Cathedral of Pamplona, cat. 83, no number, fols. 1-55. Photocopy held by Library of Iowa State University, Ames, Iowa.

In Epistolam ad Romanos. MS, Vatican Library, Ottob. Lat. 1020, fols. 348-445v. (Cf. *Augustinianum,* I (1961), pp: 273-309.)

Quaestiones Variae. MS, Library of the Royal Academy of History, Madrid, 11-2-7, fols. 445-452.

"Un cuaderno sobre si pecó venialmente la Stma. Virgen." (1568) MS, Library of the Royal Academy of History, 11-2-7.

"Memorial de Fr. Luis de León sobre el Breve en que se le comisionaba para llevar a cabo la reforma de Sta. Teresa, 17 Dic. de 1590, 19 Enero de 1591." MS, Archivo de Simancas, Patronato Eclesiástico, Leg. 21-22, num. 3, 57.

"Cartas de Fray Luis de León." (On the Discalced Carmelites and the conduct of Father Gracián.) MS, National Library, Madrid, R. 176.

"Carta de Fray Luis a don Alonzo de Zúñiga, Madrid, 2 Sept., 1586." MS, British Museum, add., 28371 (Cat. IV, 22).

"Interpretatio bullae 'Cruciate.'" MS, Library of El Escorial, 0-III, 32, fols., 1-16. (Possibly a work of Fray Luis.)

Sermons: "Pro Inventione S. Crucis." "Pro Conversione D. Pauli." "In die S. Petri." MS, Biblioteca Corderera. (LP, p. 370, ZC, #362.)

LOST WORKS OF FRAY LUIS DE LEÓN:

De Religione, De Oratio, De Juramento. (1561-1562, 1576-1577). Cf. MI, p. 64.
De Statibus. (1561-1562) Cf. *Doc. ined.*, X, pp. 279, 370, etc. Cf. MI, p. 64.
De Trinitate. (1564-1565) Cf. MI.
De Gratia et Justificatione. (1564-1565) Cf. *ibid.*
De Libero Arbitrio. (1565-1566) *ibid.*
De Angelis. (1565-1566) *ibid.*
De Simonia. (1577-1578) *ibid.*
"Declaración de la palabra del profeta Ezeciel 'Sigma tau' super frontes virorum gementium." Cf. *Doc. ined.*, X, pp. 239-240.
"Declaración del Ps. 'Usquequo Domine oblivisceris me in finem.' " Cf. *Doc. ined.*, X, p. 186.
A commentary of Apocalypse possessed by Fray Basilio Ponce de León. Cf. MI, p. 78; ZC, p. 45.
A concordance of the evangelists on the Resurrection mentioned by Fray Basilio. Cf. ZC, #47.
A computation of the year of the flood mentioned by Fray Basilio. Cf. *ibid.*
"Methodo de latinidad." Cf. LP, p. 380.
A speech dealing with contention for the Chair of St. Thomas. Cf. *Doc. ined.*, X, p. 395; XI, pp. 258, 370.
Various answers. Cf. *Doc. ined.*, X, pp. 241, 347.
"Parecer sobre la gracia de N. Señora." *Doc. ined.*, X, p. 467.

BIBLIOGRAPHICAL SOURCES USED IN THIS COMPILATION:

Biblioteca de Autores Españoles. (abbr. BAE) Madrid (Sucesores de Hernando), 1907.
E. Domínguez Carretero, O.S.A. "La escuela teológica Agustiniana de Salamanca," *La Ciudad de Dios,* CLXIX (1956), pp. 657-659.
José Goñi Gaztambide. "Catalogo de los manuscritos teológicos de la Catedral de Pamplona," *Revista Española de Teología,* XVIII (1958), pp. 66 and 85.
* David Gutiérrez, O.S.A. "Sobre la autenticidad de algunos escritos atribuidos a Fray Luis de León," *Analecta Augustiniana,* XXVII (1964), pp. 341-379.
* —. "Autenticidad de las lecturas *De Spe y De Caritate de Fray Luis de León,*" *Analecta Augustiniana,* XXV (1962), pp. 340-350.
Miguel de la Pinta Llorente, O.S.A. "Contribuciones eruditas modernas sobre Fray Luis de León y autografos del poeta agustino," *Archivo Agustiniano,* XLIV (1950), pp. 293-328.
—. "Tratados varios de Fr. Luis de León," (abbr. LP) *Archivo Agustiniano,* XVII (1953), pp. 368-396.
Salvador Muñoz Iglesias. *Fray Luis de León, teólogo.* (abbr. MI) Madrid (CSIC), 1950.
—. "Manuscritos teológicos de Fray Luis de León," *Revista Española de Teología,* XV (1955), pp. 97-99.

Antonio Palau y Dulcet. *Manual del Librero Hispano-americano*. Barcelona (Palau y Dulcet), 1954. Volume Seven, pp. 479-484.

José Torobio Medina. *Biblioteca Hispano-Americana, 1493-1810*. Amsterdam (N. Israel), 1968 (reprint).

J. Zarco Cuevas. *Bibliografia de Fray Luis de León*. (abbr. ZC) Malaga, 1928.

BIBLIOGRAPHY OF RELATED BOOKS AND ARTICLES:

Acosta, Joseph. *The Naturall and Morall Historie of the East and West Indies*. E. Grimson, trans. London (Blount and Aspby), 1604.

Agrippa ab Nettesheym, H. C. *De Occulta Philosophia*. Graz (Akademischer Druck), 1967.

Alonso, Dámaso. *Poesía española*. Madrid (Gredos), 1962.

Alvarez Turienzo, S. "Sobre Fray Luis de León, filólogo," *La Ciudad de Diós*, CLXIX (1956), 112-136.

Amador de los Ríos, J. *Historia social, politica y religiosa de los Judios de España y Portugal*. Madrid (Aguilar), 1960.

Amann, E. *et al.*, eds. *Dictionnaire de Théologie Catholique*, Paris (Letouzey), 1937. 15 Vols.

Arango y Escandón, Alejandro. *Fray Luis de León*. México (Imprenta de Andrade y Escalante), 1866.

Arias Montano, B. *Commentaria in Duodecim Prophetas*. Antwerp, 1571.

Arkin, Alexander Habib. *La influencia de la exégesis Hebrea en los comentarios biblicos de Fray Luis de León*. Madrid (CSIC), 1966.

Asín Palacios, Miguel. *Huellas del Islam*. Madrid (Espasa-Calpe), 1941.

Augustine, St. *City of God*. Abridged by V. J. Bourke. New York (Image Books), 1958.

Baer, Y. F. *A History of the Jews in Christian Spain*. Philadelphia (Jewish Publications Society of America), 1966. Two Vols.

Baruzi, Jean. *Luis de León, Interprête du Livre de Job*. Paris (Presses Universitaires de France), 1966.

Bataillon, Marcel. "Charles-Quint Bon Pasteur selon Fray Cipriano de Huerga," *Bulletin Hispanique*, L (1948), 398-406.

— Erasmo y España. Mexico (Fondo de Cultura Economica), 1950. Two Volumes.

Bell, A. F. G. *Luis de León*. Barcelona (Araluce), 1927.

Beltran de Heredia, Vicente. *Domingo de Soto*. Madrid (Ediciones Cultura Hispanica), 1961.

— "Final de la discussion acerca de la patria del Mtro. Vitoria," *Ciencia Tomista*, LXXX (1953), 275-289.

— *Los corrientes de espiritualidad entre los Dominicos de Castilla durante la primera mitad del siglo XVI*. Salamanca (Biblioteca de Teólogos Españoles), 1941.

Bension, Ariel. *El Zohar en la España musulmana y cristiana*. Madrid (Ediciones Nuestra Raza), 1934.

Bernard, G. "Le Second Procès contre Fr. Luis de León," *Revue des Questions Historiques*, (1897), 222-230.

Berthier, A. "Un Maître Orientaliste du XIIIe Siècle: Raymond Martin, O. P.," *Archivum Fratrum Praedicatorum,* VI (1936), 267-311.

Blau, J. L. *The Christian Interpretation of the Cabala.* New York (Columbia University Press), 1944.

Bordoy Torrents, P. M. "Momentos históricos de la gloria de Fray Luis de León," *La Ciudad de Dios,* CLIV (1942).

Bouwsma, William J. *Concordia Mundi: The Career and Thought of Guillaume Postel (1518-1581).* Cambridge (Harvard University Press), 1957.

Bover, José M. "Fray Luis de León, traductor de San Pablo," *Estudios Eclesiásticos,* VII (1928), 417-431.

Brettle, Sigismund. *San Vicente Ferrer und Sein Literarischer Nachlass.* Münster in Westf. (Verlag der Aschendorffschen Verlagsbuchhandlung), 1924.

Brierre-Narbonne, J. J. *Le Messie Souffrant dans la Littérature Rabbinique.* Paris (Geuther), 1940.

— *Les Prophéties Messianiques de l'Ancien Testament dans la Littérature Juive.* Paris (Geuther), 1933.

Briggs, C. A. *Messianic Prophesy.* New York (Scribner's), 1886.

Bruni, G. "Egidio Romano e la Sua Polemica Antitomista," *Rivista de Filosofia Neoscolastica,* XXXVI (1934), 239-251.

Buddei, Jo. Francisci. *Introductio ad Historiam Philosophiae Hebraeorum.* Halae Saxonum (Imp. Orphanotrophei), 1720.

Burrus, Ernest J. "Alonso de la Veracurz's Defense of the American Indians," *The Heythrop Journal,* IV (1963), 225-253.

— *The Writings of Alonzo de la Vera Cruz, O.S.A.* Rome (Jesuit Historical Institute), 1968. Three Volumes.

Cantera Burgos, Francisco. *Alvar Garcia de Santa María y su familia de conversos.* Madrid (CSIC), 1952.

Capmany y de Montpalau, Antonio de. *Teatro historico-critico de la elocuencia española.* Barcelona (J. Gaspar), 1848, Vol. III.

Carreras y Artau, Joaquín. "Arnaldo de Vilanova, apologista antijudaico," *Sefarad,* VII (1947), 49-62.

Carreras y Artau, Tomás y Joaquín. *Historia de la filosofía española.* Madrid (Real Academia de Ciencias Exactas, Fisicas y Naturales), 1943. Two Vols.

Cartagena, Alonso de. *Defensorium Unitatis Christianae.* Ed. by M. Alonso. Madrid (CSIC), 1943.

Carro, Venancio D. *Domingo de Soto y su doctrina juridica.* Madrid (Imp. Hijos E. Minuesa), 1943.

Castán Tobeñas, J. "El derecho y sus rasgos en el pensamiento espanol," *Revista General de Legislacion y Jurisprduencia.* XCVII (1949), 646-707; XCVIII (1950), 153-204.

Castro, Américo. *La realidad histórica de España.* 3rd Edition. Mexico (Porrua), 1966.

Cohn, Norman. *The Pursuit of the Millenium.* Fairlawn, N. J. (Essential Books), 1957.

Corts Grau, J. *História de la filosofia del derecho,* Part One. Madrid (Editora Nacional), 1952.

Corwin, E. S. "The Higher Law Background of American Constitutional Law," *Harvard Law Review,* XLII (1928), 149-185, 365-409.

Coster, A. "Discours Prononcé par Luis de León au Chapitre de Dueñas (15 mai 1557)," *Revue Hispanique,* L (1920), 1-60.

— "Luis de León," *Revue Hispanique,* LIII (1921), 5ff.

Crisógono de Jesus, O. C. D., Fr. "El misticismo de Fr. Luis de León," *Revista de Espiritualidad,* I (1942), 30-52.

Cuevas, Eusebio. "Fr. Alfonso de Mendoza, Agustino, primer tratadista de Cristo-Rey," *La Ciudad de Dios,* CLIV (1952), 333-362.

Dagens, Jean. *Bibliographie Chronologique de la Littérature de Spiritualité et de ses Sources (1501-1610).* Paris (Desclée de Brouwer), 1952.

Debus, Allen G. *The English Paracelsians.* London (Oldbourne), 1965.

Del Vecchio, Giorgio. *Philosophy of Law.* Trans. by T. O. Martin. Washington (Catholic University of America Press), 1953.

Diego, Sandalio. "Fray Luis de León y Francisco de Ribera en el Comentario de Abdias," *Estudios Eclesiasticos,* VIII (1929), 5-22.

Difernan, B. "Estudio especifico del Derecho natural y Derecho positivo según los clásicos agustinos españoles del siglo XVI," *La Ciudad de Dios,* CLXIX (1956), 253-285.

— "Miguel B. Salón, fundador del derecho internacional," *Revista Española de Derecho Internacional,* I (1953), 83-126.

— "La orden agustiniana y los estudios juridicos en la epoca clasica española," *Anuario de Historia del Derecho Español,* XXV (1955), 775-790.

Dionysius the Areopagite. *Mystical Theology and the Celestial Hierarchies.* N. Godalming, Surrey (The Shrine of Wisdom), 1949.

— *On the Divine Names and the Mystical Theology.* Trans. by C. E. Rolt. New York (Macmillan), 1920.

Domínguez Carretero, E. "La escuela teológica agustiniana de Salamanca," *La Ciudad de Dios,* CLXIX 1956) 638ff.

Domínguez del Val, Ursino. "La predestinación y reprobación en Francisco de Cristo y Alfonso de Mendoza," *La Ciudad de Dios,* CLIV (1942), 293-317.

— "La teología de Fr. Luis de León," *La Ciudad de Dios,* CLXIV (1952), 163-178.

Domínguez Ortiz, Antonio. *La clase social de los conversos en Castilla en la edad moderna.* Madrid (CSIC), 1955.

Dunning, W. A. "The Monarchomachs: Theories of Popular Sovereignty in the 16th Century," *Political Science Quarterly,* XIX (1904), 277-301.

Enciclopedia Universal Ilustrada, Europeo-Americana. Madrid (Espasa-Calpe), 1958, 70 Vols.

Ennis, Arthur. *Fray Alonso de la Vera Cruz, O.S.A. (1507-1584).* Louvain (E. Warny), 1957.

Espina, Alfonso de. *Fortalium Fidei contra Judeos Saracenos, aliosque Christianae fidei inimicos.* Nuremberg (A. Koberger), 1494.

Figgis, John N. *The Divine Right of Kings.* New York (Harper) 1965.

Flore, Joachim de. *Expositio in Apocalypsim.* Venice, 1527.

Folgado, Avelino. "Los tratados *De Legibus* y *De Justitia et Jure* en los autores españoles del siglo XVI y primera mitad del XVII," *La Ciudad de Dios*, CLXXII (1959), 275-302.

Froom, LeRoy Edwin. *The Prophetic Faith of Our Fathers*. Washington (Review and Herald), 1948. Vols. I and II.

Fuente, Vicente de la. *Biografia de Leon de Castro*. Madrid (Libreria de D. Eusebio Aguado), 1860.

Galatini, Petri, *De Arcanis Catholicae Veritatis Libri XII*. Frankfurt (Marnii Haeredes), 1612.

Gallo, Juan, *De Legibus*. Vatican Library MSS. Ottob. Lat. 1.004.

García, Felix, ed. *Obras completas castellanas de Fray Luis de León*. 4th Edition. Madrid (Biblioteca de Autores Cristianos), 1957, Two Vols.

García Alvarez, J. *Fray Luis de León: La paz como perfection ontológica del hombre*. Paris (Unpublished dissertation, Faculty of Philosophy, Institut Catholique), 1962.

García de la Fuente, Olegario. "Un tratado inédito y desconocido de Fr. Luis de León sobre los sentidos de la Sagrada Escritura," *La Ciudad de Dios*, CLXX (1957), 258-334.

García Miralles, O.P., Manuel. "San Vicente Ferrer, Anotador de Santo Tomás," *Revista Española de Teología*, XV (1955), 445-458.

Getino, L. C. Alonso. *El maestro Fr. Francisco de Vitoria*. Madrid (Imp. Católica), 1930.

Gilby, Thomas. *The Political Thought of Thomas Aquinas*. Chicago (University of Chicago Press), 1958.

Gilson, E. *The Christian Philosophy of St. Thomas Aquinas*. New York (Random House), 1956.

— *History of Christian Philosophy in the Middle Ages*. New York (Random House), 1955.

Gliubich, S. *Dizionario Biografico degli Uomini Illustri della Dalmazia*. Vienna (Rod. Lechner), 1856.

Gorce, M.-M. *Saint Vincent Ferrier (1350-1419)*. Paris (Plon), 1924.

Grabmann, Martin. *História de la teologia católica*. Adiciones de David Gutiérrez, O.S.A. Madrid (Espasa-Calpe), 1946.

Gutiérrez, David. "Autenticidad de las lecturas *De Spe* y *De Caritate* de Fray Luis de León," *Analecta Augustiniana*, XXV (1962), 340-350.

— "Un comentario inédito de Fray Luis de León," *Augustinianum*, I (1961), 273-309.

— "Del origen y caracter de la escuela teologica hispano-agustiniano de los siglos XVI y XVII," *La Ciudad de Dios*, CLIII (1941), 227-255.

— "Fray Luis de León y la exégesis rabínica," *Augustinianum*, I (1961), 533-550.

— "Sobre la autenticidad de algunos escritos atribuidos a Fray Luis de León," *Analecta Augustiniana*, XVII (1964), 341-379.

Gutiérrez, Marcelino. "Escritos latinos de Fr. Luis de León," *La Ciudad de Dios*, XXII (1891), 96-107, 327-332.

— *Fr. Luis de León y la filosofía española del siglo XVI*. Madrid (Gregorio del Amo), 1891.

Guy, Alain. *El pensamiento filosófico de Fray Luis de León*. Madrid, (Rialp), 1960.

Hallevi, Judah. *Kitab al Khazari*. Trans. by H. Hirschfeld. New York (B. G. Richards), 1927.

Hamilton, Bernice. *Political Thought in Sixteenth-Century Spain*. Oxford (Clarendon Press), 1963.

Hanke, Lewis, "Mas polémica y un poco de verdad acerca de la lucha española por la justicia en la conquista de América," *Revista Chilena de Historia y Geografia*, CXXXIV (1966), 5-66.

Harrisse, H. "Un Rarissme Americanum," *Bulletin du Bibliophile et du Bibliothecaire*, (1897), 71-76.

Hirsch, S. A. "Johann Reuchlin: The Father of the Study of Hebrew Among the Christians," *The Jewish Quarterly Review*, VIII (1896), 445-470.

Hart, H. L. A. *The Concept of Law*. Oxford (Clarendon Press), 1961.

Hocedez, E. "Gilles de Rome et Saint Thomas," *Mélanges Mandonnet*, I (1930), 385-409.

Hubbard, Alice P., trans. *The Perfect Wife, Translated from the Spanish of Friar Luis de León, 1583*. Denton, Tex. (The College Press), 1943.

Huddleston, Lee E. *Origins of the American Indians, European Concepts, 1492-1729*. Austin (University of Texas Press), 1967.

Ibeas, B. "El carácter de Fr. Luis de León," *Religion y Cultura*, II (1928), 350-370.

Index Librorum Prohibitorum. Antwerp (Chris. Plantin), 1570.

Jedin, Hubert. *A History of the Council of Trent*. St. Louis (Herder), 1961. Two Volumes.

— *Papal Legate at the Council of Trent, Cardinal Seripando*. St. Louis (Herder), 1947.

Juan de los Angeles. *Dialogos de la Conquista del Reino de Dios*. Madrid (Aguirre), 1946.

— *Obras Misticas del M.R.P. Fr. Juan de los Angeles*. Fr. Jaime Sala, ed. Madrid (Bailly-Bailliere), 1917. Volume 24 of the *Nueva Biblioteca de Autores Españoles*.

Kleinhans, Arduinus. "De Vita et Operibus Petri Galatini, O.F.M.," *Antonianum*, I (1926), 145-197, 327-356.

Lea, H. C. *Chapters from the Religious History of Spain*. New York (Burt Franklin), 1967.

Leob, I. "La Controverse Religieuse entre les Chrétiens et les Juifs au Moyen Age," *Revue de l'Histoire des Religions*, XVIII, 133-156.

Lewis, John U. *Man's Natural Knowledge of the Eternal Law*. Milwaukee (unpublished dissertation, Marquette University), 1966.

Lewy, Guenter. *A Study of the Political Philosophy of Juan de Mariana, S.J.* Geneva (Droz), 1960.

Llamas, José "Documental inédito de exégesis rabínica en antiguas universidades españoles," *Sefarad*, VI (1946), 289-311.

López de Toro, José. "Fray Luis de León y Benito Arias Montano," *Archivo Agustiniano*, L (1956), 5-28.

Lorenzo, Pedro de. *Fray Luis de León*. Madrid (Nuevas Editoriales Unidas), 1963.

Lowinsky, Edward J. *Secret Chromatic Art in the Netherlands Motet.* New York (Russell and Russell) 1967.

Lyra, Nicolas de. *Biblia Sacra cum Glossa Ordinaria.* Antwerp (J. Keerbergium), 1617.

Malvenda, Tomás. *De Antichristo libri undecim.* Rome, 1604.

Marcos del Rio, F. "La doctrina mistica de Fr. Luis de León," *Religion y Cultura,* II, III, IV (1928), 531-543, 205-220, 223-236 respectively.

Marianae, Joannis. *Historiae de Rebus Hispaniae Libri XXX.* Hague-Comitum (Petrus de Hondt), 1733. Four Vols.

— *Del rey y de la institucion real.* Barcelona (La Selecta), 1880.

Martène, E. and Durand, U., ed. *Thesaurus Novus Anecdotorum,* Paris, 1717. Tome II.

Martin, F. X. "The Problem of Egidio da Viterbo, a Historical Survey," *Augustiniana,* IX, X (1960), 357-379, 43-60 respectively.

Martini, Raymundi. *Pugio Fidei adversus Mauros et Judaeos.* Leipzig (Haeredes F. Lanckisi), 1687.

Mellizo, Felipe. "Fray Luis de Léon en Menéndez Pelayo," *La Ciudad de Dios,* CLXX (1957). 464-471.

Menéndez y Pelayo, Marcelino. *Discurso leído en la Universidad Central.* Madrid (Estrada), 1889.

— *La mistica española.* Madrid (Aguado), 1956.

Merino, A., ed. *Obras del M. Fr. Luis de León.* Madrid (Ibarra), 1803.

Migne, J.-P., ed. *Patrologiae Latinae,* Tomus 183. Turnhalt, Belgium (Brepols).

Millás Vallicrosa, J. M. "Algunas relaciones entre la doctrina luliana y la cabala," *Sefarad,* XV (1958), 241-253.

— *El "Liber Predicationis contra Judeos" de Ramón Lull.* Madrid (CSIC), 1957.

— "Probable influéncia de la poesia sagrada hebraicoespañola en la poesía de Fr. Luis de León," *Sefarad,* XV (1955), p. 261-285.

Milne, A. J. M. *Freedom and Rights.* London (Allen and Unwin), 1968.

Molesworth, Sir William ed. *The English Works of Thomas Hobbes.* (Scientia Aalen), 1962. Vol. III.

Moore, George. "Notes on the Name IHWH," *American Journal of Theology,* XII (1908), 34-52.

Muñoz Iglesias, Salvador. *Fray Luis de León, teólogo.* Madrid (CSIC), 1950.

Nauert, Charles G., Jr. *Agrippa and the Crisis of Renaissance Thought.* Urbana (University of Illinois Press), 1965.

Nerlich, Michael. *El Hombre Justo y Bueno: Inocencia bei Fray Luis de León.* Frankfurt a/M (Vittorio Klostermann), 1966.

Netanyahu, B. *Don Isaac Abravanel, Statesman and Philosopher.* Philadelphia (Jewish Publication Society of America), 1953.

— *The Marranos of Spain.* New York (American Academy for Jewish Research), 1966.

The New Catholic Encyclopedia. New York (McGraw-Hill), 1967.

Newman, Louis, I. *Jewish Influence on Christian Reform Movements.* New York (AMS Press), 1966.

Ong, Walter J. *Ramus: Method and the Decay of Dialogue.* Cambridge

(Harvard University Press), 1958.

O'Neil, Charles J. *Imprudence in St. Thomas Aquinas*. Milwaukee (Marquette University Press), 1955.

Orcibal, Jean. *Le Rencontre du Carmel Thérésien avec les Mystiques du Nord*. Paris (Presses Universitaires de France), 1959.

Orozco, Emilio. *Poesia y mística*. Madrid (Ediciones Guadarrama), 1959.

Peccorini Letona, Francisco. *Los fundamentos ultimos de los derechos del hombre*. San Salvador (Ministerio de Educación), 1964.

Pereña Vicente, Luciano. "El concepto del derecho de gentes en Francisco de Vitoria," *Revista Española de Derecho Internacional*, V (1952), 603-628.

— "El descubrimiento de América en las obras de Fray Luis de León," *Revista Española de Derecho Internacional*, VIII (1955), 587-604.

— "La soberania de España en America según Melchor Cano," *Revista Española de Derecho Internacional*, V (1952), 893-924.

— *La Universidad de Salamanca, forja del pensamiento político español en el siglo XVI*. Historia de la Universidad de Salamanca Series, Tomo I, Núm. 2. Salamanca (Universidad de Salamanca), 1954.

Pérez Castro, Federico. *El manuscrito apologético de Alfonso de Zamora*. Madrid (CSIC), 1950.

Perez Goyena. "Las escuelas teológicas españolas IV, la escuela agustiniana," *Razon y Fe*, LXV (1923), 215-229.

Pfandl, Ludwig. *Cultura y costumbres del pueblo español de los siglos XVI y XVII*. Barcelona (Araluce), 1959.

Phelan, John Leddy. *The Millennial Kingdom of the Franciscans in the New World*. 2nd Edition, Revised. Berkeley and Los Angeles (University of California Press), 1970.

Pico della Mirandola, G. *De Hominis Dignitate, Heptaplus, De Ente et Uno*. Florence (Vallecchi), 1942.

— *Opera*. Bologna (B. Hectores), 1496.

Picotti, G. B. *La Giovanezza di Leone X*. Milan (U. Hoepli), 1927.

Pinta Llorente, Miguel de la. "Contribuciones eruditas modernas sobre Fray Luis de León y autógrafos del poeta agustino," *Archivo Agustiniano*, XLIV (1950), 293-325.

— "Correspondencias inquisitoriales sobre Fr. Luis de León," *Archivo Agustiniano*, XLV (1951), 11-27.

— "En torno al proceso de Fray Luis de León (Contestando al R. P. Beltrán de Heredia)," *Archivo Agustiniano*, XLIV (1950), 53-66.

— *Estudios y polémicos sobre Fray Luis de León*. Madrid (CSIC), 1956.

— "Fr. Luis de León en los carceles inquisitoriales" *Archivo Agustiniano*, XLVIII (1954), 5-44.

— "Fr. Luis de León y los hebraístas de Salamanca," *Archivo Agustiniano*, XLV (1952), 147-169, 334-357.

— *Proceso criminal contra el hebraista salmantino Martin Martinez de Cantalapiedra*. Madrid (CSIC), 1946.

— "Tratados varios de Fr. Luis de León," *Archivo* Agustiniano, XLVII (1953), 368-396.

— "Unas referencias inéditas sobre Fr. Luis de León: Las regencias de gramática en Salamanca," *Archivo Agustiniano,* XLIV (1950), 409-412.

Pistorius, Johannes. *Artis Cabalisticae: hoc est Reconditae Theologiae et Philosophiae Scriptorum Tomus.* Basel (S. Henricpetri), 1587.

Poncins, Vicomte León de. *Judaism and the Vatican, An Attempt at Spiritual Subversion.* London (Britons Publishing Co.), 1967.

Postel, G. *Candelabri Typici in Mosis Tabernaculo,* Ed. by F. Secret. Nieuwkoop (De Graaf), 1966.

Quintana Fernandez, G. "Las bases filosóficas de la teología de Fr. Luis de León," *Revista de la Universidad de Madrid,* XII (1963), 746-747.

Rahner, Karl. *Nature and Grace.* New York (Sheed and Ward), 1964.

Ralegh, Sir Walter. *The Discovery of the Large, Rich and Beautiful Empire of Guiana.* Reprinted from the edition of 1596. New York (Burt Franklin).

Recasens Siches, Luis., *La filosofía del Derecho de Francisco Suarez.* Madrid (V. Suarez), 1927.

Reeves, Marjorie. *The Influence of Prophecy in the Later Middle Ages.* Oxford (Clarendon), 1969.

Renaudet, Augustin. *Préréforme et Humanisme à Paris Pendant les Premières Guerres D'Italie (1494-1517).* Paris (D'Argences), 1953.

Retratos de los españoles ilustres con un epítome de sus vidas. Madrid, (Imp. Real), 1791.

Reuchlin, Johannes. *De Verbo Mirifico (1494), De Arte Cabalistica (1517).* Stuttgart (F. Frommann), 1964.

Revilla, Mariano. "Fray Luis de León y los estudios bíblicos en el siglo XVI," *Religión y Cultura,* II (1928), 482-529.

Ricard, Robert. "Le Symbolisme de 'Château Intérieur' chez Saint-Thérèse," *Bulletin Hispanique,* LXVII (1965), 25-41.

Ríos, Fernando de los. *Religión y estado en la España del siglo XVI.* Mexico (Fondo de Cultura Economica), 1957.

Robles, Oswaldo. *Filósofos mexicanos del siglo XVI.* Mexico (Porrua), 1950.

Roth, Cecil. *A History of the Jews of Italy.* Philadelphia (Jewish Publication Society of America), 1946.

— *A History of the Marranos.* New York (Meridian), 1959.

— *The Jews in the Renaissance.* Philadelphia (Jewish Publication Society of America), 1959.

Runes, Dagobert, foreword author. *The Wisdom of the Kabbalah.* New York (Citadel Press), 1967.

Salazar de Miranda. *Vida y subcesos de Illmo. y Rmo. Sr. Fray Dn. Bartholme Carranza y Miranda.* Romero Collection MSS, Library of the University of California, San Diego, 18th Century.

Salvá, M. and Sainz de Baranda, P., eds. *Documentos para la história de España.* Madrid (Colero), 1847. Vols. X and XI.

Sánchez-Albornoz, Claudio. *España, un enigma histórico.* Buenos Aires (Sudamericana), 1956, Two Vols.

Sancho, H. "La Explanatio Symboli Apostolorum, de Raimundo Martín, O.P.," *Cientia Tomista,* XV (1917), 394-408.

Sandret, L. "Le Concile de Pise (1511): *Revue des Questions Historiques,* XXXIV (1883), 425-456.

Santa María, Pablo de. *Scrutinium Scripturarum*. Mantua, 1475.

Schmitt, Charles B. *Gianfrancesco Pico della Mirandola (1469-1533) and His Critique of Aristotle*. The Hague (M. Nijhoff), 1967.

Scholem, Gershom G. "Devekuth or Communion with God in Hasidim," *The Review of Religion*, (1950), 114-139.

— "La Signification de la Loi dans la Mystique Juive," *Diogène*, XIV (1956), 45-60; XV (1957), 76-114.

— *Les Origines de la Kabbale*. Paris (Aubier-Montaigne), 1966.

— *Major Trends in Jewish Mysticism*. New York (Schocken Books), 1961.

Schuster, Edward J. "Alonso de Orozco and Fray Luis de León: *De los nombres de Cristo*," *Hispanic Review*, XXIV (1956), 261-270.

— "Fray Luis de León and the Linguistic Approach to Epistemology," *The Kentucky Foreign Language Quarterly*, VI (1959), 195-200.

Secret, François. "Aegidiana Hebraica," *Revue des Etudes Juives*, CXXI (1962), 409-416.

— "Girolamo Seripando et la Kabbale," *Rinascimento*, XIV (1963), 251-268.

— "L'*Ensis Pauli* de Paulus de Heredia," *Sefarad*, XXVI (1966), 253-271.

— "Les Débuts du Kabbalisme Chrétien en Espagne et son Histoire à la Renaissance," *Sefarad*, XVII (1957), 36-48.

— "Le Dominicains et la Kabbale Chrétienne à la Renaissance," *Archivum Fratrum Praedicatorum*, XXVIII (1957).

— *Les Kabbalistes Chrétiens de la Renaissance*. Paris (Dunod), 1964.

— "Le Symbolisme de la Kabbale Chrétienne dans la 'Scechina' de Egidio da Viterbo," *Archivio di Filosofia*, (1958), 131-154.

— "*Le Tractatus de Ano Jubilaei* de Lazaro da Viterbo, Grégoire XIII et la Kabbale Chrétienne," *Rinascimento*, XVI (1966), 305-333.

— *Le Zohar chez les Kabbalistes Chrétiens de la Renaissance*. Paris (Mouton), 1964.

— "L'Interpretazione della Kabbala nel Rinascimento," *Convivium*, XXIV (1956).

— "Notes pour une Histoire du Pugio Fidei à la Renaissance," *Sefarad*, XX (1960), 401-407.

— "Notes sur Paulus Ricius et la Kabbale Chrétienne en Italie," *Rinascimento*, XI (1960), 169-192.

— "Pedro Ciruelo: Critique de la Kabbale et de son Usage par les Chrétiens," *Sefarad*, XIX (1959), 48-77.

Serrano, Luciano, *Los conversos D. Pablo de Santa María y D. Alfonso de Cartagena*. Madrid (CSIC). 1942.

Sicroff, Albert A. *Les Controverses des Statuts de "Pureté de Sang" en Espagne du XVe au XVIIe Siècle*. Paris (Didier), 1960.

Silver, Abba Hillel. *A History of Messianic Speculation in Israel*. New York (Macmillan), 1927.

Simon, M., trans. *Midrash Rabba, Song of Songs*. London (Soncino Press), 1951.

Sixtus of Sienna. *Bibliotheca Sancta*. Venice, 1566.

Smith, Gerard. *Freedom in Molina*. Chicago (Loyola University Press), 1966.

Soto, Domingo de. *De Justitia et Jure Libri X*. Antwerp (P. Nutium), 1567.

Sperling, H. and Simon, H., trans. *The Zohar*. London (Soncino Press), 1933. Five Vols.

Teresa de Jesús, Sta. *Obras completas*. Madrid (Biblioteca de Autores Christianos), 1954. Vol. II.

Thomas Aquinas, St. *On Kingship*. G. B. Phelan, trans. and I. T. Eschmann, rev. Toronto (Pontifical Institute), 1949.

— *Summa Theologiae*. Turin (Marietti), 1952. Three Volumes.

Torre, Alfonso de la. *Vision delectable de la história de la filosofía y de las artes liberales*. Biblioteca de Autores Españoles, Vol. 36. Madrid (Sucesores de Hernando), 1907, 341-404.

Torres Yagües, Federico. *Fray Luis de León*. Madrid (Cia. Bibliografica Española), 1964.

Trentman, John. "Vincent Ferrer on the Logician as *Artifex Intellectualis*," *Franciscan Studies*, XXV (1965), 322-337.

Urdanoz, Teofilo, ed. *Obras de Francisco de Vitoria*. Madrid (Biblioteca de Autores Cristianos), 1960.

Usque, Samuel. *Consolation for the Tribulations of Israel*. Trans. by M. A. Cohen. Philadelphia (Jewish Publication Society of America), 1965.

Valbuena Prat, Ángel. *Historia de la literatura española*. 7th edition. Barcelona (Gili), 1963. Two vols.

Vallejo, Gustavo, *Fray Luis de León: su ambiente, su doctrina espiritual, huellas de Santa Teresa*. Rome (Colegio Internacional de Santa Teresa), 1959.

Vega, Ángel C. *Cumbres Místicas*. Madrid (Aguilar), 1963.

— "IV centenario del nacimiento del venerable Agustín Antolínez, arzobispo de Santiago," *La Ciudad de Dios*, CLXVI (1954), 257-322.

Villoslada, Ricardo G. *La Universidad de Paris durante los estudios de Francisco de Vitoria, O.P. (1507-1522)*. Rome (Universitas Gregoriana), 1938.

Viterbo, Egidio da. *Agid. Vit. S.R.E. Card. P. Sent. ad Mentem Platonis*. MS, Vat. Lat. #6325.

— *Scechina e Libellus de Litteris Hebraicis*. Rome (Centro Internazionale di Studi Umanistici), 1959. Two Volumes.

Vitoria, Francisco de. *Comentario al tratado de la ley (I-II, QQ 90-108)*. Ed. by Vicente Beltrán de Heredia. Madrid (CSIC), 1952.

Vulliard, Paul. *La Kabbale Juive*. Paris (Nourry), 1923. Two Vols.

Waite, A. E. *The Holy Kabbalah*. Hyde Park, N.Y. (University Books), 1960.

Walker, D. P. *Spiritual and Demonic Magic from Ficino to Campanella*. London (Warburg Institute), 1958.

Walsh, William Thomas. *Santa Teresa de Ávila*. 3rd edition. Madrid (Espasa-Calpe), 1960.

Wang, John B. *Estudio analitico-sintetico de las poesias originales de Fray Luis de León*. (Ph. D. thesis: University of Maryland, 1967) Ann Arbor (University Microfilms), 1968.

— "La poetica de Fray Luis de León," *Revista de Estudios Hispanicos* (University, Alabama), IV (1970), 99-105.

Welsh, Robert J. *Introduction to the Spiritual Doctrine of Fray Luis de León, O.S.A.* Washington, (Augustinian Press), 1951.

Williams, G. L., trans. *Selections from Three Works of Francisco Suárez.* New York, 1964. Vol. II.

Wind, Edgar. *Pagan Mysteries in the Renaissance.* London (Faber and Faber), 1968.

Wirszubski, Chaim. *Flavius Mithridates' Sermo de Passione Domini.* Jerusalem (Israel Academy of Sciences and Humanities), 1963.

Wolfii, J. C. *Bibliotheca Hebraea.* Hamburg (Liebezeit), 1715. Four Vols.

Zarco Cuevas, Julian. *Bibliografía de Fr. Luis de León.* Malaga, 1928.

INDEX OF NAMES OF PERSONS